D1594416

Levinas Studies

Levinas Studies:
An Annual Review

Series Editor:
Jeffrey Bloechl

Editorial Board:
Marie L. Baird
Leora Batnitzky
Bettina Bergo
Robert Bernasconi
Richard A. Cohen
Edwin E. Gantt
Claire E. Katz
Jeffrey Kosky
Philippe Nemo
Adriaan T. Peperzak
Michael Purcell
Jill Robbins
Anthony Steinbock
Andrew Tallon
Rudi Visker

Levinas Studies

An Annual Review

Volume 2

Edited by
Jeffrey Bloechl

Duquesne University Press
Pittsburgh, Pa.

Published in the United States of America by
Duquesne University Press
600 Forbes Avenue
Pittsburgh, Pennsylvania 15282

Levinas Studies: An Annual Review
Volume 2

ISBN 0–8207–0385–0
ISBN-13: 978–0–8207–0385–5

ISSN 1554–7000

∞ Printed on acid-free paper.

CONTENTS

Editor's Introduction

Jeffrey Bloechl

I t is a central aim of Levinas's philosophy to free our understanding of both experience and relation from the rule of history, whether the latter is proposed in the course of an argument for the ascendancy of the concept (Hegel) or accepted into a meditation on being and destiny (Heidegger). Neither the subject who has an identity only by virtue of a deep and ongoing effort, nor the other who looks at this subject from beyond any identity that the subject might impose on the other, *belong* to history so much as find themselves compelled to reckon with it. If the subject and the other thus enter into history, indeed meeting and interacting within it from somehow outside its constraints, then the meaning of that reckoning will reside finally not in tragedy, as so many of Levinas's contemporaries would have it, but in ethics — in dialogue, where all meaning has the definition of a word that responds to an interlocutor.

These notions are familiar enough not to require further elaboration here. What is perhaps somewhat less familiar, or less frequently adopted as a site for concentrated work on Levinas's position, is what this implies for Levinas's relation to the great figures of the philosophical tradition. It is often said, not unjustly, that Levinas's interpretations of these great figures are characterized, with few exceptions (his works on Husserl come to mind), by the fecundity of a certain violence. But this is only to state the obvious: Levinas is interested considerably less in the thoughts that a great thinker has tried to impart, than in the manner in which those thoughts either reveal or occlude the primordial ethical relation in which they have been formed. Properly understood, the classical texts of a philosophical tradition, their defining insights, and the difficult arguments that bear them are first of all the content of discourse, or what in his later work he calls *the Said*. This *Said* passes in a *Saying* that responds to an other person — whether this person is present already before the act of writing, like some waiting student, or still far off in the future, yet to discover a book or an essay that has been composed *ad aeternum*.

Each of the authors contributing to this second volume of *Levinas Studies* is plainly respectful of Levinas's unique engagement with and approach to the history of philosophy, with their own sustained rigor in assessing the stakes of his particular dialogues with a host of important philosophers and thinkers. Jacques Taminiaux's essay is remarkably concentrated in this respect: Levinas's insistence that the I-other relation is prior to the subject's relation to objects or to Dasein's relation to the world does not only challenge Husserl and Heidegger, but defines the perspective from which Levinas inscribes them within his own problematic. As these developments occur early in Levinas's philosophical itinerary, Taminiaux's essay appears first in this volume.

Since, however, the notion of Levinas as phenomenologist is rightly confronted with the notion of Levinas as philosopher of religion and as Jewish intellectual, it has seemed appropriate to follow with essays on his conception of God, the important affinities of that conception with Kabbalah, and the implications for a theism that would transcend phenomenology and (onto-)theology alike. Taking up the first of these three tasks, Jean-Marc Narbonne brings the thought of Levinas into contact with that of Plotinus, one of a handful of figures with whom many would have liked Levinas to enter into extended dialogue. The thought that Levinas is at once close to Neoplatonism and removed from it at certain important points opens the way to the somewhat rumored matter of his debt to Kabbalah — a great deal of which is cleared up here, in Jacob Meskin's essay. Martin Kavka's essay then returns much of this discussion to the broader field of Jewish thought insofar as it tries to conceive of God with and without a certain classical cosmology.

If religious thought has long encompassed the idea of a God who transcends the inspired language and the created order, the matter has been complicated in recent centuries by the rise of suggestions that inspiration and the perception of order ought to be traced back to motivations that are quite plainly human — whereupon, or so the argument goes, the time has come to simply abandon them. Before Levinas was schooled in the special rigors of either phenomenology or the Talmud, he read Dostoyevsky, at home, in the original Russian. Hence the thrust of Peter Atterton's essay on Levinas and Dostoyevsky: the alleged death of God will have been known to Levinas before he found his way to the ethical relation of responsibility for the other. Likewise, Levinas would also have had such knowledge before he was able to propose that this *ethical* relation is also the *religious* relation to a God whose "passing" binds us to one another outside of our common appearance together in history.

The remaining essays in this volume are also focused on Levinas's relation to a single interlocutor, whether or not an extended engagement is to be found in his oeuvre. In bringing Levinas together with Rousseau, Claire Katz takes the latter step, imagining a dialogue that never occurred. Or rather, she constructs one that could have, and might well should have taken place around a theme of unquestioned importance to both men: moral and religious instruction, as it emanates from a tradition and is steadied by philosophy. Equally compelling is Michel Juffé's incisive study of the Levinas-Spinoza encounter that has tantalized and indeed vexed so many scholars of either figure. Juffé's essay, especially where it links the question of the absolute to the theme of moral life and thus the problem of evil, opens the way for profitable readings of two more essays putting Levinas in dialogue with modern thought: Joseph Lawrence's avowedly Schellingian approach to some of Levinas's darker concerns, and Adriaan Peperzak's analysis of the relation between ethics and politics as contested by Levinas and his constant opponent, Hegel.

The name "Hegel," it seems to me, stands for a difficulty suspended over Levinas's relation to the history of philosophy wherever it appears determined by experiences that he himself is willing to recognize as "pre-philosophical" (e.g., *OB* 20/*AE* 24). Here it is a matter not of the "non-philosophical" structure of the ethical relation antecedent to all thinking, but instead of the force by which a certain milieu opens the mind to recognizing that relation. There has never been much doubt that the prephilosophical is specifically Jewish, at least for Levinas (explicit statements abound). But then this would be a remarkable, virtuoso Judaism, sufficiently fluent in the Western tradition to challenge its basic grammar from within — and yet unable to either make itself at home there or simply speak another language altogether. Jacques Rolland captures the sense of this Judaism well when he evokes a sense of being at once a stranger to the world and its ferment.[1] Levinas is "riveted" to his Judaism, even while speaking the tongue of a tradition that does not know how to give words to Jewish experience.[2] This does not require one to think, as is sometimes suggested, that Judaism needs Western philosophy in order to understand or express itself, but it does imply that Jewish experience is not in fact wholly alien to it. Would the prephilosophical thus be *proto*-philosophical? It seems impossible to think otherwise. But then one must confront what Levinas means by *prephilosophical* with what his friend de Waelhens, writing in an unmistakably Hegelian vein, has said about the *non-philosophical*:

> Non-philosophical experience is the source of philosophy, but it is capable of this because it is itself already penetrated by philosophy. However,

this is not yet everything. The transverse relation of philosophy to non-philosophical experience is necessarily combined with a vertical relation of philosophy to its own history. This means that philosophy, if indeed it is formed in the test of an experience that is new and strange to it, becomes fully itself only in situating itself, in turn, in the development of a specifically philosophical problematic: such a philosophy defines itself as accomplishment, reform or repetition of the philosophies that have preceded it.[3]

It is far from certain that Levinas would have been willing to accept all of this, though he might well grant that the experiences that open philosophy are evidently not alien to it. Is it conceivable that the experiences that are penetrated by philosophy are no less secondary to the nonphilosophical experience of ethical responsibility than is philosophy itself? On at least one occasion when Levinas has de Waelhens explicitly in mind, this would appear to be his position:

> The ethical situation of responsibility is not comprehensible on the basis of ethics. It does indeed arise from what Alphonse de Waelhens called non-philosophical experiences, which are ethically independent. The constraint that does not presuppose the will . . . has its place between the necessity of 'what cannot be otherwise' (Aristotle, *Metaphysics*, E), of what today we call eidetic necessity, and the constraint imposed on a will by the situation in which it finds itself. (*OB* 120; 154)

Between logic and instantiation, between system and act, *before the history in which they are interwoven*, the ethical relation in which one is always already responsible for the other is thus anterior to the thinking that discovers it (or fails to do so). This would be the nonphilosophical par excellence, since by definition it is always implied in every philosophy. And philosophy, for its part, would be nourished by experiences that deserve to be called *prephilosophical* since they give rise to a thinking that is capable not only of understanding and interpreting an entire tradition, but also of questioning and indeed contesting it. What then have Levinas's prephilosophical experiences bequeathed to his defense of a nonphilosophical relation with the other person? The latter will have been impressed upon him in and through the former, so that, as he often contended, a revolt against the Western tradition was a matter of philosophical probity, ethical exigency, and fidelity to his own Judaism — all at once, and without contradiction.

ABBREVIATIONS

Works listed are primary texts by Emmanuel Levinas. Abbreviations used in individual essays for works by others authors are listed at the end of that essay.

AE   *Autrement qu'être ou au-delà de l'essence.* La Haye: Martinus Nijhoff, 1974.

AeT *Altérité et transcendence.* Paris: Fata Morgana, 1995.

AT   *Alterity and Transcendence.* Trans. Michael B. Smith. New York: Columbia University Press, 1999.

BV   *Beyond the Verse: Talmudic Readings and Lectures.* Trans. Gary D. Mole. Bloomington: Indiana University Press, 1994.

CPP *Collected Philosophical Papers.* Trans. Alphonso Lingis. Pittsburgh: Duquesne University Press, 1998.

DEH *Discovering Existence with Husserl.* Trans. R. Cohen and M. Smith. Evanston: Northwestern University Press, 1998.

DF   *Difficult Freedom: Essays on Judaism.* Trans. Seàn Hand. Baltimore: Johns Hopkins University Press, 1990.

EE   *Existence and Existents.* Trans. Alphonso Lingis. Pittsburgh: Duquesne University Press, 2001.

EI   *Ethics and Infinity.* Trans. Richard A. Cohen. Pittsburgh: Duquesne University Press, 1985.

En   *Entre nous: Essais sur le penser-à-l'autre.* Paris: Grasset, 1991.

EN   *Entre nous: Thinking-of-the-Other.* Trans. M. Smith and B. Harshov. New York: Columbia University Press, 1998.

GCM   *Of God Who Comes to Mind.* Trans. Bettina Bergo. Palo Alto: Stanford University Press, 1998.

GDT   *God, Death, and Time.* Trans. Bettina Bergo. Palo Alto: Stanford University Press, 1996.

ITN   *In the Time of the Nations.* Trans. Michael B. Smith. Bloomington: Indiana University Press, 1994.

NT   *Nine Talmudic Readings.* Trans. Annette Aronowicz. Bloomington: Indiana University Press, 1994.

OB   *Otherwise than Being or Beyond Essence.* Trans. Alphonso Lingis. Pittsburgh: Duquesne University Press, 1998.

PN   *Proper Names.* Trans. Michael B. Smith. Palo Alto: Stanford University Press, 1996.

RR   "La ruine de la représentation." In *Endecouvrant l'existence avec Husserl et Heidegger.* Paris, Vrin, 1967.

TeI   *Totalité et infini: Essai sur l'extériorité.* La Haye: Martinus Nijhoff, 1961.

TI   *Totality and Infinity.* Trans. Alphonso Lingis. Pittsburgh: Duquesne University Press, 1969.

TIHP   *The Theory of Intuition in Husserl's Phenomenology.* Trans. A. Orianne. Evanston: Northwestern University Press, 1973.

TIP   *Théorie de l'intuition dans la phénoménologie de Husserl.* Paris: Vrin, 2000.

TO   *Time and the Other.* Trans. Richard A. Cohen. Pittsburgh: Duquesne University Press, 1987.

Levinas and the History of Philosophy

Jacques Taminiaux

Levinas has sometimes been reproached for a certain laxness toward the history of philosophy. By dint of denouncing, as the central thread of this long history, the persistence or recurrence of an ambition to totalization, he would have failed to recognize the diversity of steps articulated along its course, thus ceding to the very thing he placed in question — the prestige of the same — to the detriment of the alterity of the other. I propose to submit this alleged failure to some examination.

My theme has a preliminary consideration. It is as a philosopher that Levinas interpellates the history of philosophy: he himself, in his concepts, themes, and arguments wants to be and considers himself as the inheritor of a tradition in which he has been formed, which has incited him to think in turn, and from which he will begin. This tradition has a name: phenomenology, as inaugurated by Husserl and then prolonged and transformed by Heidegger. Levinas's early works include studies of each of them, and later he reclaimed the title of phenomenologist with some force when attempting to make his own voice heard. I also heard it when, on the occasion of submitting his dissertation to the Sorbonne for the *doctorat d'État,* of which *Totality and Infinity* formed the principal thesis, he responded obstinately to Jankelevitch, who had

Translated by Jeffrey Bloechl.

heaped praise on him for having at last exorcised French thought of certain German sirens: "Mais, Monsieur, détrompez-vous: je suis phénoménologue!" And it is certainly because he claimed this title that he committed both of his principal works to the collection *Phænome-nologica,* which was founded by Fr. van Breda and conceived by him as a counterpart to the collection *Husserliana,* which for its part was to produce a critical edition of the *Nachlaß* rescued by van Breda himself during difficult times.

If Levinas's manifest claim to the title of phenomenologist merits any attention here, it will be necessary, as a preliminary consideration for my theme, to begin by distinguishing, in his earliest works, what in his treatment of the two phenomenological approaches to which he owes his philosophical initiation, belongs to the order of exposition and what belongs to the order of correction, that is, of placing at a distance. In other words, it will be a matter of discerning, in the early texts, the particular style of his relation to the historical movement of phenomenology. Bearing in mind my theme — Levinas and the history of philosophy — I will attempt to discharge this task succinctly within the strict limits of the preliminary question that I formulate as follows: does the phenomenological current evidenced by Husserl and Heidegger, each in his own way, advance it by adopting a specific relation to the history of philosophy? And if this is case, it will permit me, still in the framework of a preliminary consideration, to raise a parallel question as to whether Levinas has subscribed to the specific relations to the history of philosophy both by Husserl and Heidegger have marked for phenomenology. This will in turn permit me, moving beyond such preliminary reflections and thus beyond Levinas's early works, to make an informed determination of Levinas's relation to the history of philosophy.

We may begin with Husserl and the contact with him by which Levinas, as he often said, entered phenomenology and was formed in its discipline.[1] Husserl often repeated to him that entry into philosophy requires a generalized *epoché* that suspends all received conceptions, whether they bear on common experience, the sciences, or the history of philosophy, near or far. To the degree that it is detached from all presuppositions, the entry into phenomenology does not claim any testament. In order to open the field that it wishes to explore, all that henceforth matters in the eyes of phenomenology that takes this field as its affair — the famous *Sache selbst* — is intentional life taken in the integrality of the bipolar correlation that defines it and in all the diversity of its modes of manifestation. The very appearing of this life is the phenomenon in the phenomenological sense, and phenomenology is a matter of describing this life as it gives itself to be seen rather than according to imposed definitions or preestablished questions.

But if the purism of the *Wesenschau* renders phenomenology refractory to every heritage, it remains that in the radical initiative that Husserl assumes, the phenomenologist knows quite well that he does not arise at the first dawn of thinking, and that his awakening is not without relation to the teaching received from the mouths of masters who are not without name (such as Brentano). He knows this all the better himself, for having opened his own field of research only after first finding it necessary to criticize, nuance, or disavow as psychologism what he had already been able to say in echo of other discourses that he had adopted with as much veneration as inadvertence, and because they were current. And he also knew that the course that had brought him to this new field, far from being totally unprecedented, fell in line with a course already designated by inherited names — *Logic, Theory of Knowledge, Wissenschaftslehre* — and already surveyed by notable interrogators: empiricists or neo-Kantians. And, further, this new field to which he forcibly gained access must, if it is not to become the theme of a mute and solitary ecstasis, be expressed, patiently described, in a language that is comprehensible to other philosophers — that is, in terms and doublets that are in fact quite ancient: noesis and noema, intuition, category, fact and eidos, immanence and transcendence. Finally, to the degree that this new field reveals its articulations and its strata, it also reveals an ultimate founding instance the exploration of which cannot but call for an ancient name: first philosophy, or metaphysics. It is thus that a certain history surrounds, envelopes, and reclaims the very gesture by which phenomenology is instituted as pure gaze "*sub specie æternitatis.*"

But to be sure, the relation of Husserlian phenomenology to the history of philosophy does not limit itself to this encroachment by the tradition on its birth in spite of its principle refusal of every heritage. In fact, in the course of the exploration in which it is engaged, this phenomenology does not refrain from expressly and thematically recognizing the phenomenal validity of many inherited theses and paths. Nor does phenomenology hesitate to justify in passing — however little they lend themselves to a strictly phenomenological reappropriation — for example, the Kantian distinction between perceptual judgment and experiential judgment, or Kant's thesis on Being as a nonreal predicate, or again Descartes' clear and distinct perception at the very heart of his celebrated doubt. More generally, this phenomenology does not fail, along the way toward justifying its pretension to raise itself to the rank of first philosophy, to explicitly debate the long tradition and to freshly examine the stages that it considers the most significant for its own project: Plato's invention of philosophy as universal science submitted to the Socratic demand for radical justification, and his imposition of a teleology of reason on humanity; Aristotle's outline of both a pure logic and a universal theory of subjectivity; Descartes' discovery of the cogito as an *Archimedean point* of scientificity and as seed of transcendental subjectivity; Locke's attempt to elaborate a pure egology conceived as a genetic and intuitive discipline; the advance in Berkeley and Hume toward an intuitionist and pretranscendental problematic of pure immanence; Leibniz's sketch, in the *Monadology*, of the fundamental traits of intentionality from the intuitive elucidation of apperceptive properties of the monad;

and finally the powerful eruption of the idea of transcendental philosophy in Kant's *Copernican revolution*.

But at each step of this genealogy, Husserl's gesture is double: there is on the one hand praise for everything that promotes or is susceptible to reappropriation by transcendental phenomenology in the most scrupulous obedience to the imperatives of the reduction, while on the other hand there is also denunciation of a long succession of confusions, misunderstandings, of inattention and distracting inclinations toward dogmatism, naturalism, and constructivism. One thus sees outlined in the Husserlian corpus a certain style of properly phenomenological relation to the history of philosophy. It joins recognition of everything in this long history that anticipates, be it from quite far, *first philosophy* understood in the new sense of an eidetic exploration of the ultimate founding instance that is transcendental immanence, with disavowal of the vices of method found in each of those same happy instances of anticipation that nonetheless do grasp everything in the absence of an authentic reduction.

Still, the relation of phenomenology to the history of philosophy does not limit itself to this ambiguous gesture of recognition and methodical critique. For if one looks more closely it appears that what brings Husserl to his debate with this long history is not at all peripheral to his proper task, as if the debate itself was of a strictly introductory order, reducible to proper pedagogy at the university. It much rather implies, at the very heart of transcendental exploration not only a philosophy of the history of philosophy that consists in deciphering its course as a teleology of phenomenology, but also a general philosophy of the history of humanity — for the idea of phenomenology is supposed by Husserl to be at once the *archè* and *telos* of an authentic humanity, making of phenomenology a sort of missionary charged with healing the whole of human culture.

Holding in reserve the question of whether the proper mode of Levinas's relation to the history of philosophy belongs in some measure to all of this, we may now ask if his early works, those that introduce

Husserlian phenomenology to France — let us not forget Sartre's words: "I came to phenomenology through Levinas" — do not perhaps betray some signs of resistance to the Husserlian project of a transcendental foundation, which for its part engages, as I have just indicated, not only a certain concept of *philosophia perennis* but also a complete philosophy of history. Such signs do exist. I will attempt to locate them, drawing on Levinas's *Theory of Intuition in Husserl's Phenomenology.*

This first book proposes to "study and present Husserl's philosophy as one studies and presents a living philosophy," in which, Levinas specifies, "we must immerse ourselves and philosophize" in order to "grasp its simple, main inspiration" aided by the best among those disciples who are inspired by it (*TIHP* xxxiii/*TIP* 14–15). Now, regarding this first, simple inspiration, Levinas immediately emphasizes that it is not at all, appearances to the contrary, of an epistemological order but engages, in his terms, "a new conception of Being." Against the naturalism that had constituted the ontology dominant at the turn of the previous century and that had no other notion of Being than that of the object of physics, Husserl will have had the primary merit of giving value to a notion of Being "closely bound to that of lived experience [*du vécu*]," that is, to the very life of the consciousness that conceals but also presupposes, as its source, Being in the naturalist sense (see *TIHP* 34/*TIP* 62). This life is absolute, insists Levinas, in the sense that all Being is related to it and it bears in itself the guarantee of its own existence. He marvels at this new ontological avenue open to philosophy. He marvels still more at the fact that this life has an "intrinsic meaning," intentionality, which sees to it that, far from being tied to its own states, it is through and through relational, and does not cease "to be in the presence of transcendent Being" (*TIHP* 30/*TIP* 50), to "transcend itself," or to direct itself to what is not it (see *TIHP* 39/*TIP* 75). It is this relation, in all its phenomenological diversity that is offered to phenomenological intuition. And this results in a considerable enlargement of the field of ontology: Being is no longer limited to imposing itself as object according to the definition provided by physics.

However, this marvel is accompanied by a certain reserve. This is due to the fact that despite its enlargement of the field of ontology, Husserlian phenomenology affirms, without pause, the "primacy of theoretical consciousness" such that to exist is first of all to have the status of an object of understanding (see *TIHP* 53/*TIP* 98–99). There is thus, according to the young Levinas, who deplores it, an "intellectualism" at the heart of this intuitivism. And it is on this point that is sketched, in the conclusion of his first book, a subtle but firm refusal of the axis that determines Husserl's relation to the history of philosophy. Of the latter, he writes that "philosophy occupies the same place in the metaphysical destiny of man as does the theoretical exercise of the sciences. In this conception philosophy appears as independent of the historical situation of man as the theory that seeks to understand everything *sub specie æternitatis*" (*TIHP* 155/*TIP* 220). And he specifies how we are to understand this "historical situation of man" that he invokes in order to contest in Husserl "the supra-historical attitude of theory": "this phenomenon *sui generis* . . . that man has a specific manner of being his past that is inconceivable in the cast of a stone. Moreover, this historicity is not a secondary property of man as if man existed first and then became temporal and historical. Historicity and temporality form the very substantiality of man's substance" (*TIHP* 156/*TIP* 221). This is of course an allusion to Heidegger, to whom the young author does not fail to pay homage, for it is to him that he owes the ontological inflection of his presentation of Husserl. The moment has thus come to turn to Heidegger, and for us to ask whether the phenomenological path such as he embarks on it and assumes it, in his own way, engages a specific relation to the history of philosophy.

Such is indeed the case, as it appears in the introduction to *Being and Time*, a work which already from its publication heavily influenced the young Levinas's reading of Husserl. From the first moment, Heidegger announces that the phenomenological task he takes up is closely bound to a certain relation to the history of philosophy. This task consists in posing anew the question of what we truly mean by the word "being" (*étant*), a question that had held the work of Plato and Aristotle spellbound, but which, after them, fell into a silence, at least "as a thematic question for effective research" (*Being and Time* §1; 2), such that what they had conquered and seized after a hard-fought struggle with the phenomena fell rather to the trivial rank of commonplace, unworthy of serious consideration, under the triple pretext that the concept of Being signifies something quite general, that which is "indefinable" (§1; 4), and the comprehension of which is self-evident. It would be much too simple to conclude from this that Heidegger's relation to the history of philosophy will consist in restoring value to the origin, against a tradition that has since become sedimented and trivial. For Heidegger cautions his readers that the triple pretext commonly alleged in order to hinder a true questioning of the meaning of Being "has its roots in ancient ontology itself" (§1; 3). It is this that prefigures the mode of his relation to the history of philosophy.

This relation supports a gesture no less ambiguous than that of Husserl, when faced with his philosophical heritage. In both cases it is a matter of distinguishing at the core of this long history what is susceptible to reappropriation because it is phenomenologically justified, from what is mistakenly distracted from any sufficient phenomenological reduction. In its Husserlian definition, the latter would grant access to the fundamental phenomenon of intentionality. But Heidegger contends that this relational phenomenon could be fundamental only so long as the relation that defines it remains ontologically undetermined. More profound than the relation of noesis to noema, there is at the heart of the being endowed with intentionality, a relation not only with the beings that it is not and thus to the being that it is, but also to the being of those other beings and to its own Being. This is why the phenomenological reduction in its Heideggerian sense consists in redirecting the phenomenological gaze from the apprehension of a being to the ontological comprehension that it implies. It is through the elucidation of this comprehension at work in every human being that philosophy will attain its proper scientificity, it being understood that for Heidegger Being is definitively the sole and proper theme of philosophy. It is thus as science of Being that philosophy will merit the title of rigorous science. And this science could be constructed only by articulating in all its structures the comprehension that is at work in the being that we are, and which consists in projecting beings on Being. On this conception, phenomenology, as the science of Being, thus conjugates *reduction* and *construction*. But neither the reduction nor the construction can be accomplished unless both are intrinsically referred to the tradition. Heidegger has a name for this intrinsic relation of reduction and construction to the history of philosophy: *De-struktion*, deconstruction. When this notion is first introduced in *Being and Time* in order to define a specific relation of phenomenology to the history of philosophy, he justifies it by the historicity of Dasein, understood as that which is engaged in the elucidation of the meaning of Being. The Heideggerian deconstruction thus upholds the very thing that Levinas calls, in his first book, "the historical situation of man," invoked in order to express some reticence toward what he calls Husserl's suprahistorical attitude.

Let us briefly note some of the essential traits of Heidegger's justification for phenomenology's specific relation to the history of philosophy by appeal to the historicity of Dasein. To say that the human existent — called Dasein because Being is a question for it — is an essentially historical being, is to say that it is de facto thrown into its problematic condition in a manner that it de facto inherits from a certain preliminary articulation of this problematic, and to say that it awakens to an authentic questioning thanks to this inherited condition in which it is inscribed. But if this same awakening of all questioning about Being, however elementary or episodic it may *de facto* be, is itself characterized by historicity, this holds all the more when the questioning is taken up explicitly and methodically as a task. For this deliberate and methodical task can be dated; its birth is one with that of philosophy in the Greeks. In order to take possession of its most proper possibilities of questioning, the elaboration of the question of Being thus must necessarily be oriented toward its own history. And if this orientation is to be called deconstructive, this is not at all because it aims to destroy the past, but rather because it means to reappropriate it in a positive manner — or, in terms of good phenomenology, it is to test the past in view of the phenomenon that is its concern: Being insofar as it is the correlate of a comprehension that relates to it. If the word *Destruktion* nonetheless does bear a negative connotation, this is because the phenomenal test must decide between what in the philosophical heritage is called by the phenomenon and corresponds to it, and what covers, obliterates and diverts us from it. But, as I have already suggested, the putting into practice of this test cannot consist in opposing the original purity of a distant past to the later deposit of the long tradition that issues from the past because the test accepts as evident the adage according to which the tradition forgets its origins. For when the test is put into practice it becomes clear that the entanglement of the phenomenal and what obstructs it affects the origin as well as each of the stages that follow it. And if this entanglement is reproduced in various guises, its governance and its key are found ultimately in Dasein itself, which strives everyday to dissimulate, divert, or obstruct the comprehension of Being of which it is, properly, the titular. It is because Dasein is ontologically divided between what it is authentically and what it is not authentically, that when it undertakes philosophy, it tends to transpose into its most intimate relation to Being, conceptual structures originating in everyday relations that it maintains with what does not belong to it authentically.

Under these conditions, the relation of Heideggerian phenomenology to the history of philosophy could only be deliberately circular. It is not a matter of letting itself be taken aback by words previously unheard, but quite literally of rediscovering itself in them. Stated otherwise, it is the hermeneutical circle that governs this relation and it does so such that the comprehension of all other discourses is always preceded by the comprehension of self. This circle is totalizing not only because it authorizes Heidegger to reappropriate many of the great texts from the history of philosophy from Plato to Nietzsche, but more deeply because the principle that founds each step in this encompassing reading — Dasein itself, torn between authenticity and inauthenticity — is a principle that makes a circle with itself and thus forms a closed totality. In effect, all research into the meaning of "Being," because it will concern itself with Being insofar as it is the correlate of a comprehension that relates to it and of which Dasein is the titular, revolves in the final instance around an ultimate condition of possibility which is Dasein's capacity to be itself a whole. And Dasein has this capacity inasmuch as its end is not a term that stops it from the outside but is in fact its own most possibility, as that which permits it to reclaim what it already is, in projecting it and thus itself toward its own death. It is this potential to be a whole, and this alone, that unlocks the intelligibility of Being, of which it is known that it resides in the ec-static and finite temporality that is constitutive of Dasein.

Two indissociable formulas thus mark the effigy of the circularity that presides over Heidegger's relation to the history of philosophy. The first reads: Dasein exists for its own sake. And the second, after having substituted the question "who is time?" for the question "what is time?," responds: "time is me, I am my time," or more precisely, since Dasein is torn between the authentic and the inauthentic, and since it therefore must conquer itself against what it is not: "am I authentically my time?"

I hope now to have said enough for there to be seen some kinship of style in the relationship that both phenomenologists, Husserl and Heidegger, entertain with the history of philosophy. It matters little that Husserl does not use the word deconstruction to characterize the manner in which he approaches that history, since it is indeed a

deconstruction that he conducts, albeit elliptically and without the support of citations, when he distinguishes between what in the thinkers
of the tradition anticipates the return — or the reduction — to intentionality, and what obstructs access to it because it slides down the slope
of the natural attitude. In short, and as Husserl says literally in the language he inherited from Brentano before Heidegger took it up in turn,
it is necessary to distinguish between that which is of the order of
Eigentlichkeit, of the authentic, and that which belongs to *Uneigent-
lichkeit,* to the inauthentic.

It may be added that in Heidegger no less than in Husserl the phenomenological relation to the history of philosophy engages a philosophy of this history, since Heidegger deciphers it as a teleology of his
fundamental ontology. And in him no less than in Husserl this relation opens onto a general philosophy of history, but with the —
significant — difference that in the author of the *Crisis* the philosophy
of history is nourished on the disarming utopia that phenomenology
might be able to heal Germany of its demons, while at the same time
Heidegger's profoundly equivocal courses celebrate immanence in the
National Socialist Revolution, thanks to a Promethean conflict between
the authentic and the inauthentic, an extension of fundamental ontology into the historical Dasein of the German people, and thus a greater
renaissance of everything that had been Greek.

Did Levinas, during the period when his own works focused on
Husserl and Heidegger, subscribe to these conceptions of the relation
of phenomenology to the history of philosophy? The question is
undoubtedly without an object if it invites us to inspect his youthful
works for signs of a reading of the tradition that diverges from that
which Husserl and Heidegger practiced. Yet the question is pertinent
if instead it invites us to seek in that period some sign of a resistance
in Levinas to the very principle that founds Husserl's reading of the
past and Heidegger's reading of it.

Concerning Husserl, I have said that Levinas's first book accuses
him of intellectualism while also praising the first phenomenologist for
having recognized the functionally relational structure of intentionality,

understood as the potential of existence to transcend itself and direct itself toward what it is not. Through his intellectualism, Husserl will have upheld — citing Levinas's first book — "the proposition that at the basis of all conscious acts there is a representation" (*TIHP* 158/ *TIP* 223). At the same time, what Husserl's description of intentionality has to teach us, gaining Levinas's admiration, is that intentionality by essential title bears within itself certain implicit potentialities, that it consists in "exceeding the intention in the intention itself, thinking more than one thinks," and that it discloses a "condition of conscious actuality in potentiality" (*DEH* 117/*RR* 131), a condition that "compromises the sovereignty of representation" (*DEH* 118/*RR* 132). It is in these terms, some years before *Totality and Infinity*, that Levinas expresses his debt to Husserl under the eloquent title of "The Ruin of Representation." This essay salutes in Husserl the renewal of the concept of the transcendental and "a modification of the very concept of philosophy, which was identified with the absorption of every 'Other' by the 'Same,' or with the deduction of every 'Other' from the 'Same' . . . and where a relation between the Same and the Other does not come to invert the philosophical eros" (*DEH* 113/*RR* 127).

The result of this is that in the principle of Husserlian phenomenology, and thus of Husserl's reading of the past, Levinas discovers a fluctuation or indeed an equivocation. There is a stated principle that generalizes representation and assures it a "power of complete actualization." There is also a principle at work that ruins this power. Or again there is a solemn phenomenological reduction that proclaims "the apodicticity of the immanent sphere" and of which Levinas says that "it has never seemed to me to justify itself" (*DEH* 119/*RR* 134). And there is, on the other hand, a phenomenological reduction that is modest and no longer glorious — one that is conducted in an *esprit de l'escalier*, according to Levinas's agreeable expression [*RR* 135] — one which discovers that *Sinngebung*, far from being "the work of a sovereign ego," is an open play and, like a "simultaneity of freedom and belonging" (*DEH* 118/*RR* 133), where "the noema conditions and shelters the noesis that constitutes it" (*DEH* 119/*RR* 134), where the

potentiality conditions actuality and where one may "glimpse a relationship with the other that is neither an intolerable limitation of the
thinker, nor a simple absorption of this other into an ego" (*DEH* 121/
RR 135).

It suffices, I would say, that the teaching of this modest reduction
be taken as the guiding line in order for there to be born another reading of the past than that which Husserl reached by the light of the sole
principle of the solemn reduction.

As for Heidegger, what Levinas discovers at the heart of his early
works is a symmetric fluctuation, though one that in some sense inverts
the one I have just invoked concerning Husserl. It is undoubtedly to
Heidegger that Levinas owes his capacity to have recognized in Husserl
an operative reduction that is attentive to the "condition of conscious
actuality in potentiality," to the transcending of intention in the intention itself and to the transcendental role of noematic horizons in the
very movement of intentionality. And this is why the essay in homage
to Husserl does not fail to salute Heidegger in passing: "The horizon
implied in intentionality is thus not the still vaguely thought context
of the object, but the *situation* of the subject. A subject *in situation*
or, as Heidegger will say, in the world, is announced by this essential
potentiality of an intention" (*DEH* 117/*RR* 132). It is also why
Levinas could gather his own essays reading the two phenomenologists under the single, significant title: *En découvrant l'existence avec
Husserl et Heidegger*. Yet the Heideggerian reduction to facticity,
understood as the situation of being-in-the-world, is paradoxical insofar as its analytical and transcendental work restores and even reinforces
a sovereign and totalizing *Sinngebung*, since it is the potentiality of
Dasein, at each time mine, to be a totality in assuming its intrinsic
mortality which, for its part, forms the seat of the ultimate ontological
conditions for the intelligibility of beings.

There is thus a reduction which in principle proclaims the *situation*
of Dasein, but which in its working attributes Dasein's concernful
existence the status of an ultimate *foundation*. One might also put it
this way: there is a potentiality which, seemingly imposed at first as

a condition, is eventually elevated to the rank of *an unconditional.* It is in consideration of this discord between the principle of the Heideggerian reduction and its result that Levinas will take up anew the phenomenological description of what he calls *situation.* It is well known that this description leads him to detect at the basis of this same situation a potentiality that does not consist in the interpellation of self by self but instead of oneself by the other. It is this other description of the primordial phenomenon that will motivate another reading of the history of philosophy than that which Heidegger conducted during the period in which he articulated his fundamental ontology.

With this, we are at last to some degree capable of an informed approach to this other reading. I have already said enough for it to be presumed that at each step of the way a debate is undertaken equally with Husserl and with Heidegger. On this point, it will suffice to recall some forceful lines in *Totality and Infinity,* which Levinas referenced in his preface to the German edition (January 1987): "This book that wants to be and feels itself to be of phenomenological inspiration proceeds from long association with Husserl's texts and a constant attentiveness to *Sein und Zeit*" (*EN* 197/*En* 249). But the preface also specifies, in a transparent allusion to Heidegger, that his book puts in question the *conatus essendi* of a being that "constantly preoccupied with Being itself [as conatus essendi] and its perseverance in Being" (*EN* 199/*En* 251). The preface to the German edition also specifies, now with regard to Husserl, that the book is engaged in a "phenomenology of the face" which, without placing in question the "noetico-noematic parallelism" of theoretical, affective, axiological, or volitive intentionality, is surprised to discover a "noesis that is not the measure of its noema" (*EN* 200/*En* 252).

The Levinasian reading of the history of philosophy has no other principle than the primordial phenomenon on which this phenomenology of the face is centered. To enter into this reading is in the first place to enter into the specific articulation of this phenomenon of which we already know, it is a situation marked by a potentiality exceeding actuality, and is indissociable from a relation to the other. This potentiality, or better this potentialization, is functionally relational and *situated* in the sense that it consists of electing in its unsubstitutable unicity the person it interpellates — with this interpellation being a response to an imperative emanating from someone unique in the world. The primordial phenomenon is thus a relation of "uniqueness to uniqueness" (*EN* 199/*En* 251) which as such is without mediation and which, far from synthesizing them in a middle term, placing them in symbiosis or a generic communion where they would be joined, instead separates them, as the subtitle of Levinas's first major work clearly underlines: *Essay on Exteriority*.

The terms of this relation that refuses any synthesis are the Same and the Other. The Same is at once identity and ipseity, for it is the I who is "identity par excellence, the primordial work of identification" (*TI* 36/*TeI* 6), not in the abstract sense of the tautology I = I, but as a concrete sojourn [*séjour*] in the world, a sojourn where, through "the body, the home, labor, possession, economy," there occurs a "reversion of the alterity of the world to self-identification" (*TI* 38/*TeI* 8). In short, it is the ego as the "concreteness of egoism" (*TI* 38/*TeI* 8). But what is the Other? Its alterity cannot be that of a correlate of a representation by the same, for in that way it would be immediately absorbed into the latter. It is a matter of an alterity that is neither formal nor the "simple reverse of identity," nor "resistance" to it, but is "anterior to every initiative, to all imperialism of the Same" (*TI* 38–39/ *TeI* 9), and which remains transcendent to it. In its concreteness this alterity is unique; it is that of the face, this face here, facing the Same.

The relation of uniqueness to uniqueness, of singular event to singular event, whose point of departure is the Same as it goes toward the Other, occurs in a movement that Levinas characterizes as metaphysical and transcendent, or better trans*a*scendent — movement of a desire understood not as expectation of satisfaction, but as the hollowing out of separation between desiring and desired and thus as avowal of the authority of the Other over the Same. Concretely, this relation is produced as discourse: not *apophantic* discourse that reveals, and not *hermeneutic* discourse that interprets and comprehends, but one of *apology* of the Same in the face of the interpellation emanating from the other, that is, concretely, when faced by the other who as such signifies and expresses but without this signification and this expression ever being susceptible to falling under my power, for they remain transcendent.

If such is indeed the articulation, outlined schematically, of the primordial phenomenon, it goes without saying that the phenomenology that recognizes it must accept it as its guide for reading the history of philosophy. Envisioned in strictly formal terms, this reading, because it is phenomenological, will associate reduction, construction, and deconstruction: reduction as return to the primordial phenomenon, construction as conceptualization of the articulation of this phenomenon, and deconstruction at once as the illumination of the texts of the heritage that is founded in the primordial phenomenon and as dismantling of what occults the relation of exteriority inherent to this phenomenon, either by unduly amalgamating what belongs to one term of the relation with what belongs to the other term, or by elevating to the rank of originary what, with respect to the primordial phenomenon, could only be derived.

I will attempt now to show how by the works that Levinas has privileged, his deconstructive reading of the history of philosophy keeps up a constant debate with Husserl and with Heidegger concerning the phenomenon that he considers primordial. Two names will suffice for this purpose: Plato and Descartes, to whom Levinas refers most insistently in his relation to the history of philosophy. It would not be difficult to show that a certain reappropriation of each is underway in both Husserl and in Heidegger, as I have already suggested in passing. Nonetheless, it is more with Plato than with Descartes that one may associate the Heideggerian path to fundamental ontology, since it has been possible to speak of a "Marburg Platonism" to characterize Heidegger's teaching during the period when he articulated this ontology, and since on several occasions he was able to present his own thinking by way of a literal commentary on the Platonic myth of the cave. It is, of course, more with Descartes that one must associate the course taken by Husserl, author of the *Cartesian Meditations*.

Let us begin by considering Levinas's reading of Plato. He places it under the aegis of the well-known formula *to agathon epekeina tes ousias*, which according to Levinas signifies that the Good is beyond Being. It is also under the aegis of this formula that Heidegger places his own reading of Plato, but for him it means to say that Being is beyond beings. However striking it may be, this difference of translation remains formal and empty unless it is related to the phenomenon taken to be primordial in the respective readings. The phenomenon that Heidegger considers primordial is, I have said, the comprehension of Being of which Dasein is the proper titular. Because Levinas holds that the phenomenon which Heidegger thus considers primordial is in fact derivative and secondary with respect to the relation to transcendence going from the totalizing oneself to radical and imperious alterity of the other, his reading of Plato is led to detect a certain number of signs that demolish the primordiality proposed by the Heideggerian reading.

Let us hold fast to three of them: *theory, truth,* and *discourse.* Heidegger addresses all three of these themes with a view to the question of the meaning of Being, since it is the latter, he contends, that institutes Greek philosophy. For his part, Levinas, without failing in the slightest bit to recognize the insistence of the themes of that question in the Greeks, stresses that it is also ethics that held them in suspense, under the species of a "utopian sociality that commands . . . the humanity in us" (*EN* 199/*En* 251) and that interrupts ontology.

Theory, that is, holding in view, the gaze, a Platonic theme if there is one, represents the very fabric of the myth of the cave, a revival of which is at the heart of fundamental ontology. It consists in distinguishing within the Platonic narrative the degrees of an ascent that is proper to the gaze culminating in the solitary vision of the most authentic Being, a vision from which it turns out that Being in the sense of what is available for the self and for others, and still more in the sense of Being as event of exterior facing. Theory is thus absorbed into ontology, understood as the comprehension inherent to the Same — comprehension which, according to Heidegger, forms the only permissible content of metaphysics.

Levinas, for his part, discerns in Greek *theoria* the signs of a precedence of metaphysics, understood in the sense of transcendence, over ontology. It is only on one hand that Greek *theoria* seems to impose the precedence of the same, while on the other hand it is indeed the desire for alterity that animates it. It is this very desire that animates it first of all when it lets the being [*l'étant*] to which it is related "manifest itself while respecting its alterity," and that continues to animate it when it submits its own dogmatic spontaneity (*TI* 42/*TeI* 12), to critique — by the other. And yet the primacy of the Same leads it to relate to the Other only by way of a middle term that assures its meaningfulness that it finds in itself. It is this primacy that defined Socrates' teaching: "to receive nothing of the Other but what is in me, as though from all eternity I was in possession of what comes to me from the outside" (*TI* 43/*TeI* 13–14).

Truth, alètheia, disclosure: Heidegger did not tire of examining the theme in Plato during the decade in which he developed his fundamental ontology. It is a central theme, he says, in the *Sophist,* the *Theatetus,* and the *Republic.* But it is a conflictual theme, he adds, as is announced already in the negative structure of the word *a-lètheia,* whereby it is indicated that truth is a combat between concealment and unconcealment. The combat is ontological, he contends, between the light of Being and its obscurity by beings, but more deeply between authentic Being and inauthentic Being, for once it is led to its onto-logical site — Dasein — truth is the struggle there — between the open-ness that constitutes its exclusive potential-to-be and the closure of this openness by events or possibilities that arrive from elsewhere. This combat, he says again, forms the specific content of the Platonic notion of justice, or *dike,* saying of the *Republic* that it has its model in the soul of the wise man who struggles to distinguish between what in him is authentic and what is inauthentic.

To this, Levinas replies that justice is consideration of the other, that is to say, of a being who does not cease to face me. The comprehen-sion of Being could not dominate this relation because "the latter rela-tion commands the former," and this ethical relation to the absolute exteriority of the other, far from being contrary to the truth "accom-plishes the very intention that animates movement unto truth" (*TI* 47/ *TeI* 18). The truth thus no longer has its proper site in the appercep-tion of solitary Dasein, but in separation. For that matter, it does not even have a proper site, but is a path animated by the intentionality of transcendence. And of this, Levinas sees several signs in Plato, notably in the *Phaedrus,* when it opposes to a solitary thought proceeding from "him who 'has his own head to himself'" (*TI* 49/*TeI* 20; citing *Phaedrus* 244a) the force of a desire that is received from elsewhere (*TI* 50/*TeI* 20–21). Of Platonic metaphor, Heidegger retains only, as a matter of truth, the struggle between light and shadow, and this Levinas counters with the metaphoric of separation, and an emphasis on everything in it that exceeds the limits of inner recollection privi-leged by Heidegger.

Discourse, logos, Rede. Heidegger said it often: it is proper to dis-course that it dis-covers, that is to say, assuming the exclusively onto-logical axis of his reading of the Greeks, it makes possible "arriving at the structures of Being of the beings we encounter and in speech."[2] It is because it aims at this arrival by attempting to penetrate dis-cov-ering discourse all the way to the Being of beings that ancient ontol-ogy as Plato elaborates it is "dialectical." It is remarkable that, according to this reading of the Greek *logos,* discourse is not addressed first to anyone but instead to a theme that one evokes and around which one deliberates. It is no less remarkable that, according to this reading, discourse is only the mediator of a saturating vision to which by definition the wise man accedes alone. This is why Heidegger considers it a merit of Aristotle that he leaves dialectic behind, and channels the *logos* into pure apprehension of *noein.*[3]

It is well known that it is this absorption of discourse into an ontological perspective that Heidegger in turn radicalizes when he makes of its conscience — initially empty of all ethical connotation — the ultimate instance of discourse and of apprehension, with the former of these to be understood as the call Dasein makes to itself to assume its authentic potential-to-be, and with the latter to be understood as one's instantaneous grasp of that call. As a result of this, discourse is not only monologue, but also view of self by self.

Against all of that, Levinas contends that discourse is first of all *invocation* of someone, an address to the Other [*Autrui*] as interlocutor. Now "this 'saying to the other, . . . precedes all ontology" (*TI* 48 / *TeI* 18). It likewise precedes all disclosure, for the manner in which it presents itself, called *face* [*visage*] — in Greek, *eidos,* before this word came to designate the idea offered to an intellectual view — "does not consist in figuring as a theme under my gaze" and "at each moment destroys and overflows the plastic image that it leaves me . . .: the adequate idea" (*TI* 50, 51 / *TeI* 21). It manifests itself *kath'auto.* "It expresses itself." It is certainly at Heidegger that Levinas takes aim when he writes: "The face brings a notion of truth which, against every contemporary ontology, is not the disclosure of an impersonal Neutre, but an *expression:* a being [*l'étant*] breaks through every envelop and generality of Being [*l'être*] (*TI* 51 / *TeI* 21–22). Under these conditions, one is not surprised to find Levinas restoring to the works of Plato their character as dialogues, a feature that Heidegger for his part considered to be strictly pedagogical. Levinas writes: "For Plato, true discourse came to its own assistance: the content that is presented to me is inseparable from him who has taught it — which means that the author of the discourse responds to questions. Thought, for Plato, is not reducible to an impersonal concatenation of true relations, but implies persons and interpersonal relations" (*TI* 71/*TeI* 43). This is why, beyond the solitary discourse of the soul with itself, beyond the classical concept of the *idea* as an object that is sublimated and permeable to thought, and beyond the thesis that holds society to follow from contemplation of the true — all themes that are dear to Heidegger — Levinas contends that the ideality of the Platonic idea, far from transmuting the Other into the Same points toward "a region where beings have a face, that is, are present in their own message" (*TI* 71/*TeI* 43), and is even "tantamount to . . . the transmutation of the other into the Other [*de l'autre en Autrui*]" (*TI* 71/*TeI* 43). This is also why Levinas settles Plato's debate with rhetoric on a wholly different axis than does Heidegger. The latter holds that the sole axis for the Platonic consideration of rhetoric is an approach to the view of Being, and thus that Plato sometimes rejects rhetoric as a form of attachment to pure semblance and sometimes as a pedagogical and psychological expedient of dialectic, with intention to those who have eyes only for the everyday. As opposed to this, Levinas settles these Platonic themes on the axis of the relation with the other: if philosophical discourse seeks to overcome rhetoric, this is because the discourse that remains rhetorical "approaches the Other not to face him, but obliquely," that is, it approaches the neighbor by ruse, and approaches the neighbor's freedom with violence — all of which are contrary to justice (*TI* 70/ *TeI* 42).

If one considers the Levinasian reading of Descartes, one realizes that it too is conducted as a function of the primordial phenomenon, and that there are signs of the latter in the *Meditations on First Philosophy* that support a deconstruction of Husserl's reading of that text in his own *Cartesian Meditations*, itself a text that Levinas helped translate in 1931.

Husserl retains from Descartes little more than the project of a universal science founded on an absolute basis. From the *Meditations*, in particular, Husserl is only interested in the first two, which are enough for him to salute in Descartes the premises for an *epoché* from the natural attitude and its realism, as well as the discovery of the fact that the pure ego resists this suspension so that it must be in its that the absolute basis for knowledge is to be sought. But this does not prevent Husserl from lamenting the insufficiency of Cartesian *epoché* with respect to the intentionality that he considers the primordial phenomenon. This is a matter of the persistence, after doubt, of notions, principles, and arguments still belonging to the natural attitude — the notion of substance, the principle of causality, the deductive argument — and thus of the absence of an intuitive and eidetic elucidation of transcendental immanence, which Descartes barely discovered and left unexplored.

Levinas in his turn finds in Descartes the means to contest the Cartesianism claimed by Husserl, and this on at least two points: the apodicticity of the pure ego at the very heart of doubt, and the noetico-noematic parallel universally inherent in the intentionality of this ego. What Levinas discovers in Cartesian doubt is the impossibility of escaping doubt entirely on one's own. What Husserl superbly neglected in Cartesian doubt — the iteration of the dream, descent toward the abyss, the evil genius — is precisely what testifies that "a world absolutely silent that would not come to us from speech, be it mendacious [that is, speech of the other, as evil genius], would be an-archic, without principle, without a beginning" (*TI* 90 / *TeI* 63). Levinas writes: "In the Cartesian *cogito,* taken as the first certitude (but which, for Descartes, already rests on the existence of God), there is an arbitrary halt which is not justified of itself " (*TI* 92–93 / *TeI* 65). For doubt is a movement toward an ever-deeper abyss beyond affirmation and negation.

In this vertiginous descent, "the I . . . does not find in the *cogito* itself a stopping place. It is not I, it is the other that can say *yes*. From him comes affirmation; he is at the commencement of experience. Descartes seeks a certitude and stops at the first change of level in this vertiginous descent; in fact he possesses the idea of infinity, and can gauge in advance the return of affirmation behind the negation. But to possess the idea of infinity is to have already welcomed the Other" (*TI* 93/*TeI* 66).

What Levinas retains in the Cartesian idea of infinity is precisely what resists intuitive evidence required by Husserlian Cartesianism. Let us understand this properly. To recognize this resistance does not at all mean to uproot the phenomena in order to surreptitiously attach them to an ulterior world [*un arrière-monde*] that would be their supposed cause, and still less to abandon phenomenology for theology or critique for faith. It is in relation to the sole primordial phenomenon of separation between the Same and the Other, and the transcendence of the latter toward the former, that Levinas welcomes the Cartesian idea of infinity. He writes: "This relation of the Same with the Other, where the transcendence of the relation does not cut the bonds a relation implies, yet where these bonds do not unite the Same and the Other into a Whole, is in fact fixed in the situation described by Descartes in which the 'I think' maintains with the Infinite it can nowise contain and from which it is separated a relation called the 'idea of infinity'" (*TI* 48/*TeI* 19). Husserl for his part considers this idea of infinity as nothing more than a symptom of an insufficient *epoché* which, because it is insufficient, authorizes Descartes to massively reintroduce, at the very issue of doubt, the natural attitude that a radical *epoché* would have to place in suspense. In short, the idea of infinity signifies a nonphenomenological approach to the *cogitatio,* as a substance with content whose cause is to be sought elsewhere, and not as an intentionality to be described for itself. Levinas, no less than Husserl, rejects "the Cartesian argumentation that *proves* the separated existence of the Infinite by the finitude of the being having an idea of Infinity (for there perhaps is not much sense to proving an existence by describing a situation prior to proof and to the problems of existence)" (*TI* 49/*TeI* 19–20). But in truth, it is well and good a matter of description and not of deduction concerning the relation that is, according to him, at the heart of the Cartesian idea of infinity. And this relation is well and good an intentionality, though one that is "unique in its genre" (*TI* 49/*TeI* 20), since it is a matter of an idea whose own *ideatum* transcends it and has as its content the very distance that separates it from the idea, or to put it in Husserl's terms, it is a matter of a noesis that is not the measure of its noema.

But if the Cartesian idea of infinity has its phenomenal seat in the primordial phenomenon of the ethical transcendence of the Same toward the Other, taking it into consideration brings one to contest the privilege that the fifth of Husserl's *Cartesian Meditations* grants to theoretical intentionality when it addresses the other. Regarding the stages marked in Husserl's celebrated analysis of the *Fremderfahrung*, Levinas does not fail to emphasize that they take as their guideline the objectivity of the theoretical object in view of the totalizing Same, such that what Husserl takes as a description of the initial relation to the Other "dissimulates . . . mutations of object constitution into a relation with the other — which is as primordial as the constitution from which it is to be derived" (*TI* 67/*TeI* 39). In other words, what Husserl calls the "primordial sphere" and beginning from which he describes the degrees of disclosure — living body, body similar to my own, body of an "alter ego" — correspond to only one of the terms of the relation of separation and transcendence that Levinas takes as the primordial phenomenon. Husserl's primordial sphere is a truncated primordial phenomenon since it corresponds only to the term that Levinas calls the Same, and it is persistently unaware of the fact that far from being able to disclose the other at the limit of its own field of objectivation, the Same "turns to the absolutely other [*autre*] only on call from the Other [*Autrui*]" (*TI* 67/*TeI* 39). The Other is the radical alterity of infinity that reveals itself without disclosing itself, for it

transcends the Same from all its height rather than fulfilling a disclosive intention emanating from the Same. It is this height, Levinas
liked to say, that Descartes himself meant when he wrote to Fr.
Mersenne (January 28, 1641): "I have never treated Infinity except
to submit to it" (AT 89/*AeT* 75–76).

Precisely because the phenomenon that guides it is one of radical
exteriority, Levinas's reading of the history of philosophy turns out to
be much less cavalier and more respectful of texts than the reading that
places the first masters of phenomenology on the unilateral axis of the
Same, understood as the ego from which meaning is given or as power
to exist for one's own sake [*à dessein de soi*]. It is not Levinas but those
others that one might reproach for having submitted the history of
philosophy to the prestige of the Same to the detriment of the alterity of the Other.

Because for him the primordial phenomenon is an exterior relation
of uniqueness to uniqueness, Levinas's reading of the history of philosophy can simultaneously maintain, on one hand, that western philosophy, since Socrates, "has most often been an ontology: a reduction
of the Other to the Same by interposition of a middle and neutral term
that ensures the comprehension of Being" (*TI* 43/*TeI* 13). and, on
the other hand, locate signs of a beyond of totality at the very interior
of this totalizing absorption — and these will have been present from
the beginning, since Levinas also forcefully emphasizes that it "will have
been the imperishable merit of the 'admirable Greek people' and the
very institution of philosophy" to have "substituted for the magical
communion of species and confusion of distinct orders a spiritual relation in which beings remain at their posts but communicate among
themselves" (*TI* 48/*TeI* 19).

Yet it is by virtue of the persistent return of this same primordial phenomenon that Levinas's reading of the history of philosophy, as allied in its style as it may be with the transcendental movement that animates the reading of the tradition as we find it in the two masters of phenomenology, still does not contain any trace of a teleology of the history of philosophy and still less a general philosophy of history. If the primordial phenomenon is a face-to-face relation that always has the character of an event and where each interlocutor remains at his post, the resultant ethical eschatology is functionally pluralist and irreducible to any teleology, to any system that pretends to reveal the orientation of history in its totality. "It is not the last judgment that is decisive, but the judgment of all the instants in time," where singular beings are "called upon to answer at their trial . . . and can speak rather than lending their lips to an anonymous utterance of history" (*TI* 23 / *TeI* xi).

God and Philosophy According to Levinas

Jean-Marc Narbonne

The Levinasian Critique of Philosophical "Thematism"

L et me begin with a strong affirmation on the part of Levinas, almost a condemnation of all philosophical discourse itself, such as we find in "The Trace of the Other":

> Western philosophy coincides with the unveiling of the Other in which the Other, in manifesting itself as being, loses its otherness. Philosophy has been stricken since its infancy with a horror for the Other that remains Other — an insurmountable allergy. That is why it is essentially a philosophy of being, the understanding of being its last word and the fundamental structure of man. That is also why it becomes a philosophy of immanence and autonomy, or atheism. The God of the philosophers, from Aristotle to Leibniz, including the God of the scholastics, is a god adequate to reason.[1]

Here we have an extremely harsh diagnostic that would seem to apply to all of philosophy, or to the very essence of philosophy, incapable of getting out of the circle of being in which it confines itself and thus incapable of conceiving of the exceptional figure of the divine — the strangeness of which it would spontaneously annul, in order to have

---

Translated by Michael B. Smith.

it harmonize with reason. This pronouncement is not isolated in Levinas, who underscores elsewhere that "the history of Western philosophy has been a destruction of transcendence" (*GCM* 56). Philosophy — such is its nature, such also its problem — consists essentially in a thematization or conceptualization, the effect of which is to nullify the difference between the subject and the object, between the thinker and what is thought. The concept subsumes, homogenates, integrates the diverse, reducing it to the identical. Through thought, the real and being are made accessible and adequate to us.[2]

Moreover, the ideas of mastery and of being go hand in hand according to Levinas, since being is itself presented by the philosophical tradition as incapable of being overthrown, surpassed or circumscribed — in short, as a grip nothing can escape. "The philosophy passed down to us . . . makes all significance, all rationality, go back to being, to the 'exploits' of being carried out by beings in that they affirm themselves as being, to being *qua* being, to the *be*ing of being" (*GCM* 111–12), in which the "–ing" [the "a" of "*essance*"] evokes for Levinas the verbal aspect of being. As an all-encompassing absolute, being cannot let anything be expressed other than itself, its "undethronable royalty," as it may be called, would thus be "stronger than that of the gods" (*OB* 4).[3] In a surreptitious echo of the Aristotelian precept according to which "not to philosophize is still to philosophize," Levinas notes that "the philosophical discourse of the West claims for itself the amplitude of an all-inclusiveness or ultimate comprehension. It compels every other discourse to justify itself before philosophy" (*GCM* 55).[4] Now, to justify oneself before philosophy cannot mean anything other than to specify one's being, that is, to show oneself as one "is," — in short, to display clearly at what level one's obligatory appurtenance to *esse* is situated. God, if God has any meaning, can only have an *ontological* one, and therefore cannot "be" differently from that being the philosopher already knows and has dealings with. In a word, either God is not otherwise than being, that is, otherwise than being itself already "is," or else God absolutely is not, and is no more than nothingness. As Levinas proposes, "philosophical discourse must then be able to

include God — of whom the Bible speaks — if indeed God has a meaning. But, once thought, this God is immediately situated within the
domain of the 'exploits of being,' He is situated there as *being* [*étant*]
par excellence" (*GCM* 56).

All difference would thus be essentially *ontological difference,* understood as a difference *of* being or a difference *in* being, whether the latter takes the form of a gap between one being and another, or being
taken abstractly in relation either to all beings taken together or to one
being. This verb *to be,* "too lightly dubbed auxiliary" (*GCM* 43),
would in fact be the most weighty and oppressive of all. Now to reduce
all questioning to the common denominator of being — as we are
prompted, or even forced to do by the philosophical discourse on (the
being of) God — means, for Levinas, to let oneself be led in an endless circle, since being itself, which is perfectly polysemic, of unlimited
extension, gives no purchase for thought to grasp into, and is in fact
the absolutely Neutral. Being, as Levinas observes, "is without response.
The direction in which that response would have to be sought is
absolutely impossible to envisage" (*EE* 9). The difficulty encountered
here is not accidental but involves the character of *esse* itself, to which
no intelligible content can be assigned. Let us attempt to circumscribe
more closely the difficulty we face, which forms one of the crucial points
in Levinas's thought.

If the divine is to have any meaning, this meaning will inevitably be
able to impose itself only *beyond, otherwise than,* or *at a distance from*
that which renders the divine common to all things, that which inexorably collapses it onto the level of the *explicandi* and dilutes it, so to
speak, into the very element for which it is supposed to give an accounting. It is by its difference from being, by its enfranchisement and het-
erogeneity with respect to being, a difference that cannot (and this is
precisely the point) be reduced to a difference *of* being, that is, to a
difference subject to being — that God can claim unconditionality and
perfect absoluteness, and thus some form of explicative power. Either
God "is," and cannot furnish a reasoned account of being, or God can
furnish such an account, but it is because the primacy we have just

attributed to being yields to a higher sublimity *that can no longer be expressed in terms of being*, that is unrelated to and incommensurable with it. The difference between the divine and being has meaning only as "différance", that is, as irreducible difference from being, or else it fails in its ambition as radical explanation. At this point, all hope of thematization disappears definitively, since such a diff*er*ance is precisely that which cannot be a part of any concept or set of concepts what-soever. Now, in the absence of any thematization or conceptualization, *how* can we continue to speak of God *philosophically?*

But also, conversely, we can better understand Levinas's anxious, disturbed look at being, which is the very incarnation of the *faceless*, the impersonal, the eternally identical to itself: perfectly flat, useless, meaningless, a blind alley, dubbed by Levinas the *there is* [*il y a*]. Thus he writes:

> This impersonal, anonymous, yet inextinguishable "consumption" of being, which murmurs in the depths of nothingness itself we shall des-ignate by the term *there is*. The *there is*, inasmuch as it resists a personal form, is "being in general." We have not derived this notion from exte-rior things or the inner world — from any "being" whatever. For *there is* transcends inwardness as well as exteriority; it does not even make it possible to distinguish between these. . . . *There is*, in general, without it mattering what there is, without our being able to affix a substantive to this term. *There is* is an impersonal form, as in it is raining, or it is warm. An essential anonymity. (*EE* 52, 53)

The impersonal formula *there is* thus highlights the essential neu-trality of being itself, its characteristic anonymity. That is why "rather than to God, the notion of the *there is* leads us back to the absence of God, to the absence of all beings [*tout étant*]" (*EE* 56). That is also why, since "being rejects all specification and specifies nothing" (*EE* 2), the desire to limit ourselves to being, which in principle *contains every-thing*, comes to a dead end, and in reality leads out onto nothingness. The verb of verbs is the bearer of no particular message, the augur of nothing that can be defined. Hence the realization of the necessity of a *nonontological* way out of ontology, which domain is shown to be paradoxically reductive.

> The problem that is posed, consequently, and that shall be our own, consists in asking ourselves whether meaning [*le sens*] is equivalent to the *esse* of being; that is, whether the meaning that, in philosophy, is meaning, is not already a restriction of meaning; whether it is not already a derivation or a drifting away from meaning; whether the meaning equivalent to essence — the exploits of being, being *qua* being — is not already approached in the presence that is the time of the Same. This hypothesis can only be justified by the possibility of going back, starting from this presumptively conditioned meaning, to a meaning that would no longer express itself in terms of being, nor in terms of beings. (*GCM* 57)

In other words, Levinas's idea would be to put in play, or rather to *put back in play*, to *reactivate*, beyond the invading irruption of rationality of the philosophical type, a rationality of a different type.

> A different — or more profound — rationality, and one that will not allow itself to be led into the adventure that, from Aristotle to Heidegger, was embarked upon by theology's remaining a thought of Identity and Being, and that proved fatal to God and to the man of the Bible, or their homonyms. (*GCM* 106–07)

In Levinas, the thought of being thus characterized serves, of course, to reprove the "thematism" that mars philosophical discourse in general, but it aims more directly at the denunciation of the *ontologism* characteristic of Martin Heidegger, who, perhaps more than any other philosopher, attempted to tie his reflection to the problematic of being, and who — again, more than any other — is attached to what Levinas calls the *amphibology* of being and beings.

Levinas, tirelessly and before many others, with a mixture of admiration and bitterness,[5] denounced what seemed to him the most troubling aspects of Heidegger's thought. Moreover, he frankly states his desire to break away from the latter's neutrality. Thus he writes at the end of *Totality and Infinity:*

We have thus the conviction of having broken with the philosophy of the Neutral: with the Heideggerian Being of the existent whose impersonal neutrality the critical work of Blanchot has so much contributed to bring out, with Hegel's impersonal reason, which shows to personal consciousness only its ruses. The movements of ideas of the philosophy of the Neutral, so varied in their origins and their influences, agree in announcing the end of philosophy. For they exalt the obedience no face commands. (*TI* 298)

Gradually we come to the necessity of moving on to a "thought more thoughtful than the thought of being" (*GCN* 121), intended here in the sense of the thought of the Becalmed (*Étale*), the Same, the Identical. A thought that can truly be an exception to the indifferent regimen of being, a regimen of the *no why*, and thus rise in opposition to "an ontology of the Neutral, an ontology without morals" (*EI* 90), dominated by the sole question of the deployment of beings and their *persevering* in being, oikeiōsis and *conatus*. Hence this pressing question.

Is being its own reason for being; the alpha and omega of intelligibility, first philosophy and eschatology? Would not the "coming to pass" of being that comes to pass continue along, to the contrary, while at the same time demanding a justification, or posing a question preceding every question? (*GCM* 152)

Thus the question preceding all questions would ask, not *What is being*, by which some contend that all things began, but rather *for whom* or *for what* [is there] being, in the same way that people sometimes ask *What is the meaning of life:* "It is a question of the meaning of being: not the ontological meaning of the comprehension of this extraordinary verb, but the ethical meaning of the justice of being" (*GCM* 171). If being is understood as that which unfolds inexorably in power and enters into the domain of effectuality, to the exclusion of legitimacy, the question of the right *to* power, of what is right *in* being, immediately exceeds the limits of ontology per se, and opens up a break in the direction not simply of a *beyond* of being that would be understood as a surplus of being, but an *otherwise than* being.

In such a framework, God would no longer be expressed through ontology but obligation. God would stand in contrast with being, with its calculations and its inflexibility. Hence, once again, doubt is cast on the ability of philosophy itself to be all-embracing.

> The intelligibility of transcendence is not ontological. The transcendence of God can neither be said nor thought in terms of being, philosophy's element, behind which philosophy sees only night. (*GCM* 77)

Levinas then goes so far as to speak of a "break between philosophical intelligibility and what is beyond being" (*GCM* 77), the dimension of the beyond requiring a *signifying* of another type than the signification connected with the conceptual *logos*. In other words, this means that there would be a radical *heteronomy* between, on the one hand, absolutizing the difference between being and entities — where being has the value of an anonymous factor (Heidegger) — and on the other hand, absolutizing a (divine) *différance* in relation at once to being and to all entities (Levinas). The idea of heteronomy, then, introduces here a difference of order or of nature between what relates to being *qua* given and what rises to the level of that which is presupposed by the latter. As Levinas specifies, "The statement of being's *other*, of the otherwise than being, claims to state a difference over and beyond that which separates being from nothingness — the very difference of the *beyond,* the difference of transcendence" (*OB* 3).

The difference of transcendence is announced, therefore, as that through which *meaning* imposes its hegemony and precedence on *essence* itself. It is on the basis of that *de facto* hegemony and precedence — even if it is not always recognized by philosophy as such — that Levinas can maintain that it is ethics that is first philosophy; that if there must be first philosophy, in other words, if the *first* must be *philosophical,* this first cannot be authorized otherwise than on the basis of the question of the *should-be* or the *right-to-be,* that is, on the basis of the question *prior to* all questions, an interlocutory question capable of rescinding all the others.

If first philosophy "is an ethics" (*EI 77*), it is because it is led to question being according to a plan that can no longer be ontological, or, to borrow an expression coined by Levinas, because it proceeds from a *dis-inter-estedness*, that is, from a positive exiting from being and its orbit.

> This is what is meant by the title of the book: *Otherwise than Being.* The ontological condition undoes itself, or is undone, in the human condition or un-condition. To be human means to live as if one were not a being among beings. As if, through human spirituality, the categories of being were inverted into an "otherwise than being." Not only into a "being otherwise"; being otherwise is still being. The "otherwise than being," in truth, has no verb which would designate the event of its un-rest, its dis-inter-*estedness*, the putting-into-question of this being — or this *estedness* — of beings. (*EI* 100)

Now according to Levinas philosophy has constantly restricted itself to the totality formed by being, the modulations and types of which it has undertaken to map out, without being overly concerned about the emergence of that which, despite the polysemy of being and doubtless blinded by it, in truth broke definitively with that manifold. Whence, of course, in Levinas, the antithesis of the *totality* (of being) and the irreducible *infinite* of that totality.

If, as Levinas maintains, "the glory of God" consists precisely in "the otherwise-than-being" (*EI* 109), does it not follow that *the philosophy that speaks being* can no longer speak of God, and has in fact never been able to speak of God (an extreme accusation indeed), and that the discourse on the glory of God, if it is even possible, must take its lead from an *otherwise than philosophize?*

FROM THE *BEYOND* BEING TO THE *OTHERWISE-THAN-BEING*: A NEW ISSUE FOR THOUGHT?

It is quite obvious that the *otherwise than philosophize* is already in itself an event that belongs to philosophy, to the extent that the latter has not in fact restricted itself — as Levinas himself concedes — to a discourse on being, but has rather recorded its own over-extension. There is, consequently, an *otherwise than philosophize* that is *philosophical.* Where is it located? In several philosophical *loci,* but for Levinas primarily in Plato, and let us say in Platonism as such (I include here Neoplatonism, especially that of Plotinus, whom Levinas cites on several occasions). Its major irruption, in Plato, as we know, coincides with the appearance of the Idea of the Transcendent Good in the *Republic* 6.509b. In *Totality and Infinity,* we find:

> One of the ways of Greek metaphysics consisted in seeking the return to and the fusion with Unity. But Greek metaphysics conceived the Good as separate from the totality of essence, and in this way (without any contribution from an alleged Oriental thought) it caught sight of a structure such that the totality could admit of a beyond. The Good is Good *in itself* and not in relation to the need to which it is wanting; it is a luxury with respect to needs. It is precisely in this that it is beyond being. . . . The Place of the Good above all essence is the most profound teaching, the definitive teaching, not of theology, but of philosophy. (*TI* 102–03)

A "structure such that the totality could admit of a beyond," an admirable phrase, and one that illustrates magnificently the heart of the Levinasian message. When all is supposedly said and done, a supplement, evasive and incomprehensible, is yet added. As Levinas puts it:

> For the idea of totality, in which ontological philosophy veritably reunites — or comprehends — the multiple, there must be substituted the idea of a separation resistant to synthesis. (*TI* 293)

That "separation resistant to synthesis," that beyond separated and as if counter-distinguished from the totality — Levinas believes he can find it in Plato himself, who, contrary to the prevailing philosophical tradition which was chiefly "a destruction of transcendence" (*GCM* 56), preserved its requirement in his work.[6] Moreover, it is interesting to note that Levinas, on several occasions, spontaneously refers to Plotinus in this context. It is not just Plato, it is Plato in his Neoplatonic filiation — or more specifically his Plotinian one — that grants us access to a dimension of reality generally obfuscated in the history of philosophy. Here is one example.

> Must we not consequently think that the comprehension of being is not the most intimate work of thought and that it does not lead us toward the ultimate secret of subjectivity? In agreement with Plato and Plotinus, who dared to pose, against all good sense, something beyond being, is not the idea of being younger than that of the infinite? Should we not concede that philosophy cannot confine itself to the primacy of ontology.[7]

So it is that particularly in Plotinus, the One is not only excepted from the field of being properly so called, but neither does it belong to the "something" (*ti*), a category too ontologically determined and defined to be suitable to the ineffable and uncircumscribable *aperileptōi*. The one is consequently "before the something" *pro tou ti*, that is, *beyond* what the most general and the most indefinite verbal category of the Greek language — as well as our own — gives access to. The One is thus a "non-something" subsisting beyond all possible thinghood, a manner of *idea*, to take up Levinas's expression, to which no *ideatum* corresponds, and before which the mind remains marked with a definitive inadequation. Again, one might say that the One is a *rupture of intelligibility* for a system in which the adequation of self with self is of prime importance; in which thought takes delight in the contemplation of its own objects of thought.

To this will, common to both Neoplatonism and Levinas, to transcend ontology as such, we must nevertheless add, in the case of Levinas, a new characteristic that modifies in certain respects the properly Neoplatonic — or even Greek — issue originally at stake. That is the idea that the beyond being should be understood in an *ethical manner*, and that the economy of the Good as a properly ethical economy is different or even *opposed* as such to the economy of Being. We have here an original formulation, the equivalent of which I find in neither Plato nor any of the ancient Neoplatonists, for whom the Good does indeed eventually surpass ontology (or at least a certain determined conception of being), but without ever challenging its legitimacy or intrinsic value at its own level. The idea of an *opposition* between the order of being and that of the Good is not found in them, for the following reason: the Good is conceived as a reflection or trace of being, and cannot nullify the effects of the latter, even if it may at times moderate them. The order of the *beyond being* is not substituted in the Neoplatonic tradition for the *order of being*, as if ethics were in some way "at odds with ontology,"⁸ but rather crowns and improves it without opposing it.

Is it the same in Levinas? Does being still bear the imprint of the Good of which it is the result? Or has it suddenly lost all virtue? Are we dealing with a new type of Manichaeism in which being would appear as the locus of the annulment or eradication of the Good, rather that of its dispensation? Put differently, are the Good and calculation as diametrically opposed as it is claimed here? Moreover, what is the meaning in Levinas of the *nonontological ethical surplus* introduced by the Good? Does it refer to a transcendent mode of existence, a kind of *super-being*, a *surreal* or a hypostasis that is superior to being, as the references to the Platonic *epekeina,* the Plotinian One, and the Cartesian Infinite might perhaps lead one to suspect? And if not, how can Levinas draw his argument from a "beyond" that is derived from a philosophical reflection the nature of which is not particularly ethical but ontological, or, if you will, super-ontological, in order to show specifically that the beyond can have no other meaning but that of an *ethical beyond?* Thus we see that while Levinas's thought seems somehow *structured like a (Neo)platonism,* relying on its double architectonics to express itself, it cannot or does not think it should remain (Neo)platonic. This is a divergence that requires further explanation.

THE NEOPLATONIC VERSUS THE LEVINASIAN RUPTURE

In Levinas, the status of philosophy remains ambiguous. On one hand, since philosophy is riveted to being, it remains totalizing and "thematizing." Fundamentally rebellious toward otherness, it nullifies, by thematization, what transcends it, and integrates it as object into its endogenous economy. Yet on the other hand, as we have seen, it is the philosophers who bring us "the enigmatic message of the beyond being,"[9] and Levinas himself curiously conceives of his undertaking as a means of "returning to Platonism in a new way."[10] What does this mean? What connection can be established between the *(Neo)platonic beyond* and the *Levinasian beyond*?

.The fact that the principle of the Platonists, the Good, the One or the Ineffable, marks a manner of rupture in the order of reality and thought is undeniable. That is even one of the main points of controversy between Platonists and Aristotelians. In one sense, the rupture might be termed *entitative:* the principle is not of the same nature as that of which it is the principle. Moreover, that is why it is said to be beyond being. It does not belong to the same order as the one it governs. Whence the famous Neoplatonic axiom according to which the One gives what it does not have, in the sense that it is not a part of the network (of being) that it makes possible. One cannot, obviously, speak of an onto- logical rupture *stricto sensu,* since the Principle transcends the level of ontology. One should rather speak of a rupture *in relation to* ontol- ogy. In another sense, the rupture is of a cognitive order. The princi- ple can no longer be grasped by thought, because it is not itself of the order of thought. A certain amount of irrationalism, or shall we say of a-rationalism, is introduced at the level of the principle.

These two caesuras are important philosophically speaking, in that they involve a manner of self-limitation of thought, based on an objec- tive criterion: the irreducible difference between the term of origin and those derived from it. Nevertheless, this extreme point is not — no more in Plotinus than in Proclus — the resource or domain of a new order of things. Neither Plotinus nor Proclus introduce a heterony- mous *motive for action* of the principle in relation to that of subaltern realities, let alone an extraneous *manner of action.* From this point of view, the series remains indubitably continuous and the principle takes its place naturally atop the edifice it commands. In this sense, the One is therefore more a *respondent* (of the existence of being) than a *response* (to the meaning of being), and the Neoplatonic conviction holds that a *respondent* must itself *be otherwise* than that for which it is responsible.

On this point, Levinas's language differs, and is, moreover, not without terminological fastidiousness. *Otherwise than being*, he notes, is not simply *being otherwise*, for "being otherwise is still being," whereas *otherwise than being* is understood as designating that which attempts to free itself from the ontological condition itself, whatever the latter's more particular form may be (*EI* 100). Now what is specific to the Neoplatonic One is precisely *to be otherwise*, and not to pretend to an *otherwise than being*. This is the distinction that could be made between an *epekeina* of *transcendence* and an *epekeina* of *destitution*.[11] The philosophy Levinas favors is that of the epekeina *by* transcendence (Plato, Plotinus, etc.), but the one he strives toward is an epekeina of destitution. True, in both cases being is given second place, but in the first case it is the better to *explain* it factually, in the second the better to *justify* it axiologically, and, to a certain extent, to *relieve* it of its exorbitant authority. It is in this sense that Levinas would avoid a grave misunderstanding: to speak of otherwise than being is not simply to rectify one ontology by another.

> The reduction, the going back to the hither side of being, to the hither side of the said, in which being shows itself, in which the *eon* is hypostatized, could nowise mean a rectification of one ontology by another, the passage from some apparent world to a more real world. . . . The hither side of or the beyond being is not a being on the hither side of or beyond being. (*OB* 45)

That last formulation is the opposite of the Neoplatonic model which is characterized precisely by the establishment, at each extremity of the metaphysical system, of an "entity" distinct from that of the being situated in the middle. Now, Levinas does not want to limit himself to this *corrective* model of ontology. He uses the beyond being as a springboard to reach an otherwise than Greek being. The transcendence that he glimpses is of a different complexion. However, the Neoplatonic being otherwise is already sufficient — and this is part of its interest for Levinas — to counter some of Heidegger's objections concerning Greek metaphysics. In other words, the (Neo)platonic epekeina, in Levinas's mind, already constitutes an incipient invalidation of that Heideggerian reading of the Greek tradition that Levinas himself is struggling against, which his argument regarding the concept of *otherwise than being* will deepen and complete.[12] Yet Levinas does not simply aspire to a new or more lofty land, but to a different dimension, which is that of the ethics of responsibility for the other, a dimension into which Platonism and Neoplatonism can no longer lead him with as much certainty.

THE ARGUMENT FROM GREAT AGE

One way this can be observed, among others, is in Levinas's recourse to what I will call the *argument from great age*. For this latter, the order of being is not only, as in Neoplatonism, the order of what is henceforth demoted to second place, but it is also the order of what must be *corrected,* the order upon which a new order must be superimposed and which is no longer *ontological* but *ethical*.

The argument from great age is already adumbrated in Plato and in the Neoplatonic tradition. In Plato, especially in the famous passage from the *Republic* 6.509b, in which the Good, posited as beyond the *ousia*, is said to surpass the latter "in age (*presbeia*) and power (*dunamei*)." The first meaning of *presbeia* is in fact not *majesty* (which is in a way derived from it, and which is usually used to translate the Greek term in this passage), but *great age* properly so called. That idea recurs in a somewhat different form in *Philebus* (64e) and reappears in *Laws* (10.896c–d). The argument is taken up again by Plotinus in connection with the relationship between the Good and the Beautiful — the Beautiful being said to be younger (neōteron), and the Good older (presbuteron), not temporally, but by reason of truth and the anteriority of power.[13]

Great age is then here an eminence of truth and power and not a chronological anteriority. It is, let us say, an existential or entitative eminence. The Good is more ancient in that sense, as more powerful and truer than the Beautiful. But in Levinas, *great age* truly opens up other perspectives. In *Of God Who Comes to Mind*, for example, he writes:

> The placing in us of an unencompassable idea [i.e. the Infinite, in reference to Descartes] overturns this presence to self which is consciousness; it thus forces through the barrier and the checkpoint, evading the obligation to accept or adopt all that enters in from without. It is thus an idea signifying with a signifyingness *prior* to presence, to all presence, *prior* to any origin in consciousness. (*GCM* 64; emphasis added)

Or again:

> In the human, there is an intelligibility *older* than what is manifested as a comprehension of being, embracable and thus constitutable by consciousness, and which reigns as world. (*GCM* 121; emphasis added)

And also:

> That a human spirituality might be possible which does not begin in knowledge, or in the psyche as experience, and that the relation to the you in its purity be the relation to the invisible God, is no doubt a new view on the human psyche. . . . Yet this is also very important for the orientation of theology: the God of prayer, of invocation, would be *more ancient* than the God deduced from the world or from some sort of *a priori* radiance and stated in an indicative proposition. (*GCM* 148: emphasis added)

Anteriority in relation to consciousness, *anteriority* in relation to presence and to *esse*, but that could nonetheless be retrieved in the form of a *trace*, *anteriority* also of the God of prayer: we recognize here some of the recurrent themes of Levinasian philosophy, as opposed to "philosophy" *simpliciter*. But there is still nothing here so very far from the Neoplatonic *epekeina* itself, except perhaps the insistence on the kind of signifying implied in that great age, which we must now examine. In Levinas's preface to the second edition of *Existence & Existents*, the signifying that is in fact implied by that anteriority is described as follows:

To catch a glimpse in the "existent," in the human "being" [*étant*], and in what Heidegger will call "the being of beings [*étantité de l'étant*], not a concealment and "dissimulation" of being, but a step toward the Good and toward the relation to God, and, in the relation between beings, something other than a "declining metaphysics" [*métaphysique finissante*] — this does not mean that we simply invert the terms of the famous Heideggerian difference, favoring beings [*l'étant*] over being [*étantité*]. This overturning is but the first step in a movement that, opening onto *an ethics older than ontology*, will allow the signifying of meanings from beyond the ontological difference, which is doubtless in the final analysis the very meaning of the Infinite. That is the philosophical approach leading from *Totality and Infinity* to *Otherwise than Being*.[14]

In this text of exceptional richness, Levinas condenses in a few lines the elements of research that constitute the essence of his philosophical approach. First it is established that the research on the subject of the existent [*étant*], as a movement toward the Good and the divine, is a preparatory step toward an ethical interrogation always necessarily *prior* to the ontological. Now the existent who moves toward the Good is obviously none other than the human individual, whose existence [*étantité*] cannot — and this is Levinas's constant and categorical refusal — be banalized, as when concealed by or submitted to a higher determination that would then have to be sounded for its inner content. Next, since the human being opens onto the Good, this implies that the Platonic *epekeina* is already inscribed here below in the sensible human face, well before having to be traced in some *external* entity. Further, this inscription of the transcendent beyond *in the sensible* is not simply univocal, in the sense of an opening of the individual taken each time in isolation in relation to some beyond, but plurivocal, that is, inscribed primarily in the various ties that bind beings [*étants*] to one another. Indeed, the human face as a privileged *locus* of ethics, but especially that of the other person, the one who meets and responds to my look. These two things taken together confirm the essentially ethical character of the beyond of ontology in question, in a meontology of a different nature from the one inaugurated by the Platonic or Neoplatonic *super-being*.

Furthermore, Levinas does not waver on this point: transcendence is not simply the affair of another world, but lives *here below*, in the tie of responsibility for the other.

> We think that the idea-of-the-infinite-in-me — or my relation to God — comes to me in the concreteness of my relation to the other man, in the sociality which is my responsibility for the neighbor. (*GCM* xiv)

In one of those lapidary formulas for which he has the secret, Levinas will condense elsewhere all this teaching in noting: "All the negative attributes that enunciate the beyond essence become positivity in responsibility" (*OB* 12). The beyond exercises therefore already, and even eminently, its attraction in the positivity of the neighbor. The beyond is more enigmatic and stronger here than there. A Platonism not *over-turned*, but certainly *lowered*, that is, played out again at a lower level.

That is what *Totality and Infinity* already taught us: "The Other remains infinitely transcendent, infinitely foreign" (*TI* 194) or yet again, "The idea of infinity, the infinitely more contained in the less, is concretely produced in the form of a relation with the face" (*TI* 196). Once again invoking the theme of great age, this time in relation to the Cartesian infinite — "its *anteriority* to all finite thought" (*TI* 197; emphasis added) — Levinas articulates the elements of a singular *transcendence through immanence* of which the human face, its sole epiphany, supports and justifies by itself alone the entire structure:

> The infinite paralyses power by its infinite resistance to murder, which, firm and insurmountable, shines in the face of the Other, in the total nudity of the defenseless eyes, in the nudity of the absolute openness of the Transcendent. There is here a relation not with a very great resistance, but with something absolutely *Other*: the resistance of what has no resistance — the ethical resistance. (*TI* 199)

One can, then, always discuss, argue about, quarrel at will over the being [*étantité*] of the divine — in short, play the endless Game (*Spiel*) of being and its scintillations, but the demand for justice instituted by the face of the other suddenly leaves destitute all the tangled exploits of being.

If ontology — the comprehension, the embracing of Being — is impossible, it is not because every definition of Being already presupposes the knowledge of Being, as Pascal has said and Heidegger refutes in the first pages of *Being and Time;* it is because the comprehension of Being in general cannot *dominate* the relationship with the Other. The latter commands former. (*TI* 47)

Thus we observe that the *great age* that Levinas brings into play against being's own Play stands in truth in a relation of homonymy with the great age evoked by Plato and Plotinus. It undergoes a *metabasis eis allo genos,* a "change of genus," as Aristotle would say,[15] unequaled in the Greek arena, which also explains how the philosophy of being, the ontology of the simple *fact of being,* deaf to any other voice and especially to the *right to be,* can come to embody for Levinas — a terrible sentence — *a philosophy of injustice.* He writes, "A philosophy of power, ontology is, as first philosophy which does not call into question the same, a philosophy of injustice" (*TI* 46). Thus Levinas insists on the absence of "play" in what he himself intends.

> Nothing is more grave, more august, than responsibility, responsibility for the other, and saying, in which there is no play, has a gravity more grave than its own being or not being. (*OB* 46)

CONCLUSION

What is brought out from the preceding is that Levinas seeks in Greek philosophy the resources for a primacy that is no longer that of the Greeks. *Beyond being* becomes an *otherwise than according to the mode of being.* This otherwise is *ethics,* irreducible to being, based entirely on something that is in a sense an exception, a hole in being, namely the other as face. But the otherwise-than-according-to-Greece also has another dimension. It is a destitution of the privilege of *autarkeia,* of anamnesis, of knowledge — in short, of all that comes from the self as basis, since the other is an exception to my knowledge, to my ideal of mastery. Whence in Levinas the privilege of *humanism of the other man* over *humanism of oneself* or of *the self.* And God, and theology in all this? That too, for Levinas, derives its meaning from my meeting with the other, which is that through which *God occurs to me.*

> When I speak of the other I use the term "face." The "face" is what is behind the façade and beneath the facial expressions we put on: the mortality of our neighbor. In order to see, to know the "face," we must already look directly into the other's gaze. The "face" in its nakedness is the weakness of a unique being exposed to death, but at the same time the utterance of an imperative that obliges me not to leave him or her alone. That obligation is the first word of God.[16]

The classical ontological beyond, or if you will, the *topos*, that is, that which is immediately understood as a relation to a certain *outside* — Levinas sets this aside. The beyond is ethical, or nothing at all. The tip of being is not at the periphery of being, like the prime-mover God of Aristotle, situated at the periphery of the world; the tip of being, the surpassing of being, is on the contrary this *hole*[17] in being, this *hole* or this a*narchy*[18] instituted by the other that breaks the enchainment to the *There is* of being.

> It is through the Other that newness signifies, in being, the *otherwise than being*. Without the proximity of the other in his or her face, everything is absorbed, gets bogged down, walled into being, goes in the same direction; everything forms a whole, absorbing the very subject to which it is disclosed. (*OB* 182)

> *For it remains incomprehensible to me that another concerns me:* "Who is Hecuba to me?" Stated otherwise, "Am I my brother's keeper?" Such questions are incomprehensible within being. (*GDT* 175)

When Levinas declares, "For me, theology begins in the face of the neighbor. The divinity of God is played out in the human. God descends in the 'face' of the other,"[19] the "otherwise" in question re*acts* at once *to* being and *to* what is Greek. Now, we know that for Levinas the Greeks, too, can sometimes be "biblical,"[20] and Plato especially among the Greeks. How can we establish this? The task cannot be undertaken in detail here. But I will retain a statement that as far as I know Levinas does not quote, but that allows us a glimpse, within the

Platonic science, of something of the Levinasian concern for moral primacy, for ethics as first philosophy. On the substantive issue, I do in fact believe Levinas would not have found much to take exception to in the Platonic assertion from *Charmides:*

> What makes up happiness is neither a life of knowledge in general, nor all the other sciences, but one science only: that which has as its object good and evil.[21]

The Role of Lurianic Kabbalah in the Early Philosophy of Emmanuel Levinas

Jacob Meskin

I n 1982 the American philosopher and Levinas scholar Edith Wyschogrod conducted an interview with Emmanuel Levinas, the transcript of which she published seven years later. Early in the interview, Wyschogrod proposed to Levinas that his philosophy constituted a radical break with western theological tradition because it started not with a Parmenidean ontological plenitude, but rather with the God of the Hebrew Bible. The God Levinas began with, according to Wyschogrod, was an indigent God, a hidden God who commands that there be a world apart from God, because God needs the multiplicity of the world in order for there to be justice. Levinas responds to this proposal:

> That's quite right. Justice, I call it responsibility for the other, right? There is even in *Totality and Infinity*, the evocation of the *tzimtzum* [the idea in kabbalistic writings of the self-contraction of God in order to create the void in which creation can take place], but I won't venture into that.[1]

An intriguing remark, no doubt, but what does the phrase "evocation of the *tzimtzum*" mean exactly? Does this reply of Levinas's say anything about the nature of other work? In short, is Levinas telling us something important here, and if so, what is it?

Before addressing these questions, it is worth noting that with the Hebrew term *tzimtzum* Levinas is invoking one of the most original and influential ideas found in the writings of the famous Jewish mystic Rabbi Isaac Luria (1534–72), also known as Ha Ari, "the Lion." R. Luria's life and work inspired both an enduring revitalization of kabbalistic tradition and a truly vast, daringly imaginative, and dauntingly intricate mystical literature. While there is obviously far more to this literature than tzimtzum, the idea of God's initial act of self-withdrawal in order to, as it were, "make room for" existence different from and independent of God, certainly bears extensive implications for the Jewish mystical understanding of creation, human nature, the cosmos, and redemption.[2] It is, in addition, an idea that has long captivated the religious and philosophical imagination of Jew and non-Jew alike. Historians of western philosophy and theology have noted the surprising presence of Lurianic tzimtzum in the works of such figures as Boehme, Schelling, and Rosenzweig among others.[3] However, the concept of tzimtzum that figured in the works of these thinkers had been, for the most part, extracted both from its original context in Lurianic texts, and from the extensive speculation on tzimtzum of later Jewish mystics who came after R. Luria.[4]

To return to the questions posed above, then, one answer might be that in this interview more than 20 years after publishing *Totality and Infinity* in 1961, Levinas was in fact revealing to his readers a less than obvious, extra-philosophical source of inspiration on which he drew in composing that early masterwork. Perhaps, on the other hand, he had learned something about the Kabbalah in those intervening 20 years, and so had come after the fact to see some sort of loose affinity between his earlier philosophical approach and the Lurianic concept of tzimtzum. Perhaps on the third hand, as both philosophers and talmudists like to say, Levinas was simply enjoying an elevated intellectual conversation, and so seized an opportunity to suggest a comparison at once playful and fascinating, but with no real textual roots.

Without denying that Levinas was invariably charming in his interviews, I will nonetheless argue in this paper that the first possibility is closest to the truth. In other words, I will be claiming that Levinas actually had some knowledge of Kabbalah, in particular of Lurianic Kabbalah, when he sat down to write *Totality and Infinity* and, even more importantly, that we can find certain Lurianic notions *at work* in this classic of twentieth century philosophy. Moreover, I will identify a unique historical pathway through which Levinas may have acquired this knowledge, one very different from the usual pathway through which western philosophers have in the past gained whatever, largely decontextualized knowledge of Lurianic Kabbalah they may have possessed. This sort of twofold claim, namely that Levinas both knew something about Lurianic Kabbalah and put this knowledge to concrete use in his philosophical argumentation has not, to the best of my knowledge, been advanced before. Indeed scholars have not, for the most part, devoted a great deal of attention to the general question of kabbalistic influences in Levinas's work.[5] As we are about to see, the present claim is one that scholars in several fields are likely to find quite controversial.

For starters, there is the matter of Lurianic Kabbalah itself. Given its markedly esoteric character, and the sheer number of kabbalistic thinkers and adepts over the past 500 years who have continued to develop R. Luria's insights and practices, scholars and perhaps even initiates must venture into its truly labyrinthine depths with justified trepidation. For example, some of the most significant recent secondary work in Lurianic Kabbalah has focused on trying to untangle the immensely confusing compositional history and divergent strata of the "original" texts circulating under R. Luria's name, a *sine qua non* without which it is difficult to trace the historical flow of Lurianic texts and ideas.[6] It follows from this that claims invoking the presence (in any sense) of this multifarious and more or less esoteric body of texts will need, at the very least, considerable clarification and specificity.

Secondly and perhaps even more crucially, there is the surprising assertion that Lurianic Kabbalah played a role in the *philosophical* writings
of Emmanuel Levinas. It might well seem far more appropriate to inves-
tigate the role of such traditional Judaic mystical materials (if any) in
Levinas's *Jewish apologetic* writings, rather than in his philosophical ones.
Not only do the philosophical texts feature few references to things
Jewish, they also hew fairly strictly to the traditions and conventions
of modern philosophy, producing a thematic coherence and carefully
shaped, overarching argument utterly unlike the visionary hermeneutic and ritual texts in the Lurianic canon. The present attempt to track
down such apparently heterogeneous material in Levinas's philosophy
will, therefore, raise many a critical eyebrow.

These two points having been raised, however, this paper's central
claim may incite controversy for still other reasons, which would have
to be called disciplinary. The historian grown wary of claims suggesting "influence;" the philosopher certain that only issues of rigor and
not of provenance matter in philosophical argumentation; the Jewish
studies scholar trained to see a vast gulf separating Kabbalah from modern Jewish thought, and the modern Jewish thinker suspicious of
mysticism and appeals to what may seem irrational and irretrievably
past — all of these might proffer reasons to wonder about the value of
the present inquiry.

These are all weighty issues that must be addressed. I will return to
them shortly below, but for the moment I want to attend to a more
basic query, one that many readers may find themselves entertaining
at exactly this juncture. That question is the following: outside of the
brief passage from Levinas's interview cited above, why would anyone
think that there might be Lurianic ideas afoot in Levinas's texts in the
first place? What might make this strange notion seem even vaguely
credible? Let me then cite two short excerpts here from the pages of
Totality and Infinity itself. While these excerpts have been previously
discussed, notably by Mopsik and Ajzenstat, for the moment I invoke

them solely to underscore the presence of Lurianic motifs in Levinas's philosophy.[7]

> The Place of the Good above every essence is the most profound teaching, not of theology, but of philosophy. The paradox of an Infinity admitting a being outside of itself which it does not encompass, and accomplishing its very infinitude by virtue of this proximity of a separated being — in a word, the paradox of creation — thenceforth loses something of its audacity . . . But then it is necessary to cease interpreting separation as pure and simple diminution of the Infinite, a degradation. Separation with regard to the Infinite, compatible with the Infinite, is not a simple "fall" of the Infinite. (*TI* 103; 76)

> Infinity is produced by giving up [*en renonçant à*] the invasion of a totality, in a contraction that leaves a place for the separated being. Thus relationships that open up a way outside of being take form. An infinity that does not remain enclosed circularly in itself, but withdraws from the ontological extension so as to leave a place for a separated being exists divinely. Over and beyond the totality it inaugurates a society. The relations that are established between the separated being and Infinity redeem what diminution there was in the contraction creative of Infinity. Man redeems creation. (*TI* 104; 77; translation modified)

These rather amazing excerpts speak volumes. Here, in the first part of *Totality and Infinity* which introduces the overall framework of the book's argument, Levinas straightforwardly borrows the Lurianic idea of tzimtzum and puts it to use in two ways. In the first excerpt he draws on it to reinterpret both the Platonic idea of the *good beyond being* and the Neoplatonic scheme of emanation, arguing that both — far from representing a loss of an otherwise unitary infinity — capture the richness of a new, pluralistic, and relational form *of* infinity. In the second excerpt Levinas uses the notion of tzimtzum to help define terms which will stand at the absolute center of *Totality and Infinity's* argument, such as "totality," "separated being", and of course "Infinity." Nor do these excerpts stand alone, since there are several others like them in the book. Even more importantly, these Levinasian invocations of an infinite which divinely contracts itself to make room for separate beings clearly cannot be dismissed as mere rhetorical flourishes. To extend Wittgenstein's famous locomotive metaphor, these borrowed or adapted Lurianic concepts are working parts of the engine, and not merely "ornamental."[8] The work they do, and the way they do it, will be essential to Levinas's *philosophical* argument in *Totality and Infinity.*

This paper, then, will be devoted primarily to making an initial case for the admittedly multifarious claim stated above. In addition I will offer some reflective responses to the sharp disciplinary challenges raised above. Although it will not be possible to address all of these in detail in this paper, I hope that even the somewhat condensed responses to these challenges I offer below will convince readers that much more is at stake here than several seemingly recondite questions of intellectual history. Indeed, fundamental interpretive issues in philosophy, religious studies, and modern Judaism are involved. The vast majority of secondary work on Levinas has focused on analyzing his relation to Husserl, Heidegger, and Derrida, with some attention also to other continental figures and to classic older thinkers. This is understandable, and also immensely beneficial, given the seemingly endless richness of Levinas's relationships with these philosophers. Yet so much more remains to be said about Levinas — almost as if there were a vibrant life in the midst of his texts that, even with the revelatory power of much current secondary work, still remains in the shadows. The efforts undertaken here aim to start describing this "shadow life" and to bring it into the light, in order to appreciate its vital contribution to Levinas's thought and texts.[9] This will also have the added benefit of specifying a hitherto hidden reason that readers and critics alike find Levinas's philosophy so compelling, so powerful. This is by no means to make the fatuous assertion that Levinas was a mystic, for he was not. But it is to highlight Levinas's living receptivity to the dynamism concealed in traditional sources, and to praise his creation of rigorously philosophical texts within which we can nevertheless hear the echo of other, heterogeneous texts and insights. Here we have a vital paradigm for modern Jewish thought, both that of the past and that which must come today.

My argument in what follows falls into four parts. First of all, I will indicate at least one highly probable historical pathway through which Levinas may have learned something about the Kabbalah. Despite my relatively brief treatment here, I think it will become evident quickly that the historical details involved point to a truly engrossing and enigmatic story, one that has in fact already served as the subject of several articles and even a book. Secondly, I will describe what is, arguably, the basic structure of the overarching philosophical argument of *Totality and Infinity*. This sets the stage for the third part of the paper, in which I argue that this basic structure bears witness to the influence of Lurianic ideas. Finally, in the fourth part I attend to the aforementioned disciplinary critiques. I have also included an appendix following the text which offers some speculation about another aspect of Levinas's argument in *Totality and Infinity* that seems to possess Lurianic resonances.

WHEN PARALLEL LINES MEET

Although the following may sound fanciful or even slightly subversive, one of the most influential figures of postwar Jewish intellectual and spiritual life in the twentieth century may be an almost completely unknown individual whose works are studied neither in the academy nor in the yeshiva. This person had only a small group of students, for he never held any formal academic or rabbinic post. Yet the list of his very few dedicated disciples includes the names of some very important writers and teachers in Jewish life in the second half of the twentieth century, names such as Elie Wiesel, Rabbi Adin Steinsaltz, Emmanuel Levinas, and Shalom Rosenberg of Hebrew University. This mercurial, unpredictable, and secretive man, who cherished his obscurity and ignored what one might call the normal rules governing polite interchange possessed, according to all reports, an unsurpassed command of the full range of both talmudic and kabbalistic traditions, and an extraordinary knowledge of contemporary western mathematics and physics as well. Dressed shabbily and resembling a vagrant, he came and went as he pleased without warning or ceremony, teaching with passion, disdain, overwhelming knowledge, and endless incitation to uproot and overturn. His disciples referred to him as "the master." The name he used during his lifetime was Mordechai Shoshani. Wiesel, Rosenberg, and Levinas have each stated that it was Shoshani who made them who they were, both as a person and as a Jew.[10]

Unsurprisingly, the little that we have been able to piece together about Shoshani's life and real identity comes from the testimony of his disciples. Wiesel in particular has written about Shoshani on several occasions. He devoted a gripping chapter to his encounters with his mysterious teacher in post-war France in his early biographical work of 1968 *Legends of Our Time,* and then reproduced a version of this chapter and added new insights to it in his memoir of 1995 *All Rivers Run into the Sea.* Wiesel also did a series of interviews on the topic of Shoshani with French journalist Salomon Malka, which Malka included as the first part of his fascinating book *Monsieur Chouchani: The Enigma of a Twentieth Century Master* which he published in French in 1994. It is interesting to note that Wiesel opines that of all Shoshani's disciples, it was only Levinas who attempted to create a philosophical system that in some way captured Shoshani's teachings.

Levinas, of course, refers several times in his talmudic writings to his "pitiless master." After agreeing to meet Shoshani only as a kindness to his good friend Dr. Henri Nerson, Levinas ended up spending an entire evening talking with him. When Levinas emerged from this first encounter, he is reputed to have said that while he did not know what Shoshani knew, it was clear that Shoshani knew everything he knew. Levinas would spend five years, from 1947 to 1952, studying with Shoshani. Shoshani had a preternatural power of memory, and seemed to have memorized every text he had ever read; he would correct Levinas's readings from various texts entirely from memory without ever even glancing at the text. Levinas makes it very clear that it was Shoshani who gave him an understanding of what Jewish tradition really was, and that his own humble efforts to show his readers some of the vital possibilities and illumination to be found in talmudic passages owes everything to Shoshani, who transmitted to him a living, oral tradition. Shmuel Wygoda has devoted an impressive article to unearthing some of the methods and insights regarding the Talmud and the meaning of its study that Levinas learned from his master.[11]

Perhaps the most telling biographical details about this unique figure, however, come from the recollections of Professor Shalom Rosenberg of Hebrew University. Rosenberg was a student of Shoshani's in Montevideo, Uruguay, after Shoshani emigrated there in the mid-1950s. Rosenberg first traveled from Argentina to Uruguay to study with Shoshani in 1956, and would spend the next 12 years traveling back and forth to continue learning with him. In fact, Rosenberg was with him in rural Uruguay when Shoshani died in 1968 in the midst of a shabbat lecture. In a brief piece published in Hebrew in 1996, and in several interviews, Rosenberg has offered the most comprehensive and detailed account we have of the real identity of Shoshani. At least some independent confirmation for it can be found in Malka's book, in which the French journalist recounts a story told to him by an individual claiming to be the neighbor of one of Shoshani's relatives — a story very similar to Rosenberg's account.[12]

It seems likely, based on these sources, that Mordechai Shoshani was in reality R. Hillel Perlman, a highly accomplished talmudist and student of Kabbalah who is mentioned in glowing terms in several of Rav Kook's letters. Born probably in the late nineteenth century in eastern Europe, R. Perlman was a child prodigy who had memorized vast sections of the Talmud at a young age. Some sort of childhood trauma seems to have taken place, perhaps the tragic death of his mother in an accident, which he may have witnessed. He traveled to Jerusalem at a relatively young age and stayed there for a while. He related to Rosenberg that as a young boy he had played on Rav Kook's lap, and that later on, in the 1920s he had studied seriously with Rav Kook. R. Perlman also learned at the famed kabbalistic Beit El yeshiva in the old city, where he became well acquainted with eminent kabbalists. However, his restless personality and nature led him constantly to move beyond what he knew. Rosenberg reports R. Perlman saying that he did not agree with the kabbalists he met in Jerusalem, that he held himself to be antimystical, and that indeed the Kabbalah itself was not mysticism! R. Perlman also told Rosenberg that he had felt, even as a child, that the divide between chasidut and mitnagdut was obviously based on a false and untenable dichotomy. Eventually he departed and traveled extensively, studied every subject under the sun, gained mastery of physics, mathematics, and many languages, and came to conceal his identity so thoroughly that he assumed a new one, that of Mordechai Shoshani, itinerant vagabond, holy provocateur, and master.

THE PHILOSOPHICAL STRUCTURE OF *TOTALITY AND INFINITY*

There is much more to say about this amazing figure. Yet enough has been said already, I hope, to render this paper's basic claim historically plausible. In short, I take it as reasonable to suggest that Levinas, who spent five years studying with Shoshani, might well have picked up certain kabbalistic teachings from his master. Again, this hardly makes Levinas a kabbalist! But it does imply that Levinas may have been made acquainted, most likely in an occurrent and unplanned way, with ideas and themes found in kabbalistic texts. Of course Levinas also possessed the level of textual skill required to explore or "read around in" classic Jewish sources, including kabbalistic ones. So it is possible that he had actually looked into certain books, perhaps to track down the textual source of ideas Shoshani may have brought up spontaneously in their study sessions. Nevertheless, I have been unable to find conclusive evidence for or against this additional conjecture.[13]

This hypothetical, but reasonable genealogical account of how Levinas might have gained knowledge of Kabbalah has several interesting implications. According to the account given here, Levinas would enjoy the unique status of being a modern western philosopher who became acquainted with kabbalistic tradition *not* through Christian Kabbalah, European hermeticism, and German idealism, but rather through a Jewish teacher trained in Kabbalah and its texts in a traditional

Jewish setting. I intend no disrespect to the aforementioned Christian and European disciplines; the focus here lies rather on Levinas's more direct and Judaic conduit to Kabbalah, along with his Hebrew textual abilities. Might these help to explain why Levinas ends up deploying the Lurianic concept of tzimtzum in a way without parallel among those earlier western philosophers and thinkers influenced by this concept? For rather than taking tzimtzum as bearing only or mostly on God's life, Levinas will take tzimtzum as bearing as much on human life as it does on God's (if not more). In order to see this we must now turn to Levinas's philosophical work itself, in particular to *Totality and Infinity.*

As indicated by the citations made in the introduction to this paper, Levinas articulates the notion of "Infinity" by specifying that infinity restrains itself from invading the totality, thereby allowing there to be discrete beings — in other words, allowing there to be a world, and individual beings in that world. He adds that such an infinity, which abandons its unperturbed identity with itself, and so leaves room for a being other than itself to exist independently, is divine. While the Lurianic echo is unmistakable here, we must now ask: what *work* does all this talk of an infinity which contracts itself actually do in the philosophical argument of *Totality and Infinity?* The answer to this question lies in Levinas's concepts of the *separated being* and of the *Other,* and the role they play in his overall argument. This means, as hinted above, that Levinas will philosophically develop the implications of tzimtzum *not* inside the godhead, as it were, but rather in the space *outside* it, an exteriority with respect to the infinite brought into being through tzimtzum.[14]

As is well known, the second part of *Totality and Infinity* proceeds by describing in remarkable phenomenological detail that level of our lives on which we exist as separated beings. In now famous analyses of enjoyment, of the way our bodies bathe in the elements of air, sea, wind, sky, and so on, and of our coming to have an indispensable respite from this element through profound locatedness in a home, Levinas describes the way we exist as discrete, individualized, embodied egos.[15] These analyses portray that dimension of a person's life which is solely about her spontaneous, sensual enjoyment of the distinctly human things that nourish and nurture her life. Such a self-centered ego of enjoyment, thriving vitally in its sensations and feelings, considered purely in itself is not yet a user of language, an employer of general concepts, or a center of abstract knowledge. That is to say, Levinas restricts the level of life he calls the *separated being* to a primary sort of living egocentricity, captivated in the pulsating of its own sensations. This is an artificial distinction, since obviously even the most selfish people use language, employ abstract concepts, and so on. However, Levinas's reason for making this artificial distinction becomes clearer in the third part of *Totality and Infinity* when he brings the separated being into contact with another person.

When the separated being has a face to face encounter with the other person, it confronts a unique challenge. Levinas argues in particular that the face of the other resists the separated being's straightforward and natural attempts to enjoy it, that is, to assimilate it directly and immediately to some aspect of the environment from which it can derive nourishment and nurture. This is because the other's face is both a thing made of extended surfaces and physical depth, and also *not* a thing.

On the one hand, my power of vision brings me the face of the other as merely another thing for my potential nourishment or nurture. In this sense, as Levinas suggests, vision seems to approach an object just as it is in itself, as if it reached the object in its origins, de novo. In vision I grasp a form in a certain horizon or perspective, and so am free to search the other side or other sides of that form, continually using the power of vision to peer at the form from all angles and even to try to grasp once and for all the relationship between a thing and its form. Nothing about the thing can hide from me. In one sense, of course this is true about the face of the other — I can always try to see what her face looks like from a different angle of vision. However in another sense the face of the other is *not* a form concealing yet unseen aspects beneath itself. There is nothing hiding beneath the visible form of the face that I could discover by changing my angle of vision, nor can I grasp once and for all the relationship between the face and "its form." The face for Levinas "presents itself out of itself":

> Vision opens upon a perspective, upon a horizon, and describes a traversable distance, invites the hand to movement and to contact, and ensures them . . . To see is hence always to see on the horizon . . . Total alterity, in which a being does not refer to enjoyment and presents itself out of itself, does not shine forth in the *form* by which things are given to us, for beneath form things conceal themselves . . . If the transcendent cuts across sensibility, if it is openness preeminently, if its vision is the vision of the very openness of being, it cuts across the vision of forms and can be stated neither in terms of contemplation nor in terms of practice. It is the face; its revelation is speech. The relation with the Other alone introduces a dimension of transcendence, and leads us to a relation totally different from experience in the sensible sense of the term, relative and egoist.[16]

This powerful passage admirably states Levinas's position. Yet more detail is required, for *how* does the face of the other constitute *its own* horizon or perspective out of which it presents itself? This seems very different from the standard case of seeing an object. After all, in standard vision the viewing subject both grasps an object *and* generates her own horizon or perspective in which she grasps that object. So how and why is seeing the face of the other different?

Levinas will respond to these questions by specifying that the face of the other, *unlike an object,* "means" at us. That is to say, the face of the other is a physical thing that indicates feelings and thoughts directly through a living stream of facial movements and gestures on its surface. As Levinas puts this,

> The face, still a thing among things, breaks through the form that nevertheless delimits it . . . To speak to me is at each moment to surmount what is necessarily plastic in manifestation. To manifest oneself as a face is to *impose oneself* above and beyond the manifested and purely phenomenal form, to present oneself in a mode irreducible to manifestation, the very straightforwardness of the face to face, without the intermediary of any image.[17]

The face of the other is the way she lets us know that she is *also* something more than, something *different from* what we see when looking at her. Because the face "imposes itself above and beyond the manifested and purely phenomenal form," it no longer makes sense to talk about peering beneath the form of the face in order to uncover the true face hiding in that form. Nor does it make sense to talk about changing my angle of perception to see more of the face. To talk in these ways could refer to the face only as a thing. Yet the face *as a face* is always fully and directly given right here and right now; there is not and never could be anything more of it for my eyes to uncover, nothing more for my vision to pierce through or remove. The face *as a face* does not stand in a horizon or perspective of my making: as face it gives itself to me out of its *own* horizon, one it generates in part by challenging mine. Because of this unimpeded directness, Levinas often refers to the face of the other as "naked." The naked face of the other is the living, corporeal enactment of the irreducibility of the other to my knowledge of the other. For this reason, it is also a beginning, an inauguration.

When the separated being encounters the face of the other, the separated being is forced willy-nilly to grow beyond its limited nature as an ego self-enclosed in its voluptuous enjoyment. In human social life, the face of the other, a thing that is more than any thing could be, perpetually imparts more to the separated, egocentric being than it can contain. This endless overflow in us, wherein the face of the other always forces more into us than we can hold, enlarges each one of us — thereby inaugurating both language and with it the self-consciousness that each of us *is* a separated, egocentric being.[18] In Levinas's words:

> Language conditions thought — not language in its physical materiality, but language as an attitude of the same with regard to the Other irreducible to an intention of thought, irreducible to a consciousness of . . ., since relating to what no consciousness can contain, relating to the infinity of the Other. Language is not enacted within a consciousness; it comes to me from the Other and reverberates in consciousness by putting it in question.[19]

Here self-consciousness in a certain sense precedes and gives birth to consciousness. And of course, a *self-conscious* ego of enjoyment is no longer merely a self-centered seeker of nourishment and nurture, but rather a full person, free to restrain or postpone instinctual satisfactions, as well as to transform them into something else, or even to offer him or herself to another for that other's instinctual satisfaction.

Because the ego cannot fully contain the non-thing which is the otherness of the other person, the overflowing ignited in me by the face of the other is not the satisfaction of a need. But it is, Levinas tells us, the incitation and stoking of desire for what must always exceed my powers of assimilation. Such desire is not erotic; it is a ceaselessly reiterated moment of bring drawn to the other in his or her heterogeneous otherness. This nonerotic desire for the other in which, as Levinas says, the other puts our egocentric being into question and so teaches us, reveals that human social life is an asymptotic approach toward the infinite. Thus, it is the continual nonsatisfaction of this desire for the infinite that in fact adds intensity to it.

THE LURIANIC DEEP STRUCTURE OF *TOTALITY AND INFINITY*

According to the philosopher and Levinas scholar Rudi Visker, the philosophical structure just described depends on the idea that the infinite *has not compelled us by any sort of full, overwhelming manifestation of itself to us.* It has rather, as Visker paraphrases Levinas in *Totality and Infinity,* contracted itself and so created a separated being and granted to it "the grace of being able to ignore its Creator."[20] Here, he continues, we see Levinas's insistence on the holy, in opposition to the sacred. Commenting on Levinas's remark that "transcendence is to be distinguished from a union with the transcendent" (*TI* 77; 49), Visker says:

> But, depending on how one approaches it, a union with the transcendent could just as well mean that the finite gets absorbed in the Infinite,

or that the Infinite loses its infinity through contact with the finite . . . If the Infinite is to keep its infinity and the finite its finitude, there has to be at least one taboo: on incarnation. But it is a taboo which is issued by something which declares *itself* taboo. That something can only be a somebody: God.

This distinction between the sacred and the holy (the sacred being that which results from a taboo; the holy being that which puts a taboo *on itself*) is at work in every move that Levinas makes in developing his ethics, and not least in that first decisive statement from the opening pages of *Totality and Infinity* . . . It is not I who resist the system, as Kierkegaard thought; it is the Other.[21]

For Visker, Levinasian holiness results not from divine myth, or fusion and loss of selfhood, but rather from a God who makes himself, his infinity, "taboo." This initiation of and commitment to a relationship of uncollapsible transcendence, ensures the very *separateness* of the separated being. Perhaps we might even venture the suggestion that in the second part of *Totality and Infinity,* Levinas makes use of a brilliantly modified Husserlian phenomenological account of embodied enjoyment precisely in order to sketch the details of the "interior life" of a being sufficiently separated to be capable of this sort of holiness. Be that as it may, we still need to ask about the second category involved here, that is, the "self-removal" of the infinite. What, then, does this act, and the potential holiness it engenders, mean for our encounter with the other?

In the face to face encounter, as we undergo ever-increasing desire for an otherness that will always overflow our grasp, we once again do not participate in any sort of higher union or ecstatic experience of the sacred. Visker argues that for Levinas the other's capacity to appeal to me, to summon me, to get me caught up in concern for him, implies that the other stands not merely outside of me but also *above* me. The call of the other in the face to face encounter is, as we saw Levinas contend above, an invocation to encounter not merely another thing that can be characterized in a context, but the other person in and for herself. Visker says, "Only a personal other has enough alterity (exteriority) to shock me in such a way that I cannot adapt (to) the shock — if I don't help the other and even if I don't feel remorse, I will at least have noticed that I denied him something he demanded from me."[22] The supplicatory demand the other makes of me in the face to face encounter is *weaker* than things and forces — the ethical shock the other induces in me is not based on something present in the world, for that would merely be another thing in a context.

Here we can begin to see that in the overall argument of *Totality and Infinity,* the other, just like the separated being, gains its character precisely from the withdrawal of the infinite. The infinite, which has contracted itself to make room for a world, makes its presence felt in the same world from which it has graciously exiled itself, only through that nonpresence whose very nongraspability calls to us. The face of the other is the corporeal site of this nonpresence; the concrete face of the other person compellingly intimates to us the infinite's having withdrawn — as if the other's face draws us in the direction of the infinite's withdrawal. The face in this sense awakens us to ethical desire. Infinite ethical desire moves us beyond our egocentric and relativizing tendency to reduce things and values to our own horizon and to the sphere of our own personal feelings, sensations, and experiences. The exteriority of the other person, the ethical summons she issues through her nonpresence in her physical presence — in other words, her particular personhood in and for itself — offers us asymptotic access to the infinite that originally abandoned presence in the world. Here the impossibility of "approaching the invisible through the invisible" is surmounted in the concreteness of the other person.[23] In Visker's formulation: "Without the incessant appeal of an Other, permanently beyond my reach, the fire of the Holy could not purify me of the sacred in me and extinguish its sacrificial pyres."[24]

I think it is clear now that Levinas *needs* the idea of an *infinite* that contracts itself in order to run the basic argument of *Totality and Infinity.* And so tzimtzum must be counted as an active part of this work's philosophical structure. As surprising as this may seem, it needs to be recalled that the idea of tzimtzum itself was in fact traditionally interpreted as having significance far beyond merely describing the initial act in the cosmic drama. In a very suggestive study of different kabbalists and mystical thinkers influenced by R. Luria, Shaul Magid has shown that tzimtzum often functioned as a trope for ultimately redemptive study and practice. Magid argues that for these figures performance of the commandments, ethical actions, special ritual practices, and, above all, mystical study of the Torah were seen as opportunities to bring the infinite back into the world, to re-infinitize the world and so return it to its original form as living potential *within* the infinite, thus *undoing the self-exile of the infinite.*[25] With this Lurianic background in focus, it is now time to revisit an earlier citation; this time around, however, it needs to be cited in full, and its implications spelled out.

> Infinity is produced by giving up the invasion of a totality, in a contraction that leaves a place for the separated being. Thus relationships that open up a way outside of being take form. An infinity that does not remain enclosed circularly in itself, but withdraws from the ontological extension so as to leave a place for a separated being exists divinely. Over and beyond the totality it inaugurates a society. The relations that are established between the separated being and Infinity redeem what diminution there was in the contraction creative of Infinity. Man redeems creation. Society with God is not an addition to God nor a disappearance of the interval that separates God from the creature. By contrast with totalization we have called it religion. Multiplicity and the limitation of the creative Infinite are compatible with the perfection of the Infinite; they articulate the meaning of this perfection. (*TI* 104; 77)

In light of my argument here, and of Magid's evocation of the redemptive significance that Lurianic kabbalistic tradition interpretively derived from the notion of tzimtzum, we find that the short sentence "Man redeems creation," and the sentences immediately preceding and following it, now leap out at us. Are we not in the full presence here of a classic Lurianic formulation in which the human being, who represents the end of a long process which began in the depths of the infinite, goes on to perfect and redeem a cosmos from which the infinite has exiled itself? This is not to say that Levinas is a direct follower of R. Luria, but the parallels are striking: both figures employ a

scheme in which an initial act of withdrawal or self-exile on the part
of the infinite finds ultimate completion in the cosmic redemptive
work of human beings. Yet the passage above intimates an even deeper
parallel. This will become clearer in considering what is probably the
strongest objection against the view for which I have been arguing.

As is well known, the late Charles Mopsik, an acclaimed and pro-
lific French Kabbalah scholar, argued in an article published in 1991
that although Levinas might have taken certain formal terms from
Lurianic Kabbalah, apart from this borrowed nomenclature there was
little else in common between the twentieth century philosopher of
the other and the sixteenth century sage of Safed.[26] Mopsik does
concede that Levinas and Lurianic Kabbalah both reject the commonplace notion that divine emanation, and the "descent down-
ward" it initiates, represent a "fall" or fundamental negation. In this
sense both differ from more standard evaluations of creation through
divine emanation found in Neoplatonism. But for Mopsik the fundamental difference between the two figures far outweigh these minor
agreements in terminology and in reaching a positive appraisal of
divine emanation.

According to Mopsik the chasm between R. Luria and Levinas lies
precisely in the latter's notion of "separation." Arguing for his view
that Levinas has merely borrowed certain terms from Lurianic Kabbalah
without taking any real Lurianic content into his philosophy, Mopsik
points out that in the passage cited above, Levinas develops the idea
of tzimtzum in terms of a "contraction" and the separation it makes
possible. Mopsik insists, however, that for R. Luria tzimtzum is not
so much about separation — say between the infinite and human
beings — as it is about "nonseparation," that is, a profound and complex sort of "differentiated continuity" between the infinite and human
beings that takes shape in the ongoing process of creation. In this sense,
Lurianic contraction amounts to an all-important first moment in a
process entirely dedicated to bringing forth a cosmos and a sentient,
conscious being within it who can come to know the infinite *as* "God."
To acquire any form, even that of God, represents a limitation of the

infinite. Yet as Mopsik makes clear, when the infinite acquires the additional form of personal human being, the infinite *comes to know itself in* the human being's coming to know God, and so breaks with its transcendent solitude.[27] Mopsik concludes that in Lurianic Kabbalah the infinite contracts not for the sake of separation, but rather for the sake of continuity, or nonseparation. He therefore denies that Levinas's philosophy contains much more than a few echoes of Lurianic terms.

But here we must ask, has Mopsik really done justice to the passage we have been considering? Let us take a look again, this time just citing a few sentences from it:

> Thus relationships that open up a way outside of being take form . . . Over and beyond the totality it inaugurates a society. The relations that are established between the separated being and Infinity redeem what diminution there was in the contraction creative of Infinity. Man redeems creation . . . Multiplicity and the limitation of the creative Infinite are compatible with the perfection of the Infinite; they articulate the meaning of this perfection. (*TI* 104; 77)

It seems to me that Mopsik may not have fully grasped the philosophical significance of these lines. As I have been arguing extensively here, the structure of *Totality and Infinity* is all about my encountering the compelling and yet not-ever-finally-fully-present reality of the infinite *in* the face of the other. Is this not one of the "relationships" that "open up a way outside of being" of which Levinas speaks in this passage? Levinas tells us that these relations between the separated being and infinity "redeem what diminution there was in the contraction creative of Infinity." Think of the relations that the face to face meeting engenders in *Totality and Infinity:* patience, war, self-sacrifice for the other, the erotic, fecundity, teaching, and so on. Levinas will of course offer his own charged readings of these well known human relationships, finding unsuspected depths in them because they all bear the mark of the prior ethical meeting with the other. For Levinas these relationships, and the many separated beings who engage in them, *are* the "multiplicity and limitation . . . that articulate the perfection" of the infinite! Or to return to his earlier phrase, these relationships "redeem what diminution there was in the contraction creative of Infinity." All of this is, arguably, the essential message of *Totality and Infinity:* our original separateness is for the sake of a profound relationality in which, as Levinas himself says, true *transcendence* comes to pass; this transcendence in and through relationship "articulates" the perfection of the infinite here in the world of finitude.

I grant that this may not be exactly the same thing as the differentiated continuity Mopsik finds in Lurianic Kabbalah proper. Levinas did not endorse the acosmism that ultimately lies behind much Lurianic Kabbalah. Nonetheless there is far greater proximity here than Mopsik seems to think, since for both R. Luria and Levinas tzimtzum and separation serve as the first moment of a process through which the infinite develops or flashes forth in the midst of finitude. What has led Mopsik to miss this, I think, is that Levinas has taken mystical ideas from kabbalistic tradition and reinterpreted them using neither a rabbinic or a kabbalistic hermeneutic, but rather a philosophical one. In this sense, as I will be arguing in the conclusion, Levinas has offered a wide-ranging, modern, and momentous philosophical *articulation* of Judaism — in the sense of this word that is associated with the thought of Charles Taylor. Once we see this, it becomes clear that Mopsik has overstated the case — Levinas has in fact embraced neither Lurianic nonseparation nor rational, antimystical, atomistic separation. He has rather created a philosophical articulation of tzimtzum, of the transcendent relationality it makes possible, and of the Infinite about whom speech and knowledge become possible (at least to some degree) in and through this living, transcendent relationality.

PHILOSOPHY, JEWISH MYSTICISM, AND LEVINAS'S ARTICULATION OF MODERN JUDAISM

In this concluding section I hope to show that working through the disciplinary objections raised above does more than provide a response to them, as important as that may be. It also opens up new vistas for reading Levinas, and limns new visions of the relationship between philosophy and religious tradition in the modern world.

The first such objection would contend that some of my argument here involves matters of "influence," a concept which has become notorious among professional historians — and for good reason. In a masterful survey of this topic, Francis Oakley records the powerful negative reaction of historians to careless and overly loose arguments about influence, through which any thing could be connected to anything else. In the absence of valid criteria for differentiating legitimate instances of influence from erstwhile pretenders, the concept invited abuse. Indeed, to establish *real influence* one would need *at the very least* to ask: (1) could X have read (or known, or learned about) Y?; (2) what form did the influence of Y on X actually take, or how do we see Y in X's work?; and (3) so what? For even if one were to establish (1) and faithfully describe (2), the broader question would remain: what do we ultimately learn from (1) and (2) that we would not have already known simply by reading and understanding X in the first place? On the other hand, literary critics often found the notion of influence constricting, an overly scientifico-historical focus that tended to obliterate the literary qualities of a text itself. In particular, as texts came to be seen not so much as pure authorial products, but rather as intertexts, or weavings-together of many other texts, searching for influence became clumsy and unhelpful.[28]

I cannot deny that I have made an effort here to amass data in support of a claim of influence. However, the argument would actually work reasonably well even if I adopted the creatively deflationary strategy Oakley records — namely replacing the claim that "Y influenced X" with the generic formulation that "X made use of Y." This may seem inconsequential — but in the case of Levinas it is very interesting indeed. With Levinas the sheer fact that he is "making use of" traditional Lurianic kabbalistic motifs and texts (whether or not we claim that these materials are an "influence" on him), already forces considerable reflection, for it is hardly the norm. In this sense, does Levinas's *use* of Lurianic materials constitute a new moment in which modern philosophers and modern Jewish thinkers, having gained sufficient self-assurance in their modernity, are now free to reclaim traditional materials in a serious, learned, self-aware, and modern commerce with Jewish tradition?

This leads directly into the concerns of the philosopher. As mentioned above, many philosophers assume that so-called extra-philosophical issues and sources need to be put aside when considering a thinker's work qua philosophy. In accord with this assumption, readers of Levinas are sometimes advised to consign his Jewishness, his Jewish writings, and even the role that certain classic Jewish texts and ideas may play in his philosophical writings to what philosophers of science call the "context of discovery." This keeps such extraneous matters separate from what really counts, namely, the nature and quality of the arguments Levinas puts forward, or the "context of justification."[29] According to this assumption, the present paper and the larger project of which it is part must be considered more or less irrelevant to the study of Levinas's philosophy. In addition, those who hold this assumption may argue that it really does not matter *where* Levinas found his ideas — insofar as he presents and argues for them philosophically in a work of philosophy, they become ipso facto part of the western philosophical tradition. If on the other hand some aspect of them remains in some sense outside the work of philosophy, then this remainder cannot, by definition, be philosophy. So matters of provenance ultimately reduce to questions of philosophical formulation and conceptual definition.

This assumption certainly isolates the internal integrity of philosophical work, protecting the sort of intelligent suasion it should carry from any outside influences. What self-respecting student of philosophy could oppose this? And yet we know that works of philosophy inevitably *also* contain countless echoes of older systems of religion, myth, cultural belief and imperative. In condemning analysis of these deeper and often subterranean patterns of inheritance and filiation that shape the texture of philosophical work as irrelevant, do we not end up in the final analysis simply remaining blind to, and insufficiently aware of the way seemingly bygone tropes and the powerful convictions they embody may live on in new forms? As might be expected in the case of a thinker whose work relies on notions like authenticity, the call of conscience, and fallen-ness, this point has often been remarked in studies of the debt Heidegger's philosophy owes to various currents in Christian tradition, Catholic, Protestant, and mystical.[30] Similar important secondary work has been done on Hegel, and on Schelling, although these studies have also identified the debt their philosophies owe to theosophic, hermetic, Rosicrucian, and Masonic sources, as well as to Christian tradition.[31] These studies have clearly shown the additional depth we get in understanding the meaning and ultimate implications of these philosophers' works by seeing them as flowing from, or at least as in many respects shaped by religious traditions, mysticism, and so on. Why should we deprive ourselves of this very same advantage in understanding Levinas's works?

This in turn points to the value of considering provenance in philosophy. Levinas seems to be telling us that, at least in certain instances, the tradition of western thought stands in need of correction (even if he uses the tradition of western thought to argue for this conclusion). However, might Levinas be performing some of the correction he believes necessary through use of sources hitherto unattested in western philosophy? Might it not therefore be vital for secondary studies of Levinas to inform us about these sources? Would we not in fact end up knowing far less if we did not work hard to identify these extra-philosophical sources? Admittedly, these extra-philosophical sources would still need to be turned into philosophy. But without appealing to them, perhaps Levinas would remain unable to correct certain limitations which have arisen in the western philosophical imagination? Indeed, this paper has argued that Jewish tradition in general and Kabbalah in particular may represent one such resource, outside of the western philosophical tradition, from which to draw in seeking corrections.

Finally, let me offer some reflections on what the present undertaking may mean for modern Jewish thought and modern Judaism. I want to argue, specifically, that we can profitably read the use Levinas makes of Lurianic motifs as an *articulation* of modern Judaism. Charles

Taylor's notion of *articulation* has received an increasing amount of scholarly attention since Taylor introduced it in his *Sources of The Self* in 1989.[32] Briefly, Taylor employs this term to underline the way in which moral reflection, moral philosophy, and even philosophy more generally, in fact proceed by the progressive unfolding in words of insights into and ideas about what Taylor calls "moral sources." Moral sources come in many varieties. They nonetheless all share the capacity to motivate, direct, and orient an individual's actions *in a way that cannot be reduced* merely to a matter of that individual's idiosyncratic tastes, preferences, or hedonic proclivities. Taylor states clearly that there may well be many such moral sources, and he shows that understanding them can require extensive historical reconstruction of long-vanished contexts and ideas whose distant force continues to affect how we understand ourselves and act today. Moral sources require articulation, that is, we must attempt to spell out what we think they are, what we think they mean, ask of us, and so on. In Taylor's words:

> Moral sources empower. To come closer to them, to have a clearer view of them, to come to grasp what they involve, is for those who recognize them to be moved to love or respect them, and through this love/respect to be better enabled to live up to them. And articulation can bring them closer. That is why words can empower; why words can at times have a tremendous moral force . . . Some formulations may be dead, or have no power at this place or time or with certain people . . . Words may have power because they tap a source hitherto unknown or unfelt . . . (O)r they may have power in another way, by articulating our feelings or our story so as to bring us in contact with a source we have been longing for . . . or through seeing our struggle through the prism of the Exodus, as with the civil rights movement in America in the 1960s.[33]

Here we get a good sense of the way in which the story of the Exodus, *pace* Michael Walzer, can serve as a moral source, and indeed one whose meaning and whose ability to move us depends very clearly on the different way or ways in which it gets articulated.

Taylor adds, however, that the relationship between articulation and the moral source it "articulates" remains complex and mysterious.

Without any articulation, of course, a moral source will have no way of impinging on our lives. Let it also be granted, as mentioned above, that there are many ways in which one may articulate a moral source (think of the vast number of songs, movies, plays, and short stories which endeavor to offer us up-to-date articulations of Charles Dickens's *A Christmas Carol* — itself already an articulation for Victorian England of the religiously embedded notion of change of heart!). The problem remains, though, that articulation does not merely render or copy a moral source. Here again is Taylor on this point:

> articulations are not simply descriptions, if we mean by this character-izations of a fully independent object, that is, an object which is altered neither in what it is, nor in the degree or manner of its evidence to us by the description. In this way my characterization of this table as brown, or this line of mountains as jagged, is a simple description. On the contrary, articulations are attempts to formulate what is initially inchoate, or confused, or badly formulated. But this kind of formula-tion or reformulation does not leave its object unchanged. To give a certain articulation is to shape our sense of what we desire or what we hold important in a certain way.[34]

Articulation is both absolutely required if moral sources are to affect our lives and, at the same time, an essentially creative interpretive process, which distinctively reshapes the very same moral source it claims to present directly to us! Taylor by no means laments this fact about articulation. He points out its direct parallels in the world of art, for example, and also for that matter in the world of religion.

Here is the way we must begin to read the philosophy of Emmanuel Levinas. For Taylor, of course, philosophy is — and has always and every-where been — articulation. In the case of Levinas, however, applying this notion yields particularly intriguing results. *Might Levinas's phi-losophy be the articulation of certain Jewish moral sources, albeit in the properly philosophical and thus universalist idiom of twentieth century intellectual discourse?* Any modern Jew, or non-Jew for that matter, inter-ested in understanding Judaism — whether as one's own tradition or as another's — would need to grasp it in and through the very same modern discourse she uses to understand anything else she understands in the modern world. This does not mean of course that philosophy can in any way replace the language of Jewish tradition — but it does mean that philosophy, or modern western discourse more generally, would be required. Thus, for us today, philosophy would seem to be a necessary articulation of Jewish moral sources, though by no means a sufficient one.

However, exactly this way of reading Levinas's philosophical texts — that is, as a profound, modern articulation of Judaism — generates a great depth of interpretative possibilities. I have argued here that these possibilities will remain inaccessible as long as we continue to confine our reading of Levinas's philosophical texts solely to the proper confines and concerns of the discipline of philosophy.[35] Let me recall Taylor's comment, already cited above, that "Words may have power because they tap a source hitherto unknown or unfelt." I have tried to show that one source of the power so many people have found in the pages of *Totality and Infinity* flows from the concept of tzimtzum, one of the book's "hitherto unknown or unfelt" moral sources. Other fecund Jewish moral sources await discovery in the pages of Levinas's philosophical texts. Taken as articulations in Taylor's sense, these texts offer modern Jewish thinkers (as well as many others) a rich and much needed model for creating modern religious visions, at once philosophical *and* compelling.

APPENDIX

There is another, closely related moment in Levinas's *Totality and Infinity* that may also owe a debt to Lurianic Kabbalah.

In a wide-ranging and erudite study, Mordechai Pachter has traced the theologico-mystical reception history of a basic distinction R. Hayyim

Vital introduces and elaborates in the first of the seven gates making up the initial part of his *Etz Hayyim* (Tree of Life).[36] Noting that kabbalists possess two traditions for representing the sefirot, namely as concentric circles and as hierarchically linear gradations, R. Hayyim Vital goes on to show that the originary act of tzimtzum itself yielded an essentially circular cosmos, in that the *En Sof* (Infinite) withdrew itself in perfect equality from every place toward one central point. This was followed by the emanation of the *kav* or line, through which both the sefirot and revelation itself came into the world. And from the *kav* further circular emanations will emerge. Pachter describes the subsequent interpretation of this distinction between circles and lines in impressive detail.[37] He shows a gradual convergence toward an interpretation in which the circles metaphorically refer to natural forces and tendencies, while the line metaphorically captures that which somehow builds on yet veers away from the natural, predictable cyclicity of the circles.[38] This opens up the possibility of a human will which is free to struggle with and deviate from the natural patterns of animal life symbolized by the circles, and thus capable of choosing to conform to revelation and to ethical rules.

Now as mentioned before, Levinas defines a primary layer of egocentric existing in which we savor and delectate in the lived qualities of our interactions with the environment. It goes without saying that when a person enjoys food, sunshine, or even a good book, she is at the very same time dealing with objects, namely, the item of food she is eating, the ray of the sun warming her body, and the physical book in her hands. Yet Levinas is clear that insofar as we are talking specifically about our immediately lived relationships with these objects, we are not talking about objects at all, but rather solely about a pleasurable wallowing in the feelings and sensations we gain in interacting with such objects. In describing the background nature of this not-yet objective enjoyment, Levinas uses the term "element," saying, for example, that during such enjoyment our bodies bathe, or are "steeped" in, a vague surrounding context, such as the air, the spray of the sea, the sky, even the taken-for-granted openness of a broad street. With this conception of the element, Levinas describes the way in which, during enjoyment, our bodies are amorphously embraced by natural and unbounded expanses, such as the sky and the ocean, that neither really end nor begin. Levinas states clearly that the element, which is the natural format in which the separated, egocentric being lives, has neither sides nor direction.[39]

However, the face of the other interrupts and dispels this hedonistic miasma because, as we have said, in attempting to enjoy it we discover that it means at us. That is, it is a side or point from which meaning is directed at us. Try as we might, we cannot find the front and back of the face — it is a sheer side or surface, pointing in one direction exactly, from itself to me.[40] The face of the other introduces linearity and direction into my directionless contentment; it is a vector of responsibility that breaks into the natural, environing element and calls directly and only on me to grow beyond it. This explains why Levinas will constantly talk about the "uprightness" of the face of the other. There may well be a resonance here, again, between a strand of Lurianic tradition and Levinas's philosophy. Just as certain kabbalists interpret circles and lines as metaphors for natural cycles and the ability of human will to follow a higher call, so Levinas articulates a philosophical image of a natural, nonlinear, and directionless modality of existence, which gets challenged by a profoundly linear moment, one which grants each of us self-awareness and the freedom to choose whether we will act on our drives or not. There would seem to be reason to treat the resonance between Lurianic tradition and Levinas here as more than coincidence.[41]

Levinas Between Monotheism and Cosmotheism

Martin Kavka

We are now, I think, in the midst of a sea change in Levinas interpretation. Increasingly in the course of the last third of the twentieth century, Levinas's phenomenological ethics was seen as a resource for intellectuals to protest a certain kind of, shall we say, methodological naturalism in philosophy. Not only scientific positivism but also existential phenomenology with its apparent emphasis on immanence[1] were feared to be terminally infected with neopagan or proto-fascist elements. If the result of these movements was an embrace of (or a failure to adequately critique) modern secularized civilization and its bureaucratized projects — problematic because such a dimension of modernity was a necessary but not sufficient condition of the Holocaust, as Zygmunt Bauman has argued[2] — then the putative solution was to bend the stick toward the opposite pole. Scholars could invoke either the broadly monotheistic overtones of Levinas's discourse of the Infinite or the specifically Judaic texts of the Bible and Talmud that Levinas saw himself as translating into philosophy, in the hope that these acts of citation would persuade scholars' audiences that a return to monotheism or the Judaeo-Christian tradition could get the West past its embarrassing century-long flirtation with human-made mass death. This reading of Levinas would be coherent with a broader trend in American thought from the 1950s onward that would include Abraham Joshua Heschel, Reinhold Niebuhr, and Martin Luther King Jr., wherein secularism (especially as evidenced by communism) is the problem, religion is the solution.[3]

Now, at the beginning of the twenty-first century — whether we date it as beginning with the second intifada, the 2000 United States presidential election, the 9/11 attacks, or the beginning of hostilities in Iraq — the Levinasian model has come to be seen by some as holding less promise than might have at first appeared. A search for the reason why this has occurred seems to suggest monotheism as the culprit, insofar as monotheism necessarily takes on a certain political form that goes against Levinas's description of God as the Infinite. One might narrate this shift briefly as follows. In his 1983 article "Jewish Existence and Philosophy," Adriaan Peperzak could comment on Levinas's association of the otherwise-than-being with divine glory by writing, "Who would not recognize this God as the God of Moses and the prophets?"[4] The unwritten answer to this rhetorical question was "No one; Levinas's God is the God of the Hebrew Bible." By 2002, when Howard Caygill published *Levinas and the Political,* the answer to Peperzak's question had become, surprisingly, "Levinas." Caygill there patiently describes the way in which for Levinas, the otherwise-than-being, i.e. illeity, is unrecognizable, precisely because it is excluded from being and thus from any and all religious and political systems (including those of Moses and the prophets).[5] It is for this reason, Caygill argues, that Levinas's remarks about the State of Israel are so frustrating for interpreters and border on incoherence. On the one hand, Israel becomes for Levinas the figure for that which is inspired by that which is otherwise than being; it is "a State where the prophetic moral code [*la morale prophétique*] and the idea of its peace will have to be incarnated [*devra s'incarner*]."[6] On the other hand, Israel undoubtedly and irrevocably *is,* and it is a place and a people held up as exemplary by a philosopher who describes subjectivity as "called to leave . . . the concept of the ego [and] its extension in the people" and, thus, presumably, also called to leave behind notions of authochthonous places (*OB* 185/*AE* 232–33). A politics rooted in a God articulated in terms of an inapparent illeity thereby turns on a Jewish identity that is "at once both diasporic and tied to a nation-state."[7] Such a politics is therefore doomed, for as soon as a monotheistic politics — the articulation of a politics inspired by that which is otherwise than being — comes on the scene, it is already ripe for critique in the name of . . . monotheism.[8]

Caygill solves this problem by relegating monotheism to a memory that can become, by virtue of its distance from the present, purely an edifying discourse as opposed to an ideology that risks an explosive politics. In his closing analysis of Levinas's talmudic readings on fire, Caygill reads Levinas as "advocating" in a 1963 essay on Hanukkah "a withdrawal from the blaze of glory and its cycle of consuming, protecting and avenging fire in order to find the glory of the presence in an ember or 'a little flask of pure oil' that keeps alight 'our failing memory' for the future."[9] Monotheism: little, cute, sentimental, and now promising 100 percent less risk of violence and ethnocentrism! *Now* how much would you pay? Caygill is not alone in thinking that monotheism is a key problem in Levinas's thought. More recently, in an article in *Political Theory,* Simon Critchley explicitly cites "the idea that political community is, or has to be, monotheistic" as one of the five problems of Levinasian politics; for him, this affects not only the issue of Israel on the global stage, but also what he describes as "the neoimperial project of the US government [which] is intrinsically linked to a Zionist vision."[10] For Critchley, only a nonmonotheistic reading of Levinas can produce a Levinasian politics that recognizes "the people in their irreducible plurality."[11]

There is something wrong with these critiques, but it is not that they say anything that is *prima facie* false. (Even Critchley's diagnosis of the either covert or overt Zionism of contemporary American governance — highly unsavory on the surface — is evidenced by the recent remarks of former Undersecretary of Defense for Policy Douglas Feith about the roots of his political vision in the death of his father's siblings in the Holocaust.)[12] It is rather that these critiques are imprecise about what monotheism is, largely because Levinas himself did not offer an account of anything opposed to monotheism except a vaguely described "paganism" or "atheism." In Levinas, these words are not philosophically or historically grounded concepts; their force is rhetorical. Even more distressingly, Levinas's own accounts of monotheism are usually quite thin; it seems to be defined only as the voice of Israel — "the monotheism which the Jewish Bible brought to humanity" (*DF* 25/*DL* 44) — which, when heard, produces fraternity. The articulation of this voice is both what Levinas does and what Levinas analyzes. Monotheism is thus ethics. But in assuming this longstanding position in liberal Jewish thought,[13] Levinas also makes this equation between monotheism and ethics ahistorical. He assumes that monotheism is *naturally* ethical when one could easily show that this equation had to be *historically produced* through philosophical labor, most notably that of Hermann Cohen. Indeed, I know of only one place where Levinas's deployment of "monotheism" is significantly more complex. It can be found in the analysis of Neoplatonism that is repeated both in "From The One to the Other" and "Philosophy and Transcendence": "Neoplatonism, exalting that consummate unity beyond being and knowing, *better* than being and knowing, offered the monotheism that conquered Europe in the first centuries of our era an itinerary and stations capable of corresponding to mystical tastes and the needs of salvation." (*EN* 135; *AT* 10) Therefore, monotheism can conquer in a way that forgets the illeity of its ground and requires supplementation from outside, although to be sure, Neoplatonism only gets the form of the ground as beyond being correct, and misses out on the concern for neighbor-love and justice that is original to monotheism.[14]

So scholars on Levinas know that they have the right to think of monotheism in a more nuanced manner, but Levinas's own tendency to think of monotheism as purely redemptive, and of consisting of nothing but other-centered ethics, leads scholars writing on Levinas to analyze monotheism simplistically. What is at stake in this word, anyway? the number of divine beings? the nature of the divine? the value and ground of empirically observed nature? Claims about the role of monotheism in Levinas must depend upon an account of monotheism's history, as well as a history of the enemies that monotheism has conjured up for itself. But as I will argue in the remainder of this essay, when such an account is given — turning to the work of the Egyptologist Jan Assmann — Levinas as monotheist shows itself to be only half of the picture. Levinas is both a representative of monotheism and what Assmann has termed "cosmotheism"; or perhaps better, Levinasian thought mixes the two in such a way that it ends up somewhere between the two poles. But this is not simply an argument of Levinasian apologetics; indeed, I would like to think that given my frustration with Levinas's vague use of religious categories, it does not even rise to that level. But admittedly, it is also an apologetic argument, because I close with some remarks attesting that this space between monotheism and cosmotheism is not simply something that can be found in Levinas. It also exists in what one might ordinarily think of as a purely monotheist text, namely the Hebrew Bible, as well as in what one might ordinarily think of as a purely cosmotheist text, one from the Ramesside period of ancient Egypt (between the thirteenth and eleventh centuries BCE). It is in such a turn to the ancients that I believe the role of religion in Levinas becomes clarified outside the bounds of the Jewish and Christian traditions, and outside the contemporary politicization of a "Judaeo-Christian tradition," as the articulation of both a conjunction and a disjunction between the visible world and its invisible transcendent ground.[15] There is manifestation, a conjunction between the visible and the invisible that seems pagan or cosmotheist. But there are also good philosophical reasons to avoid predicating anything of that which manifests itself, a disjunction that is closer to monotheism.[16]

MONOTHEISM AND COSMOTHEISM

What makes monotheism problematic has little to do with the number of figures that are or are not seen as divine beings; the debates about pantheism in the seventeenth century had pointed out that the notion of one supreme God was not foreign to polytheistic cultures. Rather, as Jan Assmann has written, it has to do with the distinction between true and false religion, what he has termed the "Mosaic distinction." Even though scholarship can date such a distinction between true monotheistic religion and false religion to the Egyptian ruler Akhenaten (who, in the fourteenth century BCE, abolished polytheistic cults and limited worship only to the sun-god Aten), Assmann still insists on referring to it as the "Mosaic distinction," since "tradition ascribes it to Moses."[17] To say that this distinction is merely imaginary in the Hebrew Bible would be untrue. The protest against idolatry throughout the Five Books of Moses, the command to the Israelites to make themselves distinct from the other nations, the strict boundaries between monotheistic Israelite culture and the other cultures of the ancient Near East that are heightened in the biblical writings associated with the Deuteronomistic Reform during the reign of King Josiah in the seventh century BCE — all of this supports the claim that the Mosaic distinction is indeed something that can be found in the Hebrew Bible. (That being said, Assmann is quite explicit in *Die Mosaische Unterscheidung* that the Hebrew Bible displays both the ideology of the Mosaic distinction and the ideology that the Mosaic distinction seeks to overthrow. Monotheism should thus be understood as an ideal type that appears, but does not exhaust, real texts at the basis of Western religion.)[18] Now, the original Egyptian institution of such a distinction was a violent one; it was not a natural outgrowth out of any previous system (*pace* the positivist accounts of Comte, or Hume). Assmann describes it as a "revolution from above" that rendered the cults and temples empty and upended the customary observance of festivals: "the new religion was not promoted, it was imposed. Tradition was not questioned, it was persecuted and forbidden."[19] For this reason, Assmann describes monotheism in his work as a "counter-religion," because one of the rhetorical strategies by which monotheism dismissed earlier traditions was by recasting them as heresy or idolatry. This strategy — which is rooted in a reconceptualization of nature — has effects on epistemology, intercultural communication, and theopolitics. I will now detail this primary move and these philosophical and political effects in order.

Before Akhenaten (or before the Amarna period, to refer to the name of the city that Akhenaten founded), Egyptian religion had articulated nature as an interlocking drama of forces, the agents of which were various divine beings; humans could maximize the gain from such forces through cultic acts.[20] As a result, the world of gods "does not stand opposed to the world of cosmos, the human individual, and society" as a supernatural realm that orders the natural world, existence, and politics. Instead, the world of gods both inaugurates and is manifested in the cosmos as a process of continual renewal through the acts of the gods. For Assmann, "the cosmic process would have lost its synergistic character, if it were thought of as organization of a single, unique [*einzig*] God."[21] Such a claim seems somewhat doubtful when Assmann goes on to oppose it to monotheism; after all, many monotheists claim that God renews the work of creation on a daily basis. Even taking into consideration Assmann's claim that monotheism is an ideal type, it turns out that renewal is not the main issue separating Egyptian religion from biblical monotheism. Rather, it is that of whether the divine exists over and above the world. Assmann clarifies this point:

> [Polytheism] certainly has to do with multiplicity, but what is decisive is not the numerical principle of multiplicity, but the lack of distinction [*Nichtunterscheidung*] between God and world, from which multiplicity necessarily results. The divine has entered the world in the three dimensions of nature, state, and myth. Polytheism is cosmotheism. The divine cannot be liberated from the world. But monotheism is about such a liberation. The divine emancipates itself from its symbiotic tie with cosmos, society, and destiny and faces the world [which is understood] as a self-reliant magnitude.[22]

What is at stake in the distinction between monotheism and cosmotheism, then, is the relationship between God and nature. Cosmotheism involves an intimate nearness between the gods and social order, which makes the world a home for both the human and the divine in a way that, for Assmann, is not the case in monotheism, in which the independence or distance of God from the world means that the world can only be conceptualized in terms of its lack of the divine. In cosmotheism, nature is something to be embraced as the realm in which the gods are manifest; in monotheism, nature is something to be conquered, and the material world is understood in terms of privation.

Even with these broad brushstrokes, Assmann's characterization of monotheism parallels much in the history of Jewish philosophy[23] (and, I believe, Christian philosophy as well). Furthermore, it is implicit in the doctrine of holiness in the Hebrew Bible. Holiness is found in the divine — as Leviticus 19:2 says, "You shall be holy, as I, the Lord your God, am holy," implying that holiness is the result of a teleological process of becoming godlike, of becoming something different than what one already is. In the Hebrew Bible, holiness is pursued by separating oneself from the notion of the world as a home, as a place in which stable foundations are present at hand. Assmann associates this with a turn from cultic life to scriptural text; the book gives what nature no longer possesses.[24] The life of the monotheist is an uncanny one: "whoever stands on the ground of the Mosaic distinction does not feel totally at home in this world."[25] In *Moses the Egyptian,* Assmann codifies this distinction of nearness and distance as one between a "paradigm of manifestation" and a "paradigm of creation." The former is typical of Egyptian cosmotheism, in which at least the elements (and in some post-Amarna texts, even animals and the king) are material in which divine power is manifest, and thus animates the world. The "paradigm of creation," on the other hand, which one finds in texts of the Amarna period and especially in biblical monotheism, asserts that which the visible world "proceeds from God, but is not itself divine."[26] In the paradigm of creation, the world is ontologically independent of God, and thus distant from God; in the paradigm of manifestation, the world is ontologically bound up with God, and thus near to God.

As stated earlier, the revolutionary move of monotheism and its inauguration of the so-called "Mosaic distinction" has both philosophical and political consequences. First, there is a new theory of truth. By virtue of the nearness of the divine to the world, the gods were thus "known"[27] by both the elites and the populace in nature; we can say that nature was *prima facie* evidence for the gods' existence. During the Amarna period, nature loses this evidentiary status and becomes something that is molded by the sun-god Aten according to his will. At the end of the "Great Hymn," a text from the Amarna period, we read that "The world becomes on your hand, as you made them / When you dawn, they live / When you set, they die / You yourself are life-time, one lives by you." Assmann describes this text as embodying the disenchantment of the world during the Amarna period, in which the world is denied "its own sources of life, meaning, power, and order, which means for the Egyptians the world's own divinity."[28] One could gloss the Amarna text that leaves the world disenchanted as follows: there is no evidence that nature works according to some non-natural or supernatural mechanism, and therefore the proposition that nature and humanity lives be the sun-god (as opposed to the dramatic inter-play of natural forces) is one that has to be taken on *faith*. It is this notion of belief in a god — as opposed to knowledge — that leads Assmann to claim that the Mosaic distinction "introduces a new type of truth: the absolute, revealed, metaphysical or faith-truth."[29]

This conception of truth strongly affects intercultural communica-tion, making impossible the translation of concepts across cultures. The polytheistic systems of the ancient Near East, because they assigned determinate characteristics and functions to various deities in the pan-theon of divine beings, allowed for a deity in one culture to be trans-lated to a deity with similar characteristics in another culture; there are lists of such translated divine names from ancient Mesopotamia. This allowed for a certain globalization of religion — or whatever phrase one might use to describe the process by which interethnic bonds are formed — to take place without a theologically grounded violence.[30] Religion did not institute boundaries between peoples, but was the ground for communication between them. Assmann claims that the Mosaic distinction, however, "blocked this translatability," because the forms of worship of other cultures were not recognized as being equivalently true.[31] Because Yahweh, for example, could not be translated into the personae of Amun or Zeus — in other words, because the divine name in monotheism is not conventional, but is essentially bound up with the transcendent to which it refers — the nonmonotheist neighbors of the ancient Israelites could not understand Israelite religion. As a result, anti-Judaism, or what Peter Schäfer has termed "Judeophobia" insofar as the Jews are assigned the characteristics of xenophobia and misanthropy, begins. While stopping short of Assmann's assertion that the Mosaic distinction "brought a new form of hate into the world — the hatred of the heathen, the heretic, and the idolator,"[32] — an assertion that can be extrapolated to blame antisemitism on its victims — one can at least say that the institution of boundaries between peoples accomplished by monotheism creates the real possibility that interethnic violence will be justified by the claim that the boundary between two peoples has no right to exist, because what lays on the other side of it (wherever one stands) is simply untrue.

Finally, in the wake of the monotheistic revolution, the nature of politics also shifts dramatically. Here Assmann stops associating the monotheistic revolution of Akhenaten with biblical monotheism; his critique is aimed wholly against biblical theopolitics. The Mosaic distinction that associates false religion with Egypt also associates false politics with with Egypt, and uses divinely given law (a novum in religion) as "the instrument of deliverance from Egyptian and every other bondage,"[33] including that of the state, which had been understood in Egypt as guaranteeing the reciprocity between persons that was seen to be the base of a well-functioning society and that was the core element of the Egyptian concept of right (*Ma'at*).[34] Biblical monotheism makes all politics essentially a theopolitics:

> While people become free of the hand of Pharaoh and his debasing oppression, at the same time the divine, or grace, is emancipated from its political representation and becomes an exclusive matter of God, who here for the first time takes the scepter of historical action in hand and withholds well-being [*Heil*] from the order of worldly violence. From now on, religion and politics are different things, the interplay of which must

be negotiated with difficulty, and the unity of which can be obtained only through violence.[35]

In other words, when sovereignty is displaced from the king to God, the risk is that the law governing society becomes anti-natural (because the ground of the law is no longer in the interhuman or the natural realm). This leaves two options for the nature of the relationship of the monotheist to the state. Either the power of the state expresses itself as grounded in monotheism and thereby foists a particular and non-natural understanding of justice on the populace, or monotheism lies opposed to the state and thereby casts state agents as unethical because they practice false politics. This latter point seems to be the most relevant: what Assmann sees as the disjunction of right and nature in monotheism means that, at least in the Torah, laws are "the laws of the people of God, and they establish the justice of the people of God, not a general ethic."[36]

This suggests that monotheism is one in which the risk is that the monotheist is unable to live with the nonmonotheist. It would be easy to show how Assmann's claim that monotheism begins this conflict leads his arguments to overlap with classic anti-Judaic rhetoric (the suffering of Jews is the fault of their own maintenance of difference, etc.). Peter Schäfer has moved in this direction, charging Assmann with implicitly blaming Jews for the Holocaust in a review that appeared in the *Süddeutscher Zeitung*.[37] But despite what one might (over)charitably describe as a lack of felicity in Assmann's prose, I invoke Assmann because he gives the most expansive account of the worries that Caygill and Critchley express only obliquely with regard to Levinasian thought. They are good worries to have, I think (although I cringe at some of Assmann's language), because sacred texts contain troubling in elements. And scholars whose work resides in or touches on the discipline of modern Jewish thought have been exceptionally blind to these troubles until recently. Too often, they assume that simply conjuring up an idealized Judaism — say, one that, because of its focus on midrash, is essentially pluralist — can solve the problems of the West.[38] But think of the student who falls — and falls hard — for the utopian element of Levinasian thought, and then, after reading Levinas's remarks in the 1982 radio interview with Salomon Malka hinting that the Palestinians are not Israelis' others, wonders whether Levinasian philosophy can only articulate a utopia, but not do anything to come nearer to realizing peace.[39]

But on Assmann's terms, it makes little sense to describe Levinas as a monotheist; indeed, the risks of monotheism are minimized — but certainly not eliminated — in Levinas precisely because he is careful to articulate both the distance and nearness between the world and God in his thinking. This seems a bit counterintuitive; after all, an account of Levinas's philosophy in 25 words or less would state that Levinas finds the good *beyond* being, and so recapitulates the very problems that Assmann sees in classical monotheism, coming out of the paradigm of creation. In addition, to talk about a simultaneous distance and nearness seems incoherent, and the temptation to pick one paradigm (creation and its distance) is strong. But there are good reasons not to think of Levinas solely in this language, but to think of Levinas in terms of the paradigm of manifestation as well.

The Manifestation of the Trace of the Other

Perhaps surprisingly, I want to defend this claim with recourse to Levinas's thinking about the face of the other and the trace. The argument for the centrality of alterity in phenomenological thinking seems to be quite clear. Most succinctly in the 1951 "Is Ontology Fundamental?," Levinas argues that every conversation depends upon the exteriority of the other to me. Exteriority is the condition of the possibility of language taking place, as it does, between a donor and a recipient of a speech-act: "The person with whom I am in relation I call *being*, but in so calling him, I call to him. I do not only think that he is, I speak to him. . . . I have spoken to him, that is to say, I have neglected the universal being that he incarnates [we should understand an implicit "allegedly" here] in order to remain with the particular being that he is."[40] Conversation thereby shows there is no "we" that is already constituted before and outside of speech-acts; rather, the "we" is what language can achieve — perhaps through a process of giving and taking of reasons and testimonies — but persons are naturally monads, with language as their window. The exteriority of the other to me, in the self-attestation of his or her expression, is what Levinas calls "face" (*TI* 201ff/*TeI* 176ff).

In order to explain the origin of the other's apparent visitation to me from the beyond, Levinas in the middle of his career invokes the category of the "trace" to signify the anarchic origin of alterity, both outside the horizon of my own world and outside the horizon of any concept that I could generate by the patterns of my own thinking. If the origin of the other were a concept — say, a realm of being in which I participate as well — there would be no need to talk to another at all; we would all have the talent to read each others' minds. For this reason, it is necessary to think of the beyond in which alterity has its origin as rigorously as possible. In the 1963 essay "The Trace of the Other," Levinas writes that "the other proceeds from the absolutely absent. But the other's relationship with the absolutely absent from which he comes does not indicate, does not reveal this absent." The other cannot even motivate a surmise about the nature of its ground (as Husserl argues is the case with indicative signs); it does not give any confidence in its referent, and so Levinas concludes that the face "is in the trace of the utterly bygone [*révolu*], utterly passed absent"[41] and that "a trace consists in signifying without making appear."[42] One might do well to conclude, then, that the Levinasian rhetoric of the face and the trace obeys the logic of Assmann's paradigm of creation, in which one might be able to state that the world is created by God, but in the final analysis, the world is utterly profane and bereft of God (at least in the framework of all humanly made history). Edith Wyschogrod seems to make such a move when she writes that "it is a mistake to assume that the elsewhere that is evoked by the face can yield a meaning for investigation; to assume that is to assume that the elsewhere is world."[43]

Nevertheless, this cannot be the end of the story. The face appears, as Wyschogrod goes on to note, even though it does not appear as other phenomena do. And earlier in "The Trace of the Other," Levinas describes the appearance of the other with recourse to the language of manifestation. Ordinarily, I would be reluctant to hang too much on this point; after all, there is no assurance that Levinas means by "manifestation" what Assmann means by it. But by reconstructing the argument here (and expanding it to cover some key passages from *Otherwise than Being*), I believe that the full stakes of Levinasian manifestation can be shown to have more in common with Assmann than one might expect.

In "The Trace of the Other," the other is described as manifesting him- or herself: "the other manifests himself in the face." And Levinas means for this word to have all the overtones of presence with which the phenomenological tradition endows it: "[the] mundane signification of the face is found to be disturbed and shaken by another presence, abstract, not integrated into the world. His presence consists in coming unto us, making an entry." It is this irruption into the horizon of my world from the outside that distinguishes the other as face from other phenomena. Nevertheless, this still raises the question of what exactly is made manifest in the other; after all, if Levinas and Assmann are to be brought together, then the Levinasian other will have to manifest something else besides itself. Levinas continues to describe the difference between the face and other phenomena as follows:

> The other who manifests himself in the face as it were breaks through his own plastic essence, like someone who opens a window on which his figure is outlined. His presence consists in *divesting* [se dévêtir] himself of the form which, however, manifests him. His manifestation is a surplus over the inevitable paralysis of manifestation.[44]

It is perhaps easiest to make sense of these sentences by concluding that Levinas is here speaking of the relation between two different types of manifestation. One kind of manifestation, that realized by the face, consists in breaking through the limits of the other kind of manifestation, ordinary "immanent" manifestation. In this latter type of manifestation, claims about the nature/being of an object overlap with claims about how the object appears or is given.[45] Only against the backdrop of immanent manifestation would it make sense to speak of the face appearing as something that transcends the horizon of my world.

In the sentences from "The Trace of the Other" quoted above, it is key to see that Levinas is not arguing here that the appearance of the other takes place in two phases, the first in which the other manifests itself like other immanent objects, and then a second more reflective phase in which the philosopher understands that for the other to remain other, there can be no manifestation at all. "Divestment," which should be understood as literally as possible in terms of undressing or denuding, does not undo manifestation. The striptease is made manifest in the manifestation of the other. This is the surplus: while immanent objects are given, as it were, having already dressed themselves up in accordance with our intentional aims, the face is not given in accordance with such an as-structure. With the face, we get something more, something undressed, raw. As a result, surplus should not be understood as the attribute of some transcendent being that the other manifests in its face; all one can say about the ground of alterity is that it is a force that has the power to disrupt the contours of the world — what Levinas calls "illeity." Yet this surplus still appears in some way; otherwise, there would be no way to justify calling it a surplus at all. How does this surplus appear?

Levinas is simply not as clear as we might want on this issue. There are, to my mind, two possible ways of answering such a question. The first would be to say that "surplus" is really only a figure of speech. On such an account, what Levinas is really saying is that the other, not signaling anything at all, manifests even less in its appearance than other objects do, and therefore calls forth the idea of a surplus — an imagined version of the object that does not lack anything. (One thinks of the way in which a raw vegetable, a carrot for example, gives intimations that its flavor could be stronger. And so we cook, and discover caramelization.) Levinas's citations of Plotinus support such a claim. As is well known, the sections in the *Enneads* on the soul as containing a trace (*ikhnos*) of the good provide one of Levinas's sources for his own thinking of the trace, as evidenced by the brief mention of Plotinus near the end of "Trace of the Other," repeated at the close of "Meaning And Sense" almost a decade later.[46] The stakes of such a citation become clearer in the 1989 essay "Philosophy and Transcendence" (in a section duplicated from the 1983 essay "From The One to the Other"), in which Levinas points out that in the *Enneads,* the intellect aims at the One yet is relatively impoverished by being able only to think of multiple Platonic ideas. It cannot get to the one simple ground of various forms (beauty, tallness, etc.). As a result, the intellect is "a state of privation, compared to the unity of the One." Nevertheless, there is the semblance of positivity here: "And yet, [it is] as if the One were *sensed* in [pressenti *par*] that very privation, as if knowledge, still aspiration by the fact of the dispersion of its seeing, went *beyond* what it sees and thematizes and were precisely thereby a *transcendence.*"[47] So it seems that the very knowledge of the limits of consciousness implies that there is something beyond those limits. After all, every limit sets a boundary, and there is space on both sides of that boundary. The *terra incognita* on the other side of the boundary must always remain unknowable; for this reason, Levinas writes that it is only *as if* the One were sensed. All one can do is wait, aspire, and pray.

But this is quite a bit more minimal than another account that one could make; here, one might point to *Otherwise than Being.* There, Levinas gives a far more extensive version of the argument made in "Is Ontology Fundamental?" that being and comprehension are not fundamental. As in *Totality and Infinity,* Levinas in *Otherwise than Being* points to the phenomenon of enjoyment as an exemplar of sensibility.[48]

> Gustative sensation is not a knowing accompanying the physico-chemical or biological mechanism of consuming, a consciousness of the objective filling of a void, a spectacle "miraculously" interiorized in the "*tasting*"; it is not an epiphenomenal echoing of a physical event, nor the "reflection" of the spatial structure of filling, not the idealist constitution, in the psyche involved in sensation, of an object that would be the tooth that bites on the bread. To bite on the bread is the very

meaning of tasting. The taste is the way a sensible subject becomes a volume . . . Satisfaction satisfies itself with satisfaction. (*OB 73 / AE 92*)

The immediacy of pleasure is not bound up with representation; some-one who said "I enjoy chocolate because of its predicates" would be thought to have a more warped sense of pleasure than the person who simply bites into a piece of chocolate cake and begins to moan.[49] The immediate enjoyment we have of things around us, without a care for understanding, is evidence that the philosophical moment of cogni-tion is not essential to selfhood. Once sensibility has been detached from representation and from conceptualized accounts of sensation as intuitive knowledge, it makes more sense to understand sensibility — now the most basic stratum of subjectivity — in terms of vulnerabil-ity or exposure (*OB* 75ff / *AE* 94ff).

This argument about enjoyment plays a key role in Levinas's protest against limiting manifestation simply to its immanent meaning. Again, Levinas is vague, but in the midst of his account of enjoyment in *Otherwise than Being,* he shifts from a thoroughgoing critique of man-ifestation to a veritable rescue of it.

> Philosophy tries in the course of its phenomenology to reduce the man-ifest and the manifestation to their preoriginal signification, a signification that does not signify manifestation. There is room to think that this pre-original signification includes the motifs of origin and appearing. Yet it is not thereby shut up in a present or a representation. If it also signifies the dawning of a manifestation in which it can indeed shine forth and show itself, its signifying is not exhausted in the effusion of dissimula-tion of this light. (*OB* 65 / *AE* 82)

Levinas's philosophical articulation of the way in which the sensible signifies is an argument for this new dawn of manifestation. Insofar as the phenomenology of enjoyment shows that consciousness is not fun-damentally engaged in cognitive pursuits, the robust notion of the know-ing subject is shown to cover over the stratum of sensibility or affectivity that, for Levinas, is situated at the base of selfhood. As in Levinas's earlier writings, there is desire before there is conceptualization; the self is exposed or stretched out into its environment before it gathers it back up in the frame of that system of significations that Heidegger defined as "world" in *Being and Time*.[50] The self is for that which lies outside it — alterity — before it is a subject with an essence. These claims break with the order of immanent manifestation because they call attention to the fact of manifestation (before which the subject is passive) over and above the object that is made manifest (which consciousness can understand in the light of its intentional aims).[51] In contrast with the Husserlian discourse of sensation, which reduces sensation to a simple matter that is only given soul by the intentionality of the subject ("sensuous data present themselves as stuffs for intentive formings or sense-bestowings"),[52] Levinas sees that what Husserl has really uncovered is sensation as the ground of consciousness having any aims at all; data, not intentive form, is primary. The analysis of sensibility is more disclosive than the analysis of consciousness. By switching the focus of phenomenological analysis away from consciousness to its ground, manifestation can itself appear — raw, undressed — outside of the objects manifest themselves, and outside of the rationalist dissimulation of perception as subject-centered. The surplus of manifestation is the fact of manifestation itself, a fact that gets occluded by intentional consciousness.

But why talk about manifestation in terms of enjoyment? Why not simply talk about manifestation in terms of the face as Levinas does in *Totality and Infinity* (*TI* 66/*TeI* 37)?[53] It would seem to make sense that the new dawn of manifestation would have to do with alterity, and not the ipseity of the pleasured subject. The answer to these questions therefore cannot be simply that the analysis of enjoyment serves to describe that realm of ego-satisfaction that can be interrupted by alterity. It seems to me that, more fundamentally, the link between enjoyment and the manifestation of manifestation itself shows that ipseity is not really real; it is conjured on top of a sensibility and vulnerability that consciousness then forgets. This means that the Levinasian analysis of sensibility cashes itself out in its grounding the possibility of the ethic of substitution. Levinas wants to prove that an ethic in which the subject is "passive to the point of becoming an inspiration, that is, alterity in the same, the trope of the body animated by the soul, psyche in the form of a hand that gives even the bread taken from its own mouth" (*OB* 67 / *AE* 85) is not a utopian ethic, but rather is really possible despite its supererogatory appearance. Such a supererogatory ethic is really possible because this is what the self has been doing *all along;* "alterity in the same" is simply another name for sensibility, the desire for some X that is not me, a desire that is immediate and unthematized. If sensibility is the most fundamental stratum of subjectivity, then it would be bad faith for the self *not* to act supererogatorily.[54] In other words, Levinas is making a more radical argument than one that would say that claims about what persons *ought* to do are senseless unless they are rooted in claims about what persons *can* do. While it is true that the ethic of substitution is groundless without the account of sensibility, it is also the case that sensibility is not simply a capability of the self. We sense whether we want to or not; sensibility is the most basic fact about who we are. Levinas is making what one might best describe as an attenuated natural law argument, in which claims about the basic nature of persons are grounds for claims about what ought to be the case; the factual ground of subjectivity in sensibility is also a norm. (There are a couple of ways of extricating Levinas from the is/ought problem that some interpreters will think he falls into here; I leave some tentative remarks about these to a footnote.)[55]

Levinas describes such supererogatory ethics in terms of the "psyche" or "animation," an ensouling. The visible sign of the ethics of nonindifference to the other is "an animate body or an incarnate identity" (*OB* 71 / *AE* 89). The body displays its having-been-ensouled by the other — animation is "the other in the same" (*OB* 70 / *AE* 88) — through its ethical acts. But Levinas can only make this claim about action not being grounded in a robustly described self-sufficient subject because the ethic of substitution recapitulates the basic position of the vulnerability of the self that was already shown in the analysis of enjoyment. Therefore, readers of *Otherwise than Being* have every right to conclude that this ethical animation could not take place without a prior animation, that of the world of enjoyment by what we can call *soul.* Insofar as something in the world can affect us immediately, it entrusts anima/soul to us.[56] Soul is what alienates the self from its ego.[57] What animates — the agent of soul — is not human, and not sexed.[58] The frequent references to maternity in Levinas's discussion of sensibility and ethics in *Otherwise than Being*[59] are figures of the ethic that sensibility makes possible. In acts for another to whom I am exposed (the other in me, wounding me), what is performed in a new key is the acknowledgment of the animation or ensoulment of an object (the tasty piece of bread with its fresh flavor that wounds me, because only a porous "wounded" self can taste) by something which I cannot describe.[60] The origin or nature of this soul we do not know, but it can be figured in many ways, including (but not limited to) maternity.

Speaking of the ethics of substitution makes no sense without speaking of vulnerability. This, in turn, makes no sense without a world in which manifestation manifests itself outside of and alongside those manifested objects that are given to consciousness in its cognitive adventures. As a result, we have the right to talk about the world as manifesting something like soul, which is manifest along with objects but separable from them, both in and beyond the world. Soul would not simply be something in the world that irrupts my horizon, but would also be something beyond the world, the possibility of my having a horizon at all. But is not such talk about the simultaneity of "in" and "beyond," immanence and transcendence, incoherent? It seems to me that this dual language is the best way to talk about the surplus that is manifestation itself, a surplus that philosophy can uncover in every conversation (as Levinas showed in "Is Ontology Fundamental?"). For while we can affirm that there is manifestation, we also cannot conceptualize what manifestation is. Soul is not given in the same manner that bread is. Bread, the flavor and odor of which is sensible, can be given a list of predicates. The same cannot be said of soul, the flavorless, odorless, clandestine companion of bread. But soul is as near to us as the smell and taste of freshly baked (or week-old, rock-hard, stale) bread. As a result, one should speak of both of Assmann's religious paradigms when discussing Levinas's philosophy of religion. Insofar as manifestation manifests itself, soul is near, in accordance with the cosmotheistic paradigm of manifestation. Insofar as it cannot be given proper predicates (and is the ground of making any predications at all), it is far from the world of ordinary objects, in accordance with the paradigm of creation. This duality is implicit in Levinas's arguments about God as illeity manifesting in its traces (which are other than God). A thinking that we assume to be strictly monotheistic — simply for biographical reasons — can be shown to be far nearer to the cosmotheistic model than one might conclude at first glance.

COSMOTHEISM IN EGYPT AND ISRAEL

Finally, I would like to take some steps toward showing that this move of uncovering the cosmotheistic potential in Levinas actually gets us closer to the Egyptian material that Assmann treats, and is consonant with at least a strand of the Jewish tradition that underlies Levinas's own work.

First, the Egyptian materials. For Assmann, the most developed statement of the paradigm of manifestation is in a hymn from the Ramesside period, dating from some years after the monotheistic revolution of the Amarna period and continuous with the solar theology that developed before Akhenaten's revolt. In the first part of this hymn, the Amun, associated with the One, is seen as manifesting himself in the form of other gods: the Ogdoad, the eight creator gods associated with reptiles; Re, the god of the sun; and Atum the earth god. These other deities are described as forms or embodiments of Amun: "Another of his forms is the Ogdoad/Primeval one of the primeval ones, begetter of Re. He completed himself as Atum, being of one body with him. He is Universal Lord, who initiated that which exists." Yet, as Assmann points out only two stanzas later in this hymn, these claims about manifestation take on a different form, since Amun is now described as truly existing beyond manifestation: "[Amun] hides himself from the gods, no one knowing his nature / He is more remote than heaven / He is deeper than the underworld. / None of the gods knows his true form / His image is not unfolded in books / Nothing certain is testified about him."[61] In this text, the manifestation of the One in the world is understood as both occurring and not occurring: there is a manifestation of a surplus by which the deity associated with the One exceeds the pantheon, as well as a stratum in which all claims about the nature of this surplus are de facto rejected because the One exceeds all language ("His image is not unfolded in books"). In the oscillation between cataphatic and apophatic moments in this Egyptian, there is a logic that is analogous to Levinas's account of the structure of the relationship between the other understood as a trace and that in whose trace the other lies. The analogy is strong enough, despite the vast difference in content, to say that a philosophy described as monotheistic, such as Levinas's, is not necessarily or resolutely opposed to its apparent contradictories. Furthermore, this same Ramesside hymn mediates between the visibility and the invisibility of Amun in the world with recourse to the concept of soul. The final line of the hymn states that Amun "has the quality of *ba* [soul] hidden of name like his secrecy." It is certainly odd to say that the soul of Amun is hidden at the same time that one asserts that Amun has the quality of soul. How can one name that which is purely hidden? Assmann interprets this last line of the stanza as evidence for the Egyptian worldview in which "the visible world has a soul that animates and moves it, just as it did for the Neoplatonists."[62] In other words, it seems that the language of soul is how the Egyptians name this indeterminate surplus that is manifest in the world as that which both grounds the world (and joined to it as an animating force that is given alongside worldly forms), and lies apart from the world (disjoined from the world, radically separate from Amun's forms, and unknowable). Through recourse to the concept of animation, God is understood as both one and many, as nowhere in itself and everywhere in its traces, both in ancient Egypt and, I submit, in Levinas.

I would want to invoke this resemblance between Levinasian "monotheism" and the "cosmotheism" of Ramesside Egypt — these terms must always have scarequotes around them — as a premise in a larger argument that Jewish philosophy, at least in the heritage that stretches from Spinoza through Levinas, is composed of a set of reasoning practices by which the risks of monotheistic philosophy are minimized (but certainly not extirpated). Such a claim, however, is meaningless if these practices take one far away from the texts at the base of a religious tradition. So let me close with one brief reference to the Hebrew Bible. Assmann is clear, especially in *Die Mosaische Unterscheidung,* that the political risk of Judaic monotheism is that divinely given law makes it impossible for political structures to effect anything; the king is, at least structurally albeit not necessarily historically, subservient to Torah.[63] In Egyptian cosmotheism, on the other hand, "kingship is a cosmic energy, like light and air: the power of god that animates, takes care of, and orders the human world is manifested in it"; "the Egyptian king is, as the son of God, at the same time the mediator of well-being and the incarnation of the divine turning to the world."[64] But this is exactly how the Hebrew Bible understood its kings as well, as sons of God who mediate the divine. In the so-called "royal ideology" of 2 Samuel 7 and Psalms 2 and 89, we have a definition of the king of Israel as the one who, by virtue of being anointed as king, is seen as the son of God.

> I will raise up your offspring after you [David], one of your own issue, and I will establish his kingship. He shall build a house for My name, and I will establish his royal throne forever. I will be a father to him and he shall be a son to Me. (2 Sam. 7:12–14)

> "I have installed My king on Zion, My holy mountain!" Let me tell of the decree: the Lord said to me, "You are My son, I have fathered you this day." (Ps. 2:6–7)

> My [God's] faithfulness and steadfast love shall be with him [the king]; his horn shall be exalted through My name. I will set his hand upon the sea, his right hand upon the rivers. He shall say to Me, "You are my father, my God, the rock of my deliverance." (Ps. 89:25–27)

In these texts, it is difficult to determine the difference between Israel and the other civilizations in the Ancient Near East as seeing the king in terms of sonship. Here, too, God is accessible, manifest in the world through the actions of the king. Kingship means the manifestation of the animating force of an unknowable God.

Now these are also violent texts; the king in these passages is also a warrior who defeats the nations of the world. Remembering them is risky. But this risk takes us further than the risk of Caygill's memory. As stated earlier, at the end of *Levinas and the Political,* Howard Caygill invokes Hanukkah as the proper figure for thinking Levinas's relationship to Judaism, claiming that despite Levinas's equivocations on the relationship between monotheism and violence, there is a minor strand in Levinas that exhorts Jewish readers "to find the glory of the presence in an ember or a little flask of pure oil that keeps alight our failing memory for the future."[65] Memory must always be kept on the verge of failing (one thinks here of Simon Rawidowicz's diagnosis of a common view of Jews as "an ever-dying people")[66] so that its ember does not becoming an all-consuming fire. But how can Hanukkah ensure that such memory remains bedridden, terminal? Does Caygill propose that Jews throughout the world stop singing "Ma'oz Tzur" at Hanukkah, with its anticipation that God will have prepared the slaughter for the blaspheming foe (and that's just in the first stanza!)? The memory of Hanukkah as the memory of a military success in the name of the untranslatable God — an example of everything that Assmann sees as threatening in monotheism — cannot be extirpated. The space between the robust memory of Hanukkah as a military success and the failed memory of Hanukkah as a Jewish adaptation of Christian consumerism[67] is not nearly as stable as Caygill (and Levinas) imagines. So if less memory is unstable, then why not side for *more* memory? Would it not be better to use the cosmotheistic potential of Levinas and other Jewish philosophers as sources for a vibrant memory that articulates the contingency of the boundary between allegedly asymmetrical religious systems such as monotheism and cosmotheism? And could not the strength of such a memory, in part because its tensions call out for a philosophical referee, engender (unlike "failing memory") the possibility of thinking that a historically grounded philosophy could prevent certain monotheists from believing, for example, that God *really* endorses the Hebrew midwives' claim in the opening chapter of Exodus that "the Hebrew women are not like the Egyptian women" (Exod. 1:19) — no matter what the text goes on to say?[68]

Art, Religion, and Ethics Post Mortem Dei: Levinas and Dostoyevsky

Peter Atterton

And that is why I renounce higher harmony altogether.
— Ivan, in Dostoyevsky's *The Brothers Karamazov*

True monotheism is duty bound to answer the legitimate demands of atheism.
— Emmanuel Levinas, "Loving the Torah More than God"

Discussions of the sources for Levinas's philosophy have tended to focus on Greece and the Bible to the neglect of his Russo-Lithuanian cultural heritage.[1] Almost no work has been done examining the impact of Russian literature on Levinas's thinking. The present essay seeks to overcome this neglect by examining the influence that Dostoyevsky in particular exerted on the development of Levinas's philosophy. I am aware that the notion of "influence" is philosophically vague, and not something whose truth can easily be ascertained. Might there be nothing more than simply a confluence between the thinking of Dostoyevsky and that of Levinas? Could it be that Levinas was attracted to the work of Dostoyevsky because he found there what he was already looking for? Although Levinas credits Dostoyevsky with introducing him to philosophy, it would be facile to draw the conclusion that St. Petersburg occupies as important a place in Levinas's intellectual itinerary as

Athens or Jerusalem. Dostoyevsky provided neither an ontology nor any of the "pre-philosophical experiences" (*EI* 24) on which, according to Levinas, all philosophical thought rests. But he did give Levinas a way to think about art, religion, and, most importantly of all, ethics after the Holocaust, an event that more than any other, according to Levinas, demonstrated the absolute failure of philosophical theodicy. It was Dostoyevsky, I submit, rather than the Bible, the Greeks, or Kant who taught Levinas that the moral imperative, addressed to the singular existing individual, supersedes the religious imperative, whose validity is placed in question by the suffering of innocents and the absence of the all-powerful and providential God of theism.

My principal aim here, then, is to show this indebtedness of Levinas to Dostoyevsky. Much of what I have to say is based on Levinas's numerous references to Dostoyevsky scattered throughout his corpus and in various interviews. I will only deal with Dostoyevsky's works that Levinas explicitly uses for the purpose of literary attestation, namely, *The Brothers Karamazov* and *Crime and Punishment*. In addition, I make limited use of *The Devils*. In any case, I am interested in examining Dostoyevsky's role, as far as I can determine, in the development of Levinas's thinking, rather than inventing one.

Russian Literature and Dostoyevsky

Levinas's love of Russian literature is well documented.[2] Born in 1906 into a family of Jewish Russophiles living in Lithuania, Levinas learned to speak Russian before he learned Hebrew. His earliest childhood memory was news of the death of Tolstoy (*IR* 23) in 1910, which sent his family into mourning.[3] He taught himself to read Russian by studying the label on the cocoa that was served at breakfast (*IR* 26), and he was soon digesting the novels of the great nineteenth century Russians that lined the shelves of his father's bookshop in Kovno (*IR* 24). He owned the complete works of Pushkin (ten volumes), which he proudly displayed near the entrance of his Parisian home (*IR* 24), and he continued to read Russian late in life. Probably the last novel he read in the original Russian (*IR* 80, 89) was Vassily Grossman's *Zhizn' i Sud'ba (Life and Fate)*.[4] Levinas was greatly impressed by the work, and he would refer to it over and again in essays and interviews dating from the mid-1980s.[5]

Levinas, however, read Grossman's novel too late for it to have influenced his thinking to a major extent.[6] It was rather the Russian literature of the preceding century, particularly the work of Dostoyevsky, that made an early, powerful, and lasting impression on him. Asked in an interview what led him to philosophy, Levinas replied:

> I think that it was first of all my readings in Russian, specifically Pushkin, Lermontov, and *Dostoyevsky, above all Dostoyevsky*. The Russian novel, the novel of Dostoyevsky and Tolstoy, seemed to me very preoccupied with fundamental things. (*IR* 28; emphasis added)

Levinas, of course, is not the only philosopher to have recognized the importance of Dostoyevsky as a *thinker*. Nietzsche once said of Dostoyevsky that he was "the only psychologist . . . from whom I had something to learn; he ranks among the most beautiful strokes of fortune in my life."[7] But whereas Nietzsche discovered Dostoyevsky only late in life, in 1887, by which time he had already dismissed all moral, religious, and metaphysical speculation as thoroughly erroneous,[8] Levinas read Dostoyevsky while still young enough to be receptive to such thought. Superficially, Levinas's encounter with Dostoyevsky parallels that of Camus, who also read Dostoyevsky (and Nietzsche) during his lycée years, and who remained fascinated with the author thereafter.[9] It can hardly be forgotten that Camus's last play *Les Possédés* (1959) was an adaptation of Dostoyevsky's novel *The Devils*, described by Camus in the foreword to his play as a "prophetic book."[10] However, whereas Camus and the postwar generation of French existentialism found in Dostoyevsky's writings the epitome of modern nihilism in which "everything is permitted," Levinas discovered there something altogether different and much more meaningful — the "wholly Other."

The first explicit reference to Dostoyevsky in Levinas's published writings occurs in "Reality and Its Shadow," which appeared in *Les Temps Modernes* in 1948. There, Dostoyevsky is mentioned twice. The main tenet of the essay is that art is essentially disengaged from philosophy and life. The existence of a statue or painting, for example, is a "semblance of existing" (*CPP* 8) in which nothing comes into presence and nothing changes. Art substitutes an image for reality, and somehow manages to transform time into an *immobile* image of eternity, like a Zeno paradox. According to Levinas, "Eternally the future announced in the strained muscles of Laocoon will be unable to become present. Eternally, the smile of the Mona Lisa about to broaden will not broaden" (*CPP* 9). What is said here about the plastic arts is predicated of all art, including literature. The characters of a novel are prisoners locked in their own fate by being committed to the infinite repetition of the same acts. Their history goes on, but makes no progress (*CPP* 10). As evidence of this, Levinas cites "a few images" found in Dostoyevsky, as recalled by Proust in the fifth volume (1923) of *In Search of Lost Time*. We read:

> The plastic issue of the literary work was noted by Proust in a particularly admirable page of *The Captive*. In speaking of Dostoyevsky, what holds his attention is neither Dostoyevsky's religious ideas, his metaphysics, nor his psychology, but some profiles of girls, a few images: the house of the crime with its stairway and its *dvornik* in *Crime and Punishment*, Grushenka's figure in *The Brothers Karamazov*. It is as though we are to think that the plastic element of reality is, in the end, the goal of the psychological novel. (*CPP* 10; modified translation)[11]

According to Levinas, art not only makes time stand still, it also suspends our moral judgment: "Being unable to end, it cannot go toward the better" (*CPP* 12). What Levinas means by this is that art has no *telos* beyond itself; it does not *act* inasmuch as it does not entertain a future goal to be accomplished.[12] Levinas says, "Art, essentially disengaged, constitutes in a world of initiative and responsibility, a dimension evasion" (*CPP* 12). Artistic endeavor is "disinterestedness" (*CPP* 12), not in the sense that Levinas will later use this term in *Totality and Infinity* (*TI* 35), nor in the sense of "contemplation" (*CPP* 12), but somewhat similar to the Kantian sense where it refers to a kind of aesthetic experience that is distinguished from practical, cognitive, and moral experience.[13] Art does not challenge us to improve the world, but works to console us by giving the illusion of an imaginary triumph over evil. "Revenge," says Levinas, "is gotten on wickedness by producing a caricature, which is to take from it its reality without annihilating it" (*CPP* 12). Raskolnikov bludgeons an old woman to death with a hatchet, but strangely, we do not condemn him for it. This is because he has not quite killed Levinas's Other, who is "the stranger, the widow, and the orphan" (*TI* 251); he has killed "a stupid, senseless, worthless, wicked, and decrepit old hag" (*CP* 84), someone whose money could be used to save countless lives from poverty, decay, and sickness:

> One death in exchange for a hundred lives — why, it's simple arithmetic! And when you come to think of it, what does the life of a sickly, wicked old hag amount to when weighted in the scales of the general good of mankind? (*CP* 84)

I shall discuss later Levinas's repudiation of precisely this type of utilitarian reasoning, which is essentially the logic of theodicy. First, I wish to return to "Reality and Its Shadow," which discusses other possibilities for art than those already mentioned.

Having denounced art as an evasion of responsibility, and lacking moral and political "commitment" (*CPP* 12),[14] Levinas writes:

> But all this is true for art separated from the criticism that integrates the inhuman work of the artist into the human world. Criticism already detaches it [art] from its irresponsibility by envisaging its technique. It treats the artist as a man at work. Already inquiring after the influences he undergoes it links this disengaged and proud man to real history. (*CPP* 12)

Levinas's claim is suggestive as follows: Consider a Marxist interpretation of works of literature. Here the critic attempts to discover the movement of history, the relations of production, or class conflicts at the origin of the creative act that up until then appeared magical and unfathomable. In the calling into question of artistic production, criticism detaches art from the world of idolatry, myth, and *enthousiasmos*, integrating it into the real world of the artist that is conditioned by psychological, cultural, and historical antecedents. In this manner, criticism rejoins philosophy as the search for truth (*CPP* 13).

The criticism of art is not always external to art, but is frequently immanent to the productive activity itself. This is especially true of modernist art, whose essence, in Clement Greenberg's words, "lies . . . in the use of the characteristic methods of a discipline to criticize the discipline itself."[15] The character of modernist self-criticism leads Levinas to invoke Dostoyevsky for a second time in "Reality and Its Shadow":

> Modern literature, disparaged for its intellectualism (which nonetheless goes back to Shakespeare, the Molière of *Don Juan*, Goethe, *Dostoyevsky*) certainly manifests a more and more clear awareness of this fundamental insufficiency of artistic idolatry. In this intellectualism the artist refuses to be only an artist, not because he wants to defend a thesis or cause, but because he needs to interpret his myths about himself. *Perhaps the doubts that, since the renaissance, the alleged death of God has put into the souls,* have compromised for the artist the reality of the henceforth inconsistent models, have imposed on him the onus of finding his models anew in the heart of his production itself, and made him believe he had a mission to be creator and revealer. The task of criticism remains essential, *even if God were not dead, but only exiled.* (*CPP* 13; emphasis added)

Needless to say, Nietzsche would emphatically disagree. The assertion that Modernism coincides with the "death of God,"[16] which in section 358 of *The Gay Science* is said to begin with Luther and the Protestant Reformation, seems to misapply Nietzsche's theory, according to which the death of God signifies the possibility of "a revaluation of values" in which art takes the place of truth.[17] To assimilate art to truth and criticism, as Levinas does in the passage quoted above, precisely resembles the treatment of art that Nietzsche denounces in *The Birth of Tragedy* under the heading of "aesthetic Socratism," whose supreme law is "To be beautiful everything must be intelligible."[18] It is perhaps because Levinas suspects that Nietzscheans would have no difficulty dismissing his views on art as reactionary, one more sign that the death of God "has not yet reached the ears of men,"[19] that Levinas displaces the criticism by speaking merely of "the *alleged* death of God," and by suggesting that God may not be dead but "only exiled." In any case, Levinas emphasizes that he is not going to discuss the "logic" of the philosophical explanation of art, which would go beyond the "intentionally limited perspective" of the essay (*CPP* 13). With the following words, "Reality and Its Shadow" abruptly ends: "For one would have to introduce the perspective of the relation with the other without which being could not be told in its reality" (*CPP* 13).

"Everything is permitted" — Ivan Karamazov

Two years before Nietzsche introduced the notion of the death of God in *The Gay Science,* Dostoyevsky completed his last work, *The Brothers Karamazov* (1880). Indeed, if one were forced to name a work by Dostoyevsky that had the greatest impact on Levinas's ethics, it would be *The Brothers Karamazov* — the novel Freud called "the most magnificent in the world."[20]

The novel includes an anecdote told by Peter Miusov about Ivan Karamazov:

> at a certain social gathering, consisting mostly of ladies, he [Ivan] solemnly declared during an argument that there was absolutely nothing in the whole world to make men love their fellow-men, that there was no law in nature that man should love mankind, and that if love did exist on earth, it was not because of any natural law but solely because men believed in immortality. He added in parenthesis that all natural law consisted of that belief, and that if you were to destroy the belief in

immortality in mankind, not only love but every living force on which the continuation of life in the world depended, would dry up at once. Moreover, there would be nothing immoral then, *everything would be permitted,* even cannibalism. But this is not all: he wound up with the assertion that for every individual, like myself, for instance, who does not believe in God or in his own immortality, the moral laws of nature must at once be changed to the exact opposite of the former religious laws, and that self-interest, even if it were to lead to crime, must not only be permitted but even recognized as necessary, the most rational. (*BK 77*; emphasis added)

Ivan has often been understood to mean (A) "If God does not exist, everything is permitted." However, on closer inspection, Ivan in fact appears to be saying (B) "If there is no *belief in God,* everything is permitted." The former material conditional is a metaphysical claim, namely, that an absolute moral good or virtue presupposes the existence of God. This is the thinking behind, for example, divine command theory. The latter is a claim about human psychology, namely, that without belief in immortality (or divine punishment), there is nothing to keep egoism in check. Although the psychological claim seems to be the one that most expresses Ivan's position above, much later in *The Brothers Karamazov,* when Ivan is having his third interview with Smerdyakov — who accuses Ivan of complicity in the murder of his father because he, Ivan, instilled in Smerdyakov the idea that "if there's no everlasting God, there's no such thing as virtue, and there's no need of it at all" (*BK 743*) — the metaphysical proposition would seem to be what is at issue. In any case, I shall assume that Ivan can be understood as making both claims. The reader should note, however, that (A) and (B) are logically distinct claims, and one does not entail the other.

Levinas invokes Ivan's consequent "everything is permitted" on a number of occasions in his work, though he too seems unclear about the antecedent. Sometimes he suggests that the antecedent is a world in which both the self and the Other are assimilated to the totality in which ethical *difference* is suspended. Thus Levinas speaks in one place of "a world that constitutes a totality in its indifference to values (good and evil being of equal worth); a world that makes up a whole in the 'everything is permitted' of Dostoyevsky."[21] On other occasions, he seems to have in mind the idea of a self that is *separated* from the totality in such a way that it finds itself alone in the world, and has yet to have its natural freedom called into question by the Other. In *Totality and Infinity*, for example, we read: "To approach the Other is to put into question my freedom, my spontaneity as a living being, my emprise over things, this 'moving force', this impetuosity of the current to which *everything is permitted*, even murder" (*TI* 303; my emphasis). The separation of the I, in which it exercises its naturally arbitrary freedom outside of the criticism of the Other, is what Levinas means by "atheism":

> One can call atheism this separation so complete that the separated being maintains itself all by itself, without participating in the being from which it is separated — *eventually capable of adhering to it by belief*. . . . By atheism we thus understand a *position prior to both the negation and affirmation of the divine*, the breaking with participation by which the I posits itself as the same and as I. (*TI* 58; emphasis added)

This is not quite the same as the antecedent of (B) above. Whereas atheism for Ivan is entailed by the negation of the belief in God, here atheism is understood as "prior to both the negation and affirmation of the divine." This implies that for there to be a resumption of relations with the Other, which in *Totality and Infinity* Levinas calls "religion,"[22] the *existential* belief in God is not necessary (though, of course, possible). Thus, if we are to understand Levinas correctly, we need to realize that it is possible to be an atheist in the ordinary sense of the word, while also "religious" in Levinas's sense of being someone who is ethically bound to the Other, and thus no longer separated.

This last point would suggest that Ivan and Levinas have fundamentally different conceptions of what the religious life amounts to, as well as fundamentally different views of what motivates one to act morally rather than permissively. Ivan, the psychological egoist, appears to recognize only a providential and transcendent God, and explains compliance with the moral law in terms of the desire for personal immortality, a wish so strong that in Dostoyevsky's *The Devils* it is capable of converting the erstwhile atheist Mr. Verkhovensky on his deathbed. "If God exists, then I, too, am immortal! *Voilà ma profession de foi!*" he cries (*D* 655).[23] By contrast, Levinas, an ethical altruist, humanizes religion, and identifies the moral incentive with "the disinterestedness of goodness, the desire of the absolutely other" (*TI* 35). Levinas, then, would agree with Ivan's metaphysical claim (A), namely, "If God does not exist, then everything is permitted" (at least when parsed to mean "If the self lives outside of God, that is, in 'atheistic separation,' then everything is permitted"); yet he would not agree with Ivan's reasoning that the only thing capable of holding one's natural egoism in check is the promise of immortality. Indeed, when we turn to the Ivan's critique of theodicy in the most celebrated chapter of *The Brothers Karamazov,* entitled "Rebellion," it seems doubtful that Ivan himself really believed in his own argument.

The Face and the Love of Humanity

The chapter opens with Ivan confessing to his younger brother, Alyosha, that he has never understood how it is possible to love one's neighbor in close quarters: "To love a man, it's necessary he should be hidden, for as soon as he shows his face, love is gone!" (*BK* 276). Although this may sound like a profoundly *un-Levinasian* thing to say, it turns out that Ivan's repulsion has an ethical meaning. It is not Levinas's "neighbor" (the stranger, the widow, and the orphan) whom Ivan is saying it is impossible to love, someone defined in terms of victimhood, but the neighbor who does violence to Levinas's neighbor. To illustrate this point, Ivan delivers a monologue on the torture of children, which includes a number of horrific examples when those as young as five to eight years old are beaten, birched, kicked, locked up, starved, fed their own excrement, and murdered. These examples, by illustrating the impossibility of loving those who caused the children to suffer when their crimes are seen up close, eventually marshal a full-blown antitheodicy. Why did the children suffer? What purpose did it serve? Where was God when they needed him? Ivan says he focuses on children because of their *innocence:* "I'm not talking of the sufferings of grown-up people, for they have eaten the apple and to hell with them — let them all go to hell, but these little ones, these little ones!" (*BK* 283). Ivan's repeated references to children's innocence (*BK* 277, 278, 283, 286) are important for they are used to reject the theodicist's argument based on the redemption of sin, namely, that "all have to suffer so as to buy eternal harmony with their sufferings" (*BK* 286). The argument simply collapses in the case of children: "What have the children to do with it — tell me please? It is entirely incomprehensible why they, too, should have to suffer so as to buy harmony by their sufferings?" (*BK* 286) If the suffering of children is the price required for universal salvation, says Ivan, then salvation itself must be declined for the reason that it is too expensive.[24] This is the ground of Ivan's "rebellion":

> "I don't want harmony. I don't want it, out of the love I bear to mankind. I want to remain with my suffering unavenged. I'd rather remain with my suffering unavenged and my indignation unappeased, *even if I were wrong*. Besides, too high a price has been placed on harmony. We cannot afford to pay so much for admission. And therefore I hasten to return my ticket of admission. This I am doing. It is not God that I do not accept, Alyosha. I merely most respectfully return him the ticket."
> "This is rebellion," Alyosha said softly dropping his eyes. (*BK* 287)

From this incredibly rich passage, it is possible to pull a number of key Levinasian theses concerning religion and ethics:

1. *Love of humankind:* In course of the monologue Ivan has switched his position from that of not knowing how to love the neighbor to that of refusing heavenly bliss "out of the love I bear to mankind." The transition goes *uninterpreted* in the text, and would suggest that Ivan's position is not quite what he said it was. Recall, Miusov attributed to Ivan the claim that "there was no law in nature that we should love mankind, and that if love did exist on earth, it was not because of any natural law but solely because

men believed in immortality" (see above). Does not Ivan, in the passage just cited, relinquish the prospect of an afterlife? Evidently, when Ivan is speaking of his love for humankind, he makes himself the exception to his own philosophical theory. This makes it hard to resist the claim that Ivan's indignation in the face of the injustice of a child being tortured is ethically motivated, precisely because it leads him *to reject* the promise of eternal life by "returning his ticket." This is disinterestedness taken to the nth degree — the refusal of being in time and of being outside of time, in eternity. Ivan refuses to play the game. He will not accept Pascal's famous wager (based on the assumption that the potential benefits of believing are so great as to make betting on theism rational), thus sacrificing his own future happiness out of love of humankind. How are we supposed to make sense of such a one-sided sacrifice, especially against the backdrop of psychological egoism? I shall return to the "idiocy" of such an ethical gesture later (section 8).

2. *Suffering:* Ivan says, "I want to remain with my *suffering* unavenged." Given this fact, one might be inclined to dismiss Ivan as someone who is unhinged or even a masochist for whom suffering has become "voluptuous" (*TI* 259). But as we will see later (section 9), Ivan's "welcome" suffering has an ethical meaning insofar as it is suffering *for* (that is, due to) the suffering of the Other. There are other characters in Dostoyevsky's novels who seek out suffering too, most notably Alyosha Karamazov, and Sonya Marmelodov, as we will see.

3. *Beyond retribution:* Earlier Ivan had asked what should be done with the landowner who had an eight-year-old boy torn to pieces by a pack of wolfhounds in front of his mother: "Shoot him? Shoot him for the satisfaction of our moral feelings?" (*BK* 284) But Ivan doesn't want retribution. He repeatedly says: "I want to remain with my suffering *unavenged*." What good, he asks, is a hell for torturers if the children have already been tortured to death? (*BK* 287). What is perhaps most remarkable about this is that Ivan

renounces retribution saying "even if I were wrong." At first blush, this would seem to plunge Ivan into the depths of irrationalism. If an argument can be produced that shows that the landowner ought to be shot and sent to hell, should not a reasonable person accept it? But that would be to concede that a punishment exists that is equal or proportional to murder — and that is what Ivan simply refuses to concede. This is because it inserts the suffering of the victim into the logic and economy of the *lex talionis* where punishments compensate for crimes and are held to make satisfactory payment or reparation, whereas there is no way to cancel the debt in the case of murder. In "An Eye for an Eye" (1963), Levinas, who was against the death penalty (*IR* 51),[25] similarly asserts that: "Neither all eternity, nor all the money in the world, can heal the outrage done to man. It is a disfigurement or wound that bleeds for all time, as though it required a parallel suffering to staunch this eternal hemorrhage" (*DF* 148). The fact that Ivan refuses "even if I were wrong" what Shakespeare called "sweet revenge" — "Not Cassio kill'd! then murder's out of tune, And sweet revenge grows harsh" (*Othello* 5.2.135–36), — suggests that there are *limits* beyond which philosophical argumentation does not operate. Reason only goes so far, notwithstanding that there is a danger that it will become too remote and abstract, and thus get too far away from the actual neighbor against whom real crimes have been perpetrated. We, of course, frequently encounter this type of attention to the "face" of the uniquely individuated Other in Levinas's ethics, which is similarly "beyond ontology," and constituted "otherwise than knowledge."[26]

4. *Antitheodicy:* Ivan's rebellion consists in an absolute rejection of theodicy summed up by the statement "too high a price has been placed on harmony. We cannot afford to pay so much for admission." Presumably Ivan is also rejecting God in the manner of the atheist who uses the problem of evil to show that the idea of an omnipotent and omnibenevolent God is self-contradictory.[27]

However, showing that theodicy is untenable is not quite the same as showing that God does not exist. It is only a *providential* God that antitheodicy disproves. This might explain why Ivan appears prepared to reject theodicy but not God *per se:* "It is not God that I do not accept, Alyosha. I merely most respectfully return him the ticket." The logic of the argument would suggest that Ivan finds his religious belief called into question by the suffering of innocents, whom God did not help, but a Levinasian might be inclined to read it otherwise, and regard Ivan's rejection of theodicy and, *a fortiori*, his refusal of a providential God as precisely indicative of a faith *that is all the more profound the more it resembles atheism.* The nature of this faith bordering on atheism is the subject of the next section.

Deus Absconditus

In "Loving the Torah More Than God," a radio address he delivered in 1955, Levinas posed the question of whether it was still possible to believe in the existence of God after the Holocaust: "What does this suffering of innocents mean? Does it not testify to a world without God, to an earth where man alone is the measure of Good and Evil?" (*DF* 143; modified translation). There are two admissible responses to which Levinas is pointing. On the one hand, insofar as the existence of the suffering of innocents refutes the existence of a God who distributes rewards and punishments to people in accordance with their good or bad behavior, a God who, in effect, treats people as perpetual children, "atheism" would appear the only rational response (*DF* 143). On the other hand, the God underlying theodicy — the God of the philosophers — may not correspond to the true meaning of God. Levinas asks: "But with what lesser demon or strange magician have you therefore filled your heaven, you who claim it is empty? And, why under an empty sky, do you continue to hope for a good and sensible world?" (*DF* 143). The implication is twofold: a children's God is unworthy of belief, and, furthermore, the atheist's "negation" of such a God — Ivan's? — is perhaps religiously inspired to the extent that it seeks justice when it is absent from the world. The belief in *Deus absconditus,* "the God who hides his face" (*DF* 143), depends for its justification on a conception of God who is no longer the providential father figure who intervenes in history and keeps his promises, but the adult's God who "appeals instead to the full maturity of the responsible man" (*DF* 143).

A satisfactory specification of the nature of God, says Levinas, is not provided by theology, but ethics as learned from the Torah (*DF* 144). Levinas's immense indebtedness to Jewish sources is sufficiently familiar that there is no need for me to discuss it here. I want instead to turn to Levinas's most detailed treatment of theodicy in "Useless Suffering," a late essay appearing in 1982. The essay amplifies many of the themes adumbrated in earlier texts, though with three significant differences. Firstly, the antitheodic argument is conjoined with a full-blown phenomenology of suffering. Secondly, the Holocaust is presented as the paradigm of the suffering of innocents. Thirdly, the renunciation of a concealed (that is, authentic) God is considered *morally* culpable. I shall return to each of these themes in the next three sections.

The Holocaust and "the end of theodicy"

The heart of Levinas's critique of theodicy is his thesis that the suffering of innocents is never morally justifiable. This is summed up in "Useless Suffering" by the statement: "the justification of the neighbor's pain is certainly the source of all immorality" (*PL* 163). The neighbor's pain is precisely "useless" in that it literally serves no purpose that would justify its being used as a means. This raises, according to Levinas, the philosophical problem of "the meaning that religiosity and the human morality of goodness can still retain after the end of theodicy" (*PL* 163). Before considering this question, however, we should remark that by "the end of theodicy" Levinas means the refutation of theodicy. Thus, he speaks of "the 'final solution' where theodicy abruptly appeared impossible" (*PL* 164). Levinas does not intend to suggest that theodicy was ever true. Theodicy was no more true before the Holocaust than was the claim that light waves require the "luminiferous aether" before the Michelson-Morley experiment. However, to link "the end of theodicy" to a specific *historical* event, the Holocaust, is clearly to give an exemplary status to the suffering of Jewish people. Enumerating the worst evils of the twentieth century, including World War I, Stalinism, Hitlerism, World War II, the Holocaust, Hiroshima, the Gulag, and Cambodia, Levinas writes:

> Among these events the Holocaust of the Jewish people under the reign of Hitler seems to us the paradigm of gratuitous human suffering, where evil appears in its diabolical horror. This is perhaps not a subjective feeling. The disproportion between suffering and every theodicy was shown at Auschwitz with glaring, obvious clarity. Its possibility puts into question the multi-millennial traditional faith. Did not the word of Nietzsche on the death of God take on, in the extermination camps, the signification of a quasi-empirical fact? (*PL* 162)

As evidence for the exemplary status of the Holocaust, Levinas quotes approvingly from Emil Fackenheim's short book, *God's Presence in History*: "Negro Christians have been murdered for their race, able to find comfort in a faith not at issue. The more than one million Jewish children murdered in the Nazi holocaust died . . . because of the Jewish faith of their great-grandparents [who brought] up Jewish children" (quoted by Levinas [*PL* 162]). While it is unclear to me what is to be gained philosophically by comparing "Negro Christians" with "Jewish children," the logic is the same as that used in "Rebellion," where Ivan makes a point of repeatedly saying that he is going to focus on the suffering of children because they have "not eaten of the apple." Levinas seems to accept the logic of using the example of children to derail theodicy when he says:

> The inhabitants of the Eastern European Jewish communities constituted the majority of the six million tortured and massacred; they represented human beings least corrupted by the ambiguities of our world, *and the millions of infants had the innocence of infants.* (*PL* 163; emphasis added)

Although Levinas is undoubtedly right, one might still be inclined to question the exemplarity Levinas cedes to Jews here, which is obviously not to deny the innocence of the victims of Nazi persecution, but to question the implied loss of innocence of those individuals who were not.

"Useless Suffering" also includes a commentary of Fackenheim's notion of a 614th commandment: Jews are commanded to survive as Jews lest the Jewish people perish as Jews and hand Hitler a posthumous victory,[28] which Levinas interprets as follows:

> To renounce after Auschwitz this God absent from Auschwitz — no longer to assure the continuation of Israel — would amount to finishing the criminal enterprise of National-Socialism, which aimed at the annihilation of Israel and the forgetting of the ethical message of the Bible, which Judaism bears, and whose multi-millennial history is concretely prolonged by Israel's existence as a people. (*PL* 163–64)

If this is correct, then clearly one would have to reject atheism in the ordinary sense of the term, but it is not clear that Fackenheim's argument is as compelling as Levinas appears to suggest in the essay under discussion. One could argue, as does Michael Wyschogrod,[29] that the commandment not to hand Hitler a posthumous victory only has imperatival force for those Jews who are already believers — reducing the commandment to a redundancy. Moreover, Fackenheim's argument can also be criticized on purely ethical grounds, for it implies that all atheistic Jews, including the survivors who were atheists at the time of the Holocaust or became atheists due to their experiences, are guilty of being "accomplices" to the Hitlerian regime.

For Levinas, the Holocaust and the many other cruelties of the twentieth century, "from Sarajevo to Cambodia" (*PL* 164), present an ultimate choice not just for Jews, but all *humanity*. "Is humanity, in its indifference, going to abandon the world to useless suffering?" Or, alternatively,

> must not humanity, in a faith more difficult than ever, in a faith without theodicy, continue Sacred History; a history which now demands even more of the resources of the *self* in each one, and appeals to its

suffering inspired by the suffering of the other person, to its compassion which is non-useless suffering (or love), which is no longer suffering "for nothing," and which straightway has meaning? . . . [A]re we not all pledged — like the Jewish people to their faithfulness — to the second term of this alternative? (*PL* 164)

Two things about the second alternative are most perplexing. One wonders why the exhortation for "humanity" to be moral without any consoling theodicy requires a commitment to continue *Jewish* "Sacred History" (*l'Histoire Sainte*). What is the special relationship between Judaism and morality? Levinas, of course, would say, with Kant,[30] that he is not founding morality on faith, but his faith on morality. But he would fail to specify the conditions under which moral judgments promoted from within Judaism are arised to the status of universal moral principles. This *universalization* of responsibility is odd and without parallel in Levinas's work, and would appear to repeat the type of totalizing gesture that Levinas elsewhere calls into question.

ETHICAL SINGULARITY: "AND I MOST OF ALL"

Contrast the foregoing with Levinas's remarks on the subject of theodicy in an interview five years after the publication of "Useless Suffering":

Before the twentieth century, all religion begins with the promise. It begins with the 'Happy End.' It is the promise of heaven. Well then, doesn't a phenomenon like Auschwitz invite you, on the contrary, to think the moral law independently of the Happy End? That is the question. I would even ask whether we are not faced with an order that one cannot preach. *Does one have the right to preach to the other a piety without reward?* That is what I ask myself. It is easier to tell myself to believe without promise than it is to ask it of the other. *That is the idea of asymmetry.* I can demand of myself that which I cannot demand of the other. (*PL* 176; emphasis added)

The idea of asymmetry is the key concept of *Totality and Infinity*, where Levinas defines it as "the radical impossibility of seeing oneself from the outside and of speaking in the same sense of oneself and of others" (*TI* 53). The importance of this concept for Levinas's ethics is sufficiently obvious. But did Levinas invent it or only theorize it? Certainly he did not invent it. In the interview just mentioned, Levinas claimed that the idea is to be found in Dostoyevsky. He said:

> The idea of dissymmetry seems very important to me; it is, perhaps, the most important way of conceiving of the relation between self and other which does not place them on the same level. You know my quotation from Dostoyevsky: "Everyone is guilty in front of everyone else and me [*sic*] more than all the others." That is the idea of asymmetry. (*PL* 179)

The quotation in question is from the chapter of *The Brothers Karamazov* entitled "From the Life of the Departed Priest and Monk, The Elder Zossima, taken down from his own words by Alexey Karamazov [Alyosha]." David Magarschak's English translation runs as follows:

> S. every one of us is responsible for everyone else in every way, and I most of all. (*BK* 339)

There are numerous occasions in various published works and interviews where Levinas quotes the above[31] — sometimes twice in the same interview. Admittedly, Levinas does not always quote it the same way, and sometimes conflates it with another, closely related teaching attributed to the Elder, which Magarshack translates as:

> S' For you must know, beloved, that each of us is beyond all question responsible for all men and all things on earth, not only because of the general transgressions of the world, but each one individually for all men and every single man on this earth. (*BK* 190)

There are two significant differences between S and S' that are worth mentioning. First, S limits responsibility by speaking of it *for* humans, whereas S' speaks of a responsibility "for all humans *and all things on earth*," thereby challenging the humanist assumption made by Levinasians, though not always by Levinas himself, that ethics excludes nonhuman animals and the environment. Since I have already discussed this question elsewhere, I will not pursue it here.[32] Second, and most significantly, S underscores the asymmetry of responsibility in the sense that the ethically determined individual has more responsibility than have the others for whom he or she is responsible. Levinas takes this to mean, "I am responsible for a total responsibility, which answers for all the others and for all in the others, even for their responsibility" (*EI* 99). On the other hand, S' generalizes guiltless responsibility, and thus fails to satisfy the axiom of asymmetry. It follows that S' is *worse* than S from a Levinasian point of view. In *Otherwise than Being,* for example, Levinas calls it "criminal" to hold the Other accountable for what he or she did not do ("to accuse the innocence of the other, to ask of the other more than he owes, is criminal" [*OB* 195 n. 18]).[33] This is the ultimate ground of Levinas's antitheodicy. For were the Other justly held responsible without having done anything wrong, then the suffering of innocents would be just and justified. Indeed, it is precisely the idea that the innocent should bear the burden of guilt that is unintelligible to Ivan in the "Rebellion": "If it is really true that they [children] share their fathers' responsibility for all of their fathers' crimes, then that truth is not, of course, of this world and it's incomprehensible to me" (*BK* 286).

But the Elder's claim S is also difficult to make sense of from a philosophical point of view. If each of us is responsible for each other, how am I to be considered "more" responsible? Many people will be inclined to think that if 20 people are responsible for helping each other, then each of them is only one-twentieth responsible for the provision of help. It is as though there is only a finite amount of responsibility to go around, of which each individual has a separate share. The Elder's claim would suggest, by contrast, that responsibility multiplies in my own case, so that I am fully responsible, just as if I were acting alone in the world. The paralogistic nature of this type of ethics is frequently acknowledged by Levinas. Discussing the one exceptional case in which responsibility is imposed on a no-fault basis, he clearly states:

> This exigency . . . beyond all equity, is produced in the form of an accusation preceding the fault, borne against the self [*soi*] despite its

innocence. For the order of contemplation it is something simply demented. (*OB* 113)

As for this dementia, Levinas applauded in an interview what he called "acts of stupid, senseless goodness," citing two "feeble-minded," yet "inspired" characters from Russian literature: one was the "holy fool," Ikonnikov, from Grossman's *Life and Fate;* the other, the saintly epileptic, Prince Myshkin, from Dostoyevsky's *The Idiot* (*IR* 90).

In classical ethical theories, however different, obligations are always treated as universalizable. For example, Benthamite utilitarianism famously states that "each [is] to count for one, and none for more than one." Kantianism stipulates that we adopt only those maxims that everybody else is capable of adopting. Levinas's theory, which treats responsibility asymmetrically, thus offers for consideration an altogether different approach to ethics. But the notion of ethical asymmetry is highly debatable in a philosophical context, which is why Levinas appeals to phenomenology and literature to ground it. In the remaining section of this essay, I should like to explore further this notion as we find it attested in the work of Dostoyevsky by discussing what Levinas calls "expiatory suffering."

"EXPIATORY SUFFERING . . . SOUGHT AFTER BY DOSTOYEVSKY'S CHARACTERS" — LEVINAS

In "Useless Suffering," Levinas analyzes the phenomenon of suffering from the perspective of both the victim who is the neighbor and the ethically determined individual who suffers because of the suffering of the neighbor. He says, "It is suffering *in me,* and not as suffering in general, that *welcome* suffering . . . can signify a true idea: the expiatory suffering of the just suffering for others, the suffering that illuminates, the suffering that is sought after by Dostoyevsky's characters" (*PL* 166 n. 5). Levinas does not tell us which of Dostoyevsky's characters he has in mind, but clearly Ivan's willingness to suffer for the unpardonable suffering of children rather than attempting to palliate the injustice committed against innocents ("I want to remain with my suffering unavenged"), makes him an obvious candidate. Another character in Dostoyevsky that fits the mold of Levinas's conception of "expiatory suffering" is Alyosha Karamazov, the novel's "hero" — "a modest and unheroic hero" (*BK* xxv–vi) — who represents the embodiment of Zossima's religious teachings. "Alyosha also wondered whether his brother, a learned atheist, did not feel a sort of contempt for him, a silly novice. He knew for a fact that his brother was an atheist" (*BK* 32). In "Rebellion," interrupting his own monologue about the suffering of children, Ivan says to his brother, who is visibly distraught: "'I'm torturing you Alyosha. You're not yourself. I'll stop if you like.' 'Never mind. I want to suffer too,' murmured Alyosha" (*BK* 283). While Alyosha sometimes has doubts ("And yet I don't think I even believe in God" [*BK* 256]), ultimately his faith remains intact. This is because it is not based on theodicy, and thus cannot be refuted by examples of the suffering of innocents. Alyosha's refusal of theodicy is clear from the following passage in which his brother asks him openly:

> "Tell me frankly, I appeal to you — answer me: imagine that it is you yourself who are erecting the edifice of human destiny with the aim of making mean happy in the end . . . but to do that it is absolutely necessary . . . to torture to death only one tiny creature . . . would you consent to be an architect under those condition? Tell me and do not lie!"
> "No, I wouldn't," Alyosha said softly. (*BK* 287–88)

Both Ivan and Alyosha suffer for the unjust suffering of innocents in the absence of theodicy. However, there is a very important difference between Ivan's and Alyosha's suffering, one that perhaps suggests that Alyosha's rejection of theodicy is not quite as absolute as Ivan's. While Alyosha *welcomes* suffering, he continues to believe in the possibility of forgiveness, whereas Ivan clearly does not. Ivan tells Alyosha that he does not want the mother to embrace the landowner who killed her child: "She has no right to forgive the torturer for that, even if her child were to forgive him! And if that is so, if they [*sic*] have no right to forgive him what becomes of harmony? Is there a being in the whole world who could or would have the right to forgive?" (*BK* 287).

Alyosha replies that there is such a being — "and he can forgive everything, everyone and everything and *for everything,* because he gave his innocent blood for all and for everything" (*BK* 288). The argument is rejected by Ivan on the ground that Christ was not "the only one without sin" (*BK* 288). The interesting thing about this claim is that it pulls the rug out completely from beneath the feet of the theodicist who would still attempt to palliate injustice by an appeal to original sin. If the doctrine of original sin is not accepted (Ivan, as we know, finds it "incomprehensible"), then the Christian theology of atonement, when it does not unabashedly ignore the innocence of the victim, succumbs to the logical absurdity of "turning the clocks back," and undoing the past by retroactive forgiveness. It goes without saying that atonement comes too late for the innocent who have already been tortured, and bestowing forgiveness on behalf of the victim makes no sense if the only party qualified to forgive, that is, the victim, either refuses or, as is often the case, is already dead. Levinas too, we should add, rejects the Christian theology of atonement: "No one, not even God, can substitute himself for the victim. The world in which pardon is all-powerful becomes inhuman" (*DF* 20).

Like Alyosha, Sonya Marmeladov is selfless, innocent, sensitive, and pious, and similarly finds her faith called into question by someone she loves, in her case, Raskolnikov. In part 4, chapter 4 of *Crime and Punishment,* Sonya and Raskolnikov discuss Katerina Ivanovna, Sonya's stepmother, who is consumptive and soon to die. Sonya is in the process of defending Katerina after the Raskolnikov has *falsely* (Levinas would say, "criminally") accused her of beating Sonya:

> "Why, no! Of course not! How can you say a thing like that?" Sonya looked at him horrified.
>
> "So you are fond of her?"
>
> "Fond of her? Of course I am," Sonya said in a plaintive, drawn-out voice, folding her hands in distress. "Oh, if you — if you really knew her! She's just like a child really. She — she's almost out of her mind with grief. And what a clever woman she used to be — how generous — how kind! Oh, you don't know anything — anything!"

Sonya said this almost in despair, agitated and distressed, and wringing her hands. Her pale cheeks flushed again, and there was an anguished look in her eyes. It was plain that she had been deeply hurt, and she wanted badly to say something, to put her feelings into words, to defend Mrs. Marmeladov. A kind of *insatiable* compassion, if one may call it that, was expressed in every feature of her face. (*CP* 333) (Dostoevsky's emphasis)

In "Meaning and Sense," an essay that appeared shortly after the publication of *Totality and Infinity*, Levinas commented on the above as follows:

There is a scene in Dostoyevsky's *Crime and Punishment* where Sonya Marmaladova looks upon Raskolnikov in his despair, and Dostoyevsky speaks of "insatiable compassion." He does not say "inexhaustible compassion." It is as though the compassion that goes from Sonya to Raskolnikov were a hunger which the presence of Raskolnikov nourishes beyond saturation, increasing this hunger to infinity. (*CPP* 94)

It is almost certain that Levinas has misinterpreted the scene in question. It is not Sonya's love for Raskolnikov that Dostoyevsky is describing when he speaks of "insatiable compassion," but her love for her stepmother. Sonya's love for Raskolnikov is erotic whereas her love for her consumptive stepmother is ethical. Levinas maintains a sharp distinction between erotic love and ethics. Erotic love is constituted by the "need" for enjoyment, a need that can in principle be satisfied, while ethics is characterized by a desire that cannot be satisfied, an "insatiable Desire" (*TI* 63) ("a hunger that nourishes itself not with bread but with hunger itself" [*TI* 179]). Sonya's "insatiable compassion" is the insatiability of desire rather than the frustration of erotic love, which "resemble[s] metaphysical desire only in the deception of satisfaction or in the exasperation of non-satisfaction and desire that constitutes voluptuosity itself" (*TI* 34). Sonya may well have experienced this kind of craving for her lover Raskolnikov, but her "insatiable compassion . . . expressed in every feature of her face" for her consumptive stepmother is altogether different, and Levinas undermines his own argument considerably by getting this wrong in "Meaning and Sense."

Sonya Marmelodov's tremendous capacity to undergo what Levinas calls "expiatory suffering" is again evident a few pages later in *Crime and Punishment* when Raskolnikov informs her that her stepmother is going to die. Raskolnikov pours salt into the wound by suggesting that God does not exist to help Polya, the oldest daughter of Katerina Ivanovna from her former marriage, who will be forced to prostitute herself as she, Sonya, was:

> "No, no! It can't be! No!" she cried, like one driven to *despair*, as though someone had stabbed her with a knife. "God — God would never allow such a horrible thing!"
>
> "But he lets it happen to others."
>
> "No, no! God will protect her!" She repeated beside herself.
>
> "But what if there is no God?" Raskolnikov replied in a sort of gleeful malice, and he laughed and looked at her.
>
> Sonya's face underwent a sudden terrible change and it began to twitch convulsively. She looked at him with unutterable reproach, tried to say something, but could not bring out a single word, but just burst sobbing bitterly, burying her face in her hands.
>
> "You say Mrs. Marmeladov's mind is getting unbalanced. Well, your mind is getting unbalanced, too," he said after a short pause. (*CP* 336)

What ultimately drives Sonya into despair is the prospect of Polya's suffering without God to help her. This type of mental anguish is quite different from the despair which we find in Kierkegaard, which is over the meaninglessness of the aesthetic life, and ultimately over oneself.[34] Sonya's despair is an expression of what Levinas would be inclined to consider a just suffering in me for the unjustifiable suffering of the Other, *without hope in God*. From that moment on, the ethically determined individual realizes that he or she must help the neighbor without waiting on God.

Atheism Aufgehoben

In "Loving the Torah," Levinas writes, "the God who hides His face is, we believe, neither an abstraction of the theologians nor an image of the poets. It is the hour where the just individual finds no outside recourse, where no institution protects him, where the consolation of the divine presence in childish religious sentiment is also *refused* where the individual can triumph only in his conscience, which necessarily involves suffering" (*DF* 143; modified translation).

Levinas's philosophy rejects as illusory the search for the providential God of theism. This is not to espouse atheism, however, since *Deus Absconditus* is still something rather than nothing. When one thinks one is imagining the death of God, one is really imagining the hidden, adult's God. But that is not to imagine nothing, according to Levinas, only a situation epistemically indistinguishable from the perception of a universe in which God does not exist. "The God who hides his face" cannot be known, but is attested by an act of faith that must run the gauntlet of Ivan's form of atheism if it is not to become fanciful and abstract. As Irving Greenberg has commented: "No statement, theological or otherwise, should be made that would not be credible in the presence of burning children."[35] In "A Religion for Adults," Levinas writes, "monotheism *surpasses and incorporates* atheism, but it is impossible unless you attain the age of doubt, solitude, and rebellion [*révolte*]" (*DF* 16; modified translation; emphasis added). Although few atheists would see the negation of God as something to be *aufgehoben* in this way, but we find a similar claim made by the monk Tikhon in "Stavrogin's Confession," a chapter from *The Devils* that Dostoyevsky omitted from the first edition of the novel, and which was not published until 1923:

> Complete atheism is much more acceptable than worldly indifference. . . . The absolute atheist stands on the last rung but one before the most absolute faith (*whether he steps higher or not*), while an indifferent man has no faith at all, nothing but dismal fear, and that, too, only occasionally, if he is a sensitive man. (*D* 679; emphasis added)

"The absolute atheist" is neither Alyosha nor Sonya, two characters who retain their faith despite the suffering of innocents, but Ivan, who loses his because of the suffering of innocents. Is Ivan, then, on the threshold of absolute faith "whether he steps higher or not"? I am not so sure. It should be borne in mind that the negation of the children's God no more attests to the existence of "the God who hides his face" than the absence of money on one's pillow is evidence of the existence of an insolvent tooth fairy. It may be true that the atheist's commitment to justice when it is absent from the world is inspired (Levinas would say "commanded" [*PL* 177]) by "the God who hides his face." But we may well ask whether an air of *messianic optimism* still hovers above Levinas's account, as though God remained a source of comfort in the process of withdrawal from the world. As Juliet says, "Good night, good night! Parting is such sweet sorrow" (*Romeo and Juliet* 2.2.185). Who can forget Levinas's parting words at the end of *Totality and Infinity* (before the "Conclusions")?

> Messianic triumph is pure triumph; it is secured against the revenge of evil whose return the infinite time does not prohibit. Is this eternity a new structure of time, or an extreme vigilance of messianic consciousness? The problem exceeds the bounds of this book. (*TI* 285)

But this takes us well beyond the scope of the present essay.

CONCLUDING REMARKS

The connection between Levinas's ethics and the treatment of many of the themes we find in the work of Dostoyevsky is, I trust, clear. The continued belief in justice when justice is absent from the earth, the refusal to abandon the neighbor when the heavens appear empty, the *rebellion* against the idea that the suffering of innocents is ever justified, the rejection of theodicy, the suffering for the unjust suffering of the Other, and finally, ethical asymmetry, are all transparently Dostoyevskian. If the Holocaust taught Levinas the failure of theodicy, so utterly invalidated by such an event "that it makes waiting for the saving actions of an all-powerful God impossible without degradation" (*PL* 159), we must surely grant that reading Dostoyevsky taught Levinas a way to think about ethics without theodicy. The idea that the ethically determined individual commits him or herself to the Other regardless of whether or not God exists, would become the hallmark of Levinas's philosophy, both middle and late, and it undoubtedly bears the stamp of the influence of Dostoyevsky. If what I say is correct, it is the case that art, religion, and ethics *post mortem dei* retained their meaning for Levinas after the Holocaust not only because of his Jewish faith, but also because of Dostoyevsky, a Russian novelist who made on him the deepest impression of all — almost as deep as the scribes of Babylon.[36]

ABBREVIATIONS

For works by Levinas, see the list of abbreviations at the front of this volume.

BK   Fyodor Dostoyevsky. *The Brothers Karamazov*. Trans. David Magarshack. London: Penguin, 1984.

CP   Fyodor Dostoyevsky. *Crime and Punishment*. Trans. David Magarshack. London: Penguin, 1984.

D   Fyodor Dostoyevsky. *The Devils*. David Magarshack. London: Penguin, 1987.

IR   Jill Robbins, ed. *Is It Righteous to Be? Interviews with Emmanuel Levinas*. Stanford: Stanford University Press, 2001.

PL   Robert Bernasconi and David Wood, eds. *The Provocation of Levinas*. London: Routledge, 1988.

Educating the Solitary Man: Levinas, Rousseau, and the Return to Jewish Wisdom

Claire Katz

Man is born free; and everywhere he is in chains.
— Jean-Jacques Rousseau, *The Social Contract*

No one is more self-sufficient than Rousseau.
— Levinas, *De l'evasion*

Jean-Jacques Rousseau (1712–1778) opens his book *The Social Contract* (1762) with his famous statement, "Man is born free; and everywhere he is in chains."[1] An Enlightenment thinker, Rousseau understands himself to be responding to the two dominant traditions of political thought at this time: the voluntarist tradition of Hobbes, Pufendorf, and Grotius; and the liberal tradition of Locke and Montesquieu.[2] The latter group argues that civil society exists to protect certain natural rights, one of which is liberty.[3] The former group supports an absolute monarchy (benevolent or not), with the famous statement by Hobbes, as its signature: in the *State of Nature*, life is nasty, poor, brutish, and short. The only solution is to surrender one's freedom to the sovereign and thus escape the brutality and depravity of life in the state of nature.

Rousseau's philosophical thought draws ideas from both traditions, while also demonstrating that he disagrees with both in significant ways. His goal in *The Social Contract* is to explain how humankind might accentuate its freedom through the institutions that form civil society. However, Rousseau realizes that the most formidable threat to this kind of freedom might not be another person per se. Instead, we are threatened by our dependency on others, which is cultivated through *amour-propre*, a form of self-love exemplified by greed, vanity, and selfish desire. This dependency then contributes to political decisions and political alliances that are not based on justice, but rather on our fear that we might lose those tangibles or, worse, the flattery, that we believe we now need. In turn, these social institutions, rather than enhancing our freedom as Rousseau believes they should, contribute to what makes us appear unfree. This threat thus accounts for our reluctance to enter willingly into the social contract; we are reluctant to exchange our so-called "natural" freedom for the civil freedom that would justify the chains that we construct for ourselves in any event. As Rousseau describes it, the social contract is a human artifice that is meant not to remove our chains but rather to justify them. Dependence on others becomes voluntary.

Rousseau's *Emile* (1762), the educational treatise that is meant to complement his political thought, is by his own admission not a textbook on education; nor did he intend it to be put into practice as described.[4] However, it does follow the development of the child, Emile, whom Rousseau hopes will be the exemplar of an individual raised to be self-sufficient, that is, not dependent on others for things that might lead him to make decisions that will violate his integrity. Although the ambiguous conclusion of the book leads us to wonder if such an education, even in this fictional account, is possible or even desirable, the practicality of this process is not the essential point. Instead, Rousseau wishes to complete his political thinking by providing its educational supplement.

However, in Rousseau's efforts to ensure that Emile is educated such that he not become a victim of *amour-propre*, he risks educating Emile to be incapable of having or sustaining any relationships at all. In other words, Rousseau is so concerned that Emile not become a victim of dependency such that he might sell his soul for vanity, that Emile seems unable to sustain any healthy elements of being dependent on others. Rousseau thus implies that there are no healthy attendants of dependency. Moreover, Rousseau's own bad faith leads him to believe that he can reject, or undo, the most obvious example of dependency — our original relationship to our mothers.

I turn to the work of Emmanuel Levinas to see if his project can help us out of the quandary in which Rousseau's theory leaves us. We might call Levinas (1905–1995) a post-Enlightenment figure, in the sense that his project responds to what he believes is the failure of the Enlightenment, in which he would include some elements of Judaism.[5] Levinas's response is not simply an intellectual position about the Enlightenment, as we might hold when we read Rousseau and conclude that his project is flawed — the value of rational thinking simply responding to a rational position. That is, his response was not simply academic. As a prisoner of war in World War II and as a Jew who lost both his own and his wife's immediate families in the Shoah, Levinas was both an heir to and a victim of the Enlightenment. His project begins at this rupture.

In 1934 he published the essay, "Reflections on the Philosophy of Hitlerism," in the French, personalist journal, *Esprit*. This essay, which develops a critique of radical transcendence and immanence, reveals Levinas's dissatisfaction with both extremes; the former is tied to a view that escape from this world is primary while the latter reduces us to mere materiality and ultimately produces the blood kinship and racist philosophical position that informs Hitlerism. At the end of this essay, Levinas warns us that in this philosophical debate between immanence and transcendence, the very humanity of man is at stake — and this is the problem that concerned him for the next 60 years until his death in 1995.

Because Levinas saw the Enlightenment as a failure, he does not look to the familiar philosophical sources in the canon of the history of modern philosophy for support. Instead, he turns to literary sources such as Dostoyevsky and Shakespeare, and the Jewish sacred texts such as the Torah, Talmud, and midrash. The Jewish philosophy of, for example, Franz Rosenzweig and Hermann Cohen, provides the theoretical framework for his new way of thinking: ethics as first philosophy. As a response to the virility of the *conatus essendi* that dominates Enlightenment philosophy, Levinas rhetorically employs these sources to construct Judaism as that which stands against philosophical rationality and autonomous thinking. The image of the feminine, which pervades his work for 50 years, and his unique construction of Judaism set his project apart from the modern Enlightenment mission which promoted a philosophy that supposedly was independent of any particular tradition, culture, or religion. Ultimately, Levinas exposes not only the Enlightenment's bad faith in its emphasis and glorification of the autonomous, self-serving male, but also its inability to see the limits of reason and to anticipate the betrayal of its own promise.

In what follows, I illuminate the strengths and weaknesses of Rousseau's educational project and I demonstrate that philosophical questions raised in Rousseau's project actually point to the tradition of Jewish education as their solution. By examining Rousseau's *Emile* and Emmanuel Levinas's ethical project, I explore their respective views of our relationship to and dependency on others. Although Rousseau believes that dependency, or rather, our knowledge of being dependent, is unhealthy, Levinas's writings on education and his unique view of the ethical relation return us to a tradition of Jewish education that provides an example of healthy dependency and an incentive for us to embrace it. To accomplish this task, I trace the use of the "feminine" in their respective projects. I begin by briefly sketching the role of Sophie, Rousseau's "woman," in this complex educational process.

Sophie's presence illuminates Rousseau's ambivalence about dependency, and how this ambivalence is tied to his views of sexual difference and the education of the man, Emile. I then contrast Rousseau's emphasis on autonomy with the account of gender and subjectivity, which is found generally in Jewish philosophy, but here I focus specifically on Levinas's project.[6] Finally, I briefly explore how dependency influences Levinas's philosophical emphasis on responsibility for the other and thus how it would inform an educational program.[7] My suggestion at the end of the paper is that Levinas's ethical project, which is founded on a Jewish humanism and a Jewish model of education, supplies the missing link not only that Rousseau needs to fulfill his political project but also what is needed by the Enlightenment in general.

THE SOLITARY MAN

At the beginning of book 1 of *Emile,* Rousseau addresses his audience by saying, "Tender, anxious mother, I appeal to you." The author's footnote to this address begins as follows:

> The earliest education is most important and it undoubtedly is woman's work. If the author of nature had meant to assign it to men he would have given them milk to feed the child. Address your treatises on education to the women, for not only are they able to watch over it more closely than men, not only is their influence always predominant in education, its success concerns them more nearly, for most widows are at the mercy of their children.[8]

This statement is noteworthy for several reasons. First, we begin book 1 of *Emile* immediately with the question of the identity of Rousseau's audience. In the body of the text he directly addresses women, or more specifically, mothers; but the footnote indicates that while the treatise might be written for mothers, he does not think — at least initially — that it is mothers who are reading it. Second, even if we grant that he is addressing mothers, their role is limited and instrumental, since they are to hand Emile (the child) over to the tutor who will complete his education. The original influence and importance of the nursing mother is subordinated to the significance of Emile's "real" education, which begins when the child is handed over to the tutor to be educated in near isolation. These originary intersubjective relations that reveal humanity as dependent and vulnerable, Rousseau either overlooks or forgets when he moves Emile to his new life with the tutor, a relationship in which Emile is supposed to be kept ignorant of the dependency that is nonetheless cultivated.

Similar to other models of education, and views of women, Rousseau's discussion in book 1 of *Emile* leads us to believe that the role of women in this contrived environment is to bear and nurse the child only to turn that child over to the tutor. And again, similar to other models of education, the educational model described by Rousseau implies that women — or at least, mothers — are not fit to be tutors. The tutor needs to be someone who will not stand in the way of the student by projecting onto the student his or her own interests, desires, and needs. It would seem that a distant observer, a disinterested tutor, is the ideal candidate. Where the mother would fail in the endeavor to raise Emile with immunity to the corrupting forces of society, Rousseau believes the tutor will succeed.

Rousseau acknowledges that some dependency is non-negotiable. As we see at the end of the book, Emile does become dependent on the tutor; the significant point is that Emile developed unaware of this dependency. Thus, for all his concern about dependency, Rousseau's educational model relies on a relationship of dependency. In light of the corruption that Rousseau fears dependent relationships will yield, ought he not fear that this child is at the complete mercy of the tutor? What is to prevent the tutor from taking advantage of the child? Rousseau presupposes that the tutor is in fact a "mensch," without providing any explanation for his origin. Additionally, he invests all of this dependency in one relationship — that between the child and his tutor. The goodhearted tutor whom Rousseau conjures up is not only overdetermined, he is nothing short of magical.[9]

Having abandoned the female influence early in *Emile*, Rousseau reintroduces it to us in book 5, when we meet Sophie, the woman to whom Emile is matched. Book 5 tells the story of Sophie's education, a discussion that complicates the status of the woman in this educational project. In fact, although Emile is the one who is formally educated and ostensibly educated away from the corrupting forces of society — including the mother — his encounter with Sophie indicates that his entire education has been intended to culminate in this one event: how to be a man in a relationship with a woman. Additionally, Sophie is charged with the responsibility to oversee Emile's behavior. Emile is educated by a man to be a man; Sophie's education "must be planned in relation to man" for she is the one who tends to him as a parent tends to a child.[10] Her teaching efforts model the tutor's. But there is an important difference — Sophie must speak and act such that she *leads* Emile to do what is expected of him:

> Thus the different constitution of the two sexes leads us to a third con-
> clusion, that the stronger party seems to be master, but is as a matter
> of fact dependent on the weaker, and that, not by any foolish custom
> of gallantry, nor yet by the magnanimity of the protector, but by an inex-
> orable law of nature. For nature has endowed woman with a power of
> stimulating man's passions in excess of man's power of satisfying those
> passions, and has thus made him dependent on her goodwill, and com-
> pelled him in his turn to endeavor to please her, so that she may be will-
> ing to yield to his superior strength.[11]

Sophie is "educated" to win Emile's affections, and ultimately to have mastery over him by keeping his affections; it is a dependency that Rousseau applauds. Thus, it is Sophie who knows much more about *who* Emile is than he knows about himself. The layers of knowledge and self-knowledge that go without comment or discussion are remarkable in light of this book's focus on education. Rousseau subscribes to the classic, and old-fashioned, view that it is women who *really* have the power in the home, even if that power is both implicit and ephemeral. We should not forget that the law enforces Emile's power. Nonetheless, Rousseau leads us to believe that through her wily ways, it is Sophie who really wears the pants — by, in fact, wearing dresses.[12]

Insofar as Emile is dependent on Sophie, his dependency is unknown to him, and, Rousseau believes, this lack of knowledge regarding his dependency is crucial. In fact, this dependency is denied by all parties in order to maintain the noble illusion of male independence. Sophie must continue to win his affections and have Emile believe his actions issue from his own choice, rather than because she has tricked him, for whatever reason, into acting according to her own wishes. Emile's love for Sophie is the result of a careful manipulation, and Sophie successfully "pleases" him. In spite of Rousseau's display of contempt for the coquettishness and manipulations of French women, it is clear that he needs Sophie to be manipulative since Emile cannot know that he is in fact dependent on her. So just as Emile finds himself "falling" for her — potentially hopelessly devoted to her — the tutor arranges for Emile to travel abroad so that he can return to Sophie "worthy" of her — that is, as the autonomous male he was educated to be, one who believes he can live without her. In the end, it is Sophie to whom the tutor transfers his guardianship of Emile even though this dependency is kept secret, thus undermining any fact that Emile is truly independent of her.[13]

The layered complexity of dependency is underscored by the very last few lines of the book, in which Emile embraces his tutor and tells him that he is more dependent on the tutor than ever before, now that he, Emile, is on the verge of becoming a father.

> My master, congratulate your son; he hopes soon to have the honor of being a father. What a responsibility will be ours, how much we shall need you! Yet God forbid that I should let you educate the son as you educated the father. God forbid that so sweet and holy a task should be fulfilled by any but myself, even though I should make as good a choice for my child as was made for me! But continue to be the teacher of the young teachers. Advise and control us; we shall be easily led; as long as I live I shall need you. I need you more than ever now that I am taking up the duties of manhood.[14]

Here, however, Emile is aware of his dependency on the tutor, in part because the tutor confessed the truth of how he raised him. This dependency appears more profound than the tutor anticipated. In the end, as revealed in the sequel to *Emile, Émile et Sophie, ou Les Solitaires,* Emile turns out to be far more dependent on the tutor than he might have been in any "normal" relationship between a parent and child.[15] There is a strange sense in which Rousseau has both inverted and perverted the originary parent-child relationship and then later the relationship between lovers. The unhealthy dependency that develops between the tutor and Emile ultimately prevents Emile from developing a healthy relationship of dependency on Sophie.

Rousseau delivers an educational model that while accentuating the independent male, relies on at least a minimal dependency; Emile is serially and "monogamously" dependent, one person at a time with a limited number of people on whom he can form this type of relationship. If we follow the gender analysis through to its end then we see how Rousseau identifies the limits of the original relationship of dependency on the mother in order to emphasize Emile's dependency on the tutor, and then ultimately on Sophie. Rousseau's wish to avoid all unhealthy dependent relationships in order to be immune to forces of corrupt institutions, leads to an educational system precisely as he describes it. But central to this educational model is Rousseau's reliance on the magical, goodhearted tutor, who enters into the relationship with Emile prepared to help him flourish and always with Emile's best interests in mind. That is, Rousseau's educational model presupposes not only Emile's dependency, but a mensch on whom he depends. This presupposition requires us to ask after the origin of the mensch. The relationship that Rousseau imagines between the tutor and the student is more similar to one that he could not have imagined — that found within the tradition of Jewish education as illuminated by Emmanuel Levinas.

Judaism, Dependence, and the Return to Jewish Wisdom

At the beginning of his 1935 essay *De l'evasion*, Emmanuel Levinas asserts that "there is no one more self-sufficient than Rousseau."[16] As we see from the discussion above, this statement accurately and succinctly characterizes Rousseau's thoughts on education — and it directs our attention to the fundamental problem with that philosophical position as sponsoring an approach to education. Among other themes explored in this essay, the most noteworthy one is Levinas's emphasis on the body and the role that embodiment plays in the formation of our identities. This early essay continues Levinas's exploration of our enchainment to our body and our simultaneous need to escape that enchainment that he first identified in the essay on Hitlerism. Levinas's phenomenological description reveals that our embodiment requires vulnerability and dependence.[17] Our bodies demand our attention, and thus, our first responsibility is to feed them, clothe them, and protect them. Our primary needs betray our belief that we are free in the sense that Rousseau celebrates.

Levinas's writings follow the trajectory that begins with this early essay. They advance the view that we *are* dependent and it is our dependence that makes us human. Subjectivity for Levinas is defined by one's ethical response to the other, not by one's freedom or ability to make autonomous decisions. Interestingly, this thread entwines with another, that of his treatment of the feminine.

In Levinas's early formulation of the ethical relation, the feminine inaugurated the experience of alterity and then developed into a transcendental condition for the possibility of the ethical, that is, it provided the means for the subject to transcend to the level of the ethical, while not participating directly in the relation.[18] He ultimately names the feminine, defined as the maternal body, as the paradigm for the ethical relationship itself.[19] However, Levinas does not expect that it is only women who either are or should be capable of ethical response. His use of the maternal as a simile — "the psyche is *like* the maternal body" — assures us of that (*OB* 67; translation altered). Rather, it is the feminine, in this case, the maternal body, that provides us with the best description of that which he cannot otherwise describe — an unwilled, irrecusable responsibility. He uses the feminine to define the ethical, but it is the ethical that defines us, all of us — men and women — as human. His view of subjectivity, then, simultaneously endorses and rejects a rigid emphasis on sexual difference. And it is this originary dependency, revealed by our own primary needs and our original relationship to the maternal body that Levinas exploits for his philosophical project.

It should not surprise us that Levinas's ethical model explicitly assumes a dependent relationship. In his writings on Judaism we find frequent references to "we will do and we will hear," to Judaism as a religion for adults, to religion as a risk, and so forth.[20] Levinas's repeated use of these phrases indicates that he sees something unique in the way that Judaism begins and sustains itself. As we know from the commentaries, Judaism begins with a risk — a group of people are offered and accept the Torah without knowing what it involves. This risk resembles the kind of gamble that Rousseau hopes we will all take in accepting the social contract, though he cannot identify the institution that will persuade us to do so. According to Rousseau, we somehow need to develop the psychological and emotional maturity that will advance us to the stage of accepting a commitment without knowing what the commitment will yield, and we need to do this voluntarily. For example, those of us who are married know what it means to be married; we know that the rhetoric of those who are single and believe themselves to be "more free" is in one sense simply rhetoric; in another sense it is accurate. Although unmarried people are able to act in ways that a married person cannot (or maybe should not), this kind of freedom is not the kind of freedom promised or delivered by the institution of marriage. The same can be said of having children or going to school. From the outside, the people on the "inside" appear constrained, in "chains." Indeed, the outsiders are not mistaken; the insiders are in chains. Rousseau never promised to remove the chains, only to justify them. We choose them because we understand them to be the conditions of something more fulfilling than natural freedom. We know something that the outsiders can know only by first taking that leap and entering the institution. And they can get there only if there is an institution to help them along. What does this mean for an educational project?[21]

One might at first wonder about Levinas's commitment to education because his specific references to education and teaching are not only scattered but also brief. However, several facts of his biography attest to Levinas's deep commitment to education: his dedicated attendance, from 1957 and for almost 30 years after, at the annual conferences on talmudic texts at the Colloquia of the French Jewish Intellectuals, where he presented his unique readings of select talmudic texts; his teaching, beginning in 1930, at the *Alliance Israélite Universelle du Bassin Méditerranéen,* an organization whose goal was to foster Jewish education in the Mediterranean and North African countries; and in 1947, his appointment as director of the *Ecole Normale Israélite Orientale,* a branch of the *Alliance,* which trained teachers of Jewish education in France. Finally, he wrote several essays devoted to the theme of education, published in a collection under the title, *Difficult Freedom: Essays on Judaism.* The original publication venue of these essays on education indicates that at times they were intended for an audience of Jewish educators and at other times they were directed at French Jewish intellectuals. Their purpose was, on the one hand, to convince their audience of the need to return to a traditional model of Jewish education, specifically, a model that includes instruction in the Hebrew language and literature, and, on the other, to reassure this audience that "returning" to Jewish education did not mean turning away from French culture and modern life — the original mandate of the *Alliance.*

In his 1956 essay, "For a Jewish Humanism," Levinas reassures his audience that the Jewish school does not betray the ideals of the secular school. By supporting what he calls "Jewish humanism" — "that which cannot remain indifferent to the modern world in which it seeks a whole humanity" — the Jewish school lends support to what gives meaning to Judaism in the modern world (*DF* 273; 273–76).[22] The aim of the Jewish school, then, is not simply to bring a Jewish education to Jewish children in order to maintain Judaism as a religion; the aim of the Jewish school is to bring children into the kind of education that will reinforce the Jewish humanism found in and promoted by the Jewish sources.

Levinas identifies the problem with assimilation and the homogeneity that Jews desired and for the most part achieved as the loss of that which made them unique — "the secret of their science" (*DF* 275). Later, he claims that "the Hebrew language and the texts, to which it is substantially linked and which are revealed only through it, is the vehicle for a difficult wisdom concerned with truths that correlate to virtues. The unique nature of Judaism itself is that it consists in promoting as one of the highest virtues the knowledge of its own sources" (*DF* 276). Judaism's uniqueness consists not only in that it commands the teaching of itself, but also that this teaching has built into it the discovery, preservation, and enactment of a Jewish humanism. As a result, Levinas sees Judaism not as parochial, nor as a mechanism for separation, but as precisely the opposite — as that which is indispensable to human harmony.

In 1973, almost 20 years after the publication of "For a Jewish Humanism," Levinas published his essay "Antihumanism and Education," in which he argues that we are in a crisis of humanism for which Jewish education is ultimately the solution.[23] With the emancipation and principles of 1789, he explains, Jewish education succumbed to the "hermeneutic methods of the west," which disqualify rabbinic exegesis. Judaism became sanitized of the very element that might have allowed it to contribute to modern culture in a meaningful way. It was precisely because Jews did not want to be seen as different that they lost any means to enact the ideas that are still expressed in the Jewish schools and that still serve to separate Jews from the homogenous society into which they entered.

> [Jewish education] becomes religious instruction in which ideas detached from the civilization that nurtured them, express in abstract and bloodless form, the ultimate difference still separating Jews from the homogeneous society into which they entered. This is an ultimate difference that many Jews no longer want because they do not want any difference and because in the society in which religion lost its social effectiveness and its intellectual meaning, to be of Mosaic confession was to be ruled out by the uncertain, the outdated and the subjective. (*DF* 280)

Hence, Judaism became only a "mental reserve" rather than a religion that would be an organic part of daily life. Religious instruction was reduced to a few hours a week and to a *bar* or *bat mitzvah* where the student recites basic elements of reading and a few quickly forgotten gestures; it became separated from the very humanism that informed it in the first place.[24]

In order for Jewish education to mean something other than religious instruction narrowly construed, Levinas claims that we needed a crisis of humanism such as we have seen in the inhumanities of the twentieth century: World War I, the Russian Revolution refuting itself in Stalinism, fascism, Hitlerism, World War II, atomic bombings, genocide, and most certainly the philosophical discourse of Heidegger, which subordinates the human to the anonymous gains of Being.[25] Thus what did Western liberalism promise and what did humanism deliver? The fragility of humanism pushed for a new humanism, one that does not allow us to become persecutors. For Levinas, it led us to an *antihumanism*, which is not to be confused with an abandonment of all human ideals. Rather, antihumanism puts into doubt the humanism that he has just described, a humanism that is sanitized of religion and devoid of everything that is in fact human.[26]

This crisis revealed the loss incurred by Jews as they embraced a so-called secular life and adopted the modern liberal tradition of France. Instead of being the echo of the surrounding civilization, Levinas implores French Jews to take the lead. Thus, in the face of these atrocities, Levinas proclaims that "the opportunity for Jewish education is valuable precisely because it swims against this current of homogeneity that appears to be carrying us along" (*DF* 285). In Levinas's view, "[anti-humanism] is the declamation that takes the place of necessary activities, against the human decency that covers hypocrisy, the antiviolence that perpetuates abuse; but equally against the violence of the verbal indignation of revolutionaries themselves who immediately become inverted into a cultural pastime as they turn themselves into revolutionary literature" (*DF* 282–83). What distinguishes Jewish education from other forms of education, for example, *les belles-lettres*, is that it contains within it, not simply a few geniuses whose work we try to repeat, but also the breadth of experience amassed over thousands of years; it calls us to return to its wisdom — the Word, when elevated, is the Word of God.[27] It calls for a new (or old) relationship to the law and moral obligation.

These themes are repeated in Levinas's philosophical work. For example, in "The Transcendence of Words," Levinas writes, "The presence of the Other is a presence that teaches; that is why the word as teaching is more than the experience of the real, and the Master more than a midwife of minds" a reference to Socrates, no doubt.[28] Levinas's description of the pedagogical dimension regarding the self's relationship to the other is similar to his understanding of Jewish education.[29] For example, in this philosophical essay, he affirms that teaching is not simply about the transmission of truth, the search for the forms, or the knowledge of true beauty; teaching is about assuming responsibility for the Other.

It is worth noting that this statement comes after Levinas's discussion of Robinson Crusoe, which presents a rather different interpretation of this story than the one we find emphasized by Rousseau in *Emile*. If we recall, the only book that Emile is allowed to read is *Robinson Crusoe*, since it apparently emphasizes the solitary, self-sufficient man. Levinas, however, reads this story differently. Not only does he notice, as do most of us, that Crusoe is not alone, but in fact has the company of Friday, Levinas also emphasizes the significance of speaking.

> Contemporary philosophy and sociology have accustomed us to undervalue the direct social relations between persons speaking, and to prefer the silence or the complex relations determined by the framework of civilization, mores, law, culture. A disdain for the word, derived no doubt from the degeneration that menaces language, from the possibility of it becoming idle chatter or empty formalities. But it is a disdain that cannot gainsay a situation whose privileged nature is revealed to Robinson Crusoe when, in the tropical splendor of nature, though he has maintained his ties with civilization through his use of utensils, his morality, and his calendar, he experiences in meeting Man Friday the greatest event of his insular life — in which a man who speaks replaces the ineffable sadness of echoes.[30]

We find a similar view expressed in *Totality and Infinity*, where Levinas tells us that the Other "is manifested in a Mastery that does not conquer, but teaches. Teaching is not a species of a genus called domination, a hegemony at work within a totality, but is the presence of the infinite breaking the closed circle of totality" (*TI* 171; translation altered). Not surprisingly, then, Levinas describes the ethical relation in *Totality and Infinity* in terms of teaching. This description appears most significantly in his discussion of the relationship between the father and the son, which he refers to in this book as the paradigmatic ethical relation. Teaching, as indicated by the citation just above, is the presence of the Other as revealed in the face of the other. That is, the face of the Other is a face that calls to us and teaches.[31] Education and transcendence meet in the ethical relation to the Other. For Levinas, then, the biblical commands that enjoin the "I" to respond to the Other exemplify the ethical relationship: "Thou shalt not kill"; "Thou shalt love the stranger"; and "Thou shalt love thy neighbor as thyself." These biblical commands require that the ego project out of itself toward the other. Transcendence is connected both to God and to ethics.[32]

I have argued elsewhere that Levinas's employment of the midrashic tradition and biblical narratives serve a pedagogical function.[33] For example, Levinas's reading of the Cain and Abel story is not a straightforward interpretation that one finds in the Hebrew Bible. Levinas's reading of Cain in terms of Cain's failure to acknowledge his own responsibility for Abel is a unique interpretation. Levinas's strategic placement of these references obliges us to pay attention to his distinctive use of Cain rather than to see Cain's actions in the usual manner.[34]

Levinas uses a similar strategy in *Otherwise than Being*, where he exchanges the citations from the Bible (characteristic of his early work) for citations from the prophets. Similar to the interpretation that Abraham Joshua Heschel provides in his book, *The Prophets*, Levinas employs the prophetic tradition as a disruption. His occasional references to Isaiah and Ezekial provide some insight into the political nature of this later work. With the insertion of these prophetic citations, Levinas asks us to be disrupted, to think about the society in which we live, and, like the prophets, to respond accordingly — simply put, he asks us to refuse injustice, to feed the hungry, and to clothe the poor.[35] If we recall the dedications at the beginning of *Otherwise than Being* — in French, to those who were persecuted by the same antiSemitism, and in Hebrew, to those members of his family and his wife's family who died in the Shoah — we can assume that the task Levinas sets before us is no ordinary, or easy one. Like the prophets, we are also called to respond to the everyday injustice, the so-called small injustices, so that we are prepared to respond to the horrific ones.

The pedagogy at work in Levinas's writings reflects Levinas's own interest in Jewish education and it provides an implicit path of moral education. Levinas's view of the ethical relation, then, points to a pedagogy that would include reading the biblical narratives Jewishly. Through Levinas's incorporation of these texts into his philosophical argument, each reader is introduced to the readers who came before him or her. The confrontation with the text is therefore a confrontation with the whole of the past.[36] Repeating in 1994 a theme found in his 1973 essay on Jewish education, Levinas says,

> hence the way that readings continually refer to origins across history going from pupil to master; hence the discussion in gatherings between colleagues questioning one another from century to century, the whole thing integrating itself as tradition into commented Scripture, and always calling anew for a reading that is both erudite and modern. Hence the commentaries of commentaries. (*ITN* xiii)

Levinas sees the conversation that takes place within midrash *as modeling the very conversation that he hopes his philosophy can promote,* a conversation he outlined as the distinguishing feature of Jewish education. If he can incorporate this model of commentary into his philosophical work, then he can connect his readers to the larger interpretative conversation of both Judaism and humanism. We, his readers, thereby become part of the history and the history lessons that have been taught, and we do so prior to our choosing to do so. We, his readers, participate in Levinas's understanding of Jewish education, without ever setting foot in a Jewish dayschool![37]

For Levinas, then, this Jewish way of reading the text might be the most effective way, though certainly not the only way, to expose our students to the *idea* of alterity, that is, to other voices and the voices of the other.[38] At the very least, this method would expose them to the idea that there are voices, in the text and in the world, that are often muted if not outright silenced. Moreover, the process of questioning that we find particularly in the talmudic tradition is intended not only to teach students to question in order to be attuned to the material at hand. The Jewish tradition of learning also recognizes something unique about the journey one takes in the educational process. The questioning between the two study partners requires each participant to admit that there is always something more to be known. This process intends to develop humility and a certain integrity regarding truth. And the interaction between the study partners aids in developing the respect one has for the other, in addition to building a close bond of friendship. And the interaction between the study partners aids in developing the respect one has for the other, in addition to building a close bond of friendship. But most importantly, even if they learn nothing else, the study partners learn that dependence is healthy and productive. All of this is grounded in the initial obligation to the other that informs the relationship. The agent who enters into this tradition does so as a "we," in partnership with an Other. Finally, it explicitly recognizes that education has a transcendent moment and that to study is to be in touch with the Divine — sentiments expressed by educators, though not usually in these words.[39]

CONCLUSION

Although Levinas's project appears to promote a model of sexual difference that views women as naturally ethical and men as those who need to learn, I argue instead that the significance of Levinas's project is the underlying claim regarding dependence and vulnerability — and we can understand this view as a response to the extreme individualism and autonomy emphasized during the modern period as a

legacy of the Enlightenment. If we take Levinas's view of the masculine and the feminine to be placeholders, then it is both men and women
who need to cultivate attributes of femininity and to be careful when
occupying positions marked as masculine or virile. Here again we see
another inversion of the gendered values that emerged out of modernity.
It is both men and women who need to engage in the process of
education. The model of talmudic learning that Levinas assumes in his
project need not be for men only. If we believe that we are all in need
of moral cultivation and if we believe that critical reading and an
engagement with the other promote this kind of cultivation, then we
ought to think about this model in terms of education as such and not
in terms of the sex-specific, or even religion-specific, nature of the traditional model. At the end of "Antihumanism and Education," Levinas
tells us that it is the Talmud, through the problems of the Law and
through the question *What must be done?*, that manages to approach
difficult questions of daily life:

> Jewish education does not rely on the ineffective brutality of constraints
> imposed by the totalitarian state in order to maintain a law within free-
> dom and guarantee freedom through law. The practices in which Jews
> engage, practices that are carried out to please God are done so only
> to the extent that they allow one to safeguard the human in man. Is
> this a particularism? Of course. But it involves no separation from man.
> (*DF* 288)

Levinas locates this model of dependency and vulnerability in the
return to Jewish wisdom. His construction of Judaism and Jewish
education reminds us that with its focus on the future, the past is kept
alive in the present. Rather than reject modernity, Levinas believes that
we need to bring the prophet into its midst — the State needs
prophetism to resist the injustice that inevitably accompanies the State.
Hence he doe not dispense with the values of modernity but rather
inverts them, altering the emphasis and revealing underlying assump-
tions of which modernity does not admit.

Although I profoundly appreciate, even sympathize with, Rousseau's
fear of *amour-propre,* the extreme independence that he wished to

cultivate as a defense to it does not provide an adequate solution. He has done all that one can do to make an individual independent, and he at once succeeded and failed. What we need however is an individual who does not lose the self in the other, but rather who becomes who he is in the context of a vulnerable and dependent self. Marriage, family, teaching — they were never opposed to freedom; they only seemed that way. If as Levinas suggests, politics is derivative of ethics, then it is the Jewish tradition from which Levinas's own ethical/philosophical project emerges that may provide us with an effective model for education, one that encourages us first to engage with each other face to face and with texts that demand that we engage the difficult questions of daily life, in a way that would help us raise the *mensch* that Rousseau could never produce in *Emile*.

Levinas as (mis)Reader of Spinoza

Michel Juffé

In a certain respect, one can say that Emmanuel Levinas's ethics, as asserted mainly in *Totality and Infinity* and *Otherwise than Being,* but also partially in *Existence and Existents* and *Time and the Other,* constitutes a rebuttal of Benedict de Spinoza's *Ethics.* Levinas offers a succinct account of his thinking on this issue in *Totality and Infinity,* at the end of a section called "Separation and the Absolute," which concludes the first part of the book "The Self and the Other": "Thought and freedom come to us from separation from the consideration of the Other — this thesis is at the antipodes of Spinozism" (*TI* 105). In all likelihood, what has provoked him at such a moment would have to be Spinoza's pretense to reach the infinite by means of understanding, while for him, Levinas, the essence of created existence consists in its separation from the Infinite (in other words, as especially his later philosophy begins to make clear, from "God"). Let us nonetheless begin with the question itself: Why this intolerance toward Spinoza?

LEVINAS AS A CRITIC OF SPINOZA

Levinas never made Spinoza the subject of detailed analysis, as he did for Husserl and Heidegger, but also Buber, Rosenzweig, and even

Translated by Beatriz Bugni.

Gabriel Marcel. He does speak directly about him in two short articles: "The Case of Spinoza" (1955; *DF* 106–10),[1] which deals with the anathema (*Schammatha*) imposed on him in 1656 by the Amsterdam rabbinate, and "Have You Re-read Baruch?" (1966; *DF* 111–18),[2] is occasioned by Sylvain Zac's theses on Spinoza. In the first text — written at a time when Israel's head of state, Ben Gurion, had recommended lifting the anathema — Levinas gladly acknowledges that one could not blame Spinoza for paying tribute to Reason: "Rationalism," he observes, "does not menace the Jewish faith" (*DF* 107). However, because of his "theology without God," Spinoza does exercise "a influence on the history of ideas that was decisive and anti-Jewish" (*DF* 107). Yet there is something worse in this: Spinoza subordinates "the truth of Judaism to the revelation of the New Testament. The latter is, of course, surpassed by the intellectual love of God, but Western being involves this Christian experience, even if it is only as a stage" (*DF* 108). In fact, then, "thanks to the rationalism patronized by Spinoza, Christianity is surreptitiously triumphing, bringing conversions without the scandal of apostasy" (*DF* 108). Do the Jews who admire Spinoza "still know that our great books, which are increasingly ignored, reveal a Synagogue that in no way tries to act as a blindfold? Do they know that Spinoza, in his Jewish studies, perhaps only had teachers of little caliber?" (*DF* 109). Conclusion: Ben Gurion's recommendation that the anathema be repealed did not promise to serve Israel, because this was tantamount to acknowledging Christianity as the heir to Judaism.

The second text is significantly richer in nuances: though Spinoza did not properly understand the subtleties of scripture, since he obviously did not know the Talmud, he did admit that they lead to the Word of God, and sometimes acknowledged the superiority of the Old Testament over the New Testament. Moreover, by showing that the scripture does not have the same scope as philosophy, because it teaches "a doctrine of salvation, God's Word, composed of faith and charity" (*DF* 112), he protects them from the search for proofs characteristic of philosophical investigation. Yet this was unintentional on Spinoza's part, for he also believed that "enquiring about the author of a biblical text and the circumstances surrounding its writing allows one to isolate the meaning of the *statement* and to separate the temporal from the permanent" (*DF* 112). This provides Levinas an opportunity for a cutting remark on Spinoza: "The idea of applying the historical method to the Bible is therefore born from a concern to protect the true philosophy in the City, just as America was discovered by navigators who were expecting to reach the East Indies" (*DF* 112). Moreover, this exegetic method presupposes the possibility of understanding "a discourse without the vision of the truths enlightening it" (*DF* 113). In other words, Spinoza believes that he does not need the oral transmission (of the Talmud), which otherwise, on Levinas's account, provides us with the necessary keys for reading biblical texts. Moreover, Spinoza thinks that philosophy has nothing to say about the future, while prophets, inspired by the word of God, can foresee it and their words "echo in the hearts of men"; they transmit an ethical message, a practical rule of life, precepts one follows for "motives of an affective order, such as fear, hope, fidelity, respect, veneration, and love" (*DF* 114). In short, though Spinoza does consider the scriptures to be somewhat useful, he denies them any ontological significance, any access to the truth of God and of Creation.

And so Spinoza limits himself to a literal reading of the Bible, which is nothing but an "infantile representation of the Revelation" (*DF* 116) to which he has "reduced" a vastly richer reality. Indeed, when in search of this message [i.e., the meaning of Revelation]:

> a Jew nowadays can bring many more resources . . . than Spinoza could have dreamed of. The theoretical formulations of his tradition carry within themselves the gains of a long inner experience. The Talmud and rabbinical literature are neither folklore nor "purely human inventions," as Spinoza still thinks; not a process by which to enclose the Bible in some philosophical system of the day, or to confer a logical order on the alluvium of Jewish history. They subsume many centuries of effort

attempting to go beyond the letter and even the apparent dogmatism of the text, and restore a wholly spiritual path even those passages of Scripture called historical, or ritual, or thaumaturgical. (*DF* 116; translation corrected)

Furthermore, where Spinoza thinks he finds only confusion and a disorganized compilation, one must rather see a bubbling thinking that rejects any schematism and puts into movement everything that seems solid and stable. This "secret" of the Talmud can only result from the encounter with an "exceptional teacher," for "if they are taken out of the context of talmudic discussions, the very notions evoked become bloodless" (*DF* 298, n. 5). Yet it would be asking too much from the philosopher "who wishes to think *sub specie aeterni* to demand that he allow lived experience to be one of the conditions for a just appreciation of a text, or allow the historical relativism of ideas to be one of the causes of their fertility" (*DF* 116).

All the same, let us not forget that Spinoza himself admits that one cannot go through God's Word with the fine comb of Reason, that is, with ideas belonging to the second and third order of knowledge. He therefore considers Judaism to be not a theology but a revealed law. Implicitly, Spinoza accepts that "philosophy does not engender itself. To philosophize is to move toward the point where one sees the light as it illuminates the first meanings, which nonetheless already have a past. What Spinoza calls the Word of God projects this light and carries language itself" (*DF* 118).

Now, if this comes down to nothing more than accusing Spinoza of a lack of talmudic culture, one would find him in a situation similar to that of many authors, Jews and non-Jews alike, who misjudge the scope of scripture. But in the eyes of Levinas his error is much more serious than that: Spinoza is the philosopher of immanence, of Being conceived as the enclosed sum of everything, and of a perseverance in being beyond which one cannot go. In short, Spinoza, as Levinas sees him, sentences humanity to be nothing but itself, in the middle of a closed and completed, albeit eternal, world. That said, it is true that Levinas never writes that what offends him most is the *Deus sive Natura* at the base of Spinoza's philosophy. His criticism will instead focus with a remarkable persistence and coherence on eternity, perseverance in being (*conatus essendi*), and privilege of thought (as well as, in this connection, the unity of will and reason).

Of these, eternity is what one might consider as Levinas's *bête noire*, because it brings about all the other errors of Spinoza. For Levinas, eternity is immobility, lack of development, fixation in the Same, idealization of the undifferentiated One such as it is proclaimed first by Parmenides — the ancestor of Spinoza and Hegel. Spinoza is a good example of this tendency, but he is hardly alone, since this longing for identity pervades all metaphysics: "How can we give a meaning to time, when for philosophy, identity is identity of the Same, enjoys being in its stability of the Same, enjoys assimilating the Other to the Same, when any alteration is pointless, when understanding assimilates the Other to the Same? . . . That is when anything which is not identical with oneself, everything, which is still in the process of becoming, must be considered as purely subjective and romantic."[3] Now, this eternity is not completeness, but abstraction, poverty, even inanity:

> [Eternity], the idea of which, without borrowing anything from lived duration, the intellect would claim to possess a priori: the idea of a mode of being, where the multiple is one and which would confer on the present its full sense — is it not always suspect of only dissimulating the fulgurating of the instant, its half-truth, which is retained in an imagination capable of playing in the intemporal and of deluding itself about a gathering of the nongatherable? In the final account, would not this eternity and this intellectual God, composed of these abstract and inconstant half-instants of the temporal dispersion, be an abstract eternity and dead God? (*TO* 31)

In another context, speaking of Rosenzweig and the notion of redemption as future, as eternity of accomplishment, Levinas castigates this eternity-being that annihilates any singularity: "Eternity is therefore not conceived as a logical ideality in which the individual is absorbed, but as the penetration of the world by love, as the accession of every creature to the word 'we' but without the creature vanishing utterly into this community."[4] This of course leads to a forceful and irrevocable rejection of empty eternity, which one might assimilate to the horror of the "there is" (*il y a*), of pure being, conceptualized in Levinas's own original philosophical works. In opposition to this impersonal eternity, one must assert the richness of a lived existence, of time as a connection to the Other, — *infinitely* Other, — to that which one cannot understand, and indeed which does not allow itself to be assimilated to experience. One might even say that *Totality and Infinity*, where and to the degree that it thus promotes the transcendence of the Other, is altogether a rejection of this eternity which, for Levinas, is nothing but a totality that leaves no space to the in-finite, to development, otherness, and, finally, divinity.

Levinas is equally severe, and for the same reasons, with the notion of a "perseverance in being," or *conatus essendi*. He returns to it time and again, and in the end states with the greatest clarity: "the very emergence of the human within being is the interruption of the being that perseveres in its being, along with the connotation of violence in the notion of perseverance and *conatus essendi* — the dis-interest-edness possible through humans awakening thought to an order higher than knowing."[5] For Levinas, this perseverance of being is "obstination," a war of all against all, a refusal to let the Other break in, solipsistic auto-affirmation, and therefore malfeasance: "The being that persists in being, egoism or Evil, thus outlines the dimension of baseness itself, and the birth of hierarchy. Here begins the axiological bipolarity."[6] Selfishness, solipsism: it is a matter of the Self "whose existing consists in identifying itself, in recovering its identity through all that happens to it" (*TI* 36). Far from bringing plenitude or even a satisfactory

realization of the human, this identification pushes it into pure existing, without a soul — for Levinas, psyche is sensitivity, maternity, fraternity — therefore into the horror of the *il y a:* "Essence stretching
on indefinitely, without inhibition, without any possible halt or interruption, the equality of essence not justifying, in all equity, any instant's
halt, without respite, without any possible suspension, is the horrify-
ing *there is* behind all finality proper to the thematizing ego" (*OB* 163).
For the subject trapped in Essence, the alternative is dreadful. On the
one hand, there is the commingling with the universal, "the ultimacy
of essence, the immanence without exit from the play that encloses it,
the Stoic wisdom in its variations from Zeno to Spinoza and Hegel, a
wisdom of resignation and sublimation" (*OB* 176). On the other
hand, there is drunkenness, drugs, eroticism, and the quest for a second state: "The dilemma is without resolution; essence has no exits:
to the anxiety of death is added the horror of fatality, of the incessant
bustling of the *there is,* and the horrible eternity at the bottom of essence"
(*OB* 176). Eternity, essence, perseverance in being: these are terms closely
associated, in alliance against "the humanism of the other human
being." As maintained by Spinoza, one avatar of *conatus essendi* is the
supremacy of desire, which leads to the contemporary nihilism: struc-
turalism and psychoanalysis are targeted, as "Never, in the new science
of man, shall value serve as a principle of intelligibility. . . . One must
remember Spinoza, that great demolisher of ideologies . . .; it is
the desirable that is valued, it is not value that gives rise to desires"
(GCM 6). This leads to theories of impulse, to the death of the subject, and to the death of God.

Beyond Spinoza and Hegel, Greek thinking itself is targeted:

> What is Europe? It is the Bible and the Greeks. The Bible: an ontolog-
> ical inversion? The original perseverance of realities in their being — iner-
> tia of material objects, the enrootedness of plants, the struggle between
> wild animals, the war among "owning and interested men" as Bossuet
> calls them — is inverted in the man announced to humanity in Israel.
> Thus, for being that is dedicated to being, for the being that has no other

purpose than to be, the human self might also signify the possibility of interrupting his *conatus essendi*, the possibility of answering for the other, who is none of my business, "who is nothing to me."[7]

As Levinas sums it up in his lectures of 1975–76, "The human *esse* is not *conatus* but disinterestedness and farewell;" ethics is not "a level above being, but gratuity where the conatus, or perseverance in being, un-does itself."[8] It is in *Otherwise than Being* that Levinas's break with the *conatus essendi* is most apparent: "This book interprets the subject as a hostage and the subjectivity of the subject as a substitution breaking with being's essence" (*OB* 184). To be the hostage of the other implies, contrary to Spinoza, placing passivity (sensibility, susceptibility, vulnerability) as the supreme value: "It is the subjectivity of a man of flesh and blood, more passive in its extradition to the other than the passivity of effects in a causal chain, for it is beyond the unity of apperception the *I think*, which is actuality itself. It is a being torn up from oneself for another in the giving to an other of the bread of one's own mouth. This is not an anodyne formal relationship, but all the gravity of the body extirpated from its *conatus essendi* in the possibility of giving" (*OB* 142).

The identification of will with reason is the third "mistake" committed by Spinoza, because this implies the negation of any personality, of any freedom, absorbing the being in a anonymous totality, without a face. Again the triumph of the Same!

> The I can, to justify itself, . . . endeavor to apprehend itself in its totality. This seems to us to be the justification of freedom aspired after by the philosophy that, from Spinoza to Hegel, identifies will and reason, that, against Descartes, removes from truth its character of being a free work so as to situate it where the opposition of the I and the non-I disappears, in an impersonal reason. Freedom is not maintained but reduced to being the reflection of a universal order which maintains itself and justifies itself all by itself, like the God of the ontological argument. . . . Knowing would be the way by which freedom would denounce its own contingency, by which it would vanish in totality. In reality this way dissimulates the ancient triumph of the same over the other. (*TI* 87)

Through this identity, human suffering disappears, as does all the human pathos:

> If the will can aspire to reason in one way or the other, it is reason, reason seeking or forming itself; its true essence is revealed in Spinoza or in Hegel. This identification of will and reason, which is the ultimate intention of idealism, is opposed by the entire pathetic experience of humanity, which the Hegelian or Spinozistic idealism relegates to the subjective or the imaginary. (*TI* 217)

Spinoza in fact makes this even worse, as if that were possible, when he eliminates affectivity:

> When the I is identified with reason, taken as the power of thematization and objectification, it loses its very ipseity. To represent to oneself is to empty oneself of one's subjective substance and to insensibilize enjoyment. By imagining this anesthesia to be limitless, Spinoza conjures away separation. (*TI* 119)

It is thus clear that for Levinas, when Spinoza virtually equates will and reason, the result is that will and desire disappear.

Spinoza, then, is the philosopher who, at the forefront of occidental metaphysics, worked the hardest — no doubt together with Hegel, or perhaps even harder than Hegel — to empty humanity from itself in order to reabsorb it in being. And this would be a sort of being that neither enjoys nor suffers, a being that ignores the other, is frozen in the certainty of oneself, that leaves no access to otherness. It would be a being that amounts, in the final instance, to a totalitarian sum that leaves space only for a false infinite since, after all, the infinity that it claims is an eternity. Moreover, this eternity is "produced" by the being that perseveres in its being (or in which it produces itself, since one might say: "to be eternal, in other words to persevere in one's being").

This being is not lacking anything, and that is why it is terrifying. Yet in reality, human life is not a less-than-being but a different-from-being, a *pathetic* and therefore *ethical* experiment which is more than plain being or immutable being, because it is separated from being by the infinite, which is to say by the infinite experience of being affected, of being responsible for every other person. *Will*, therefore, cannot be *reason:* a perfect being, centered in itself, cannot "serve as ontological touchstone for a life, a becoming, capable of renewal, of Desire, of society. . . . *The individual and the personal are necessary for Infinity to be able to produced as infinite*" (*TI* 218). A person, then, cannot be reduced simply to a "being." Hence one translation of Levinas's title in 1947: *De l'existence à l'existant,* or "From living to endurance (or perseverance)."

When I began reading Levinas seriously, at the beginning of the 1990s, I thought that I finally had found an alternative to Spinoza, precisely because Levinas was bringing openness to a world that was perfectly closed on itself — a world that, it seemed to me, was the world of Spinoza. Though I did not follow Levinas's scathing criticism, I accepted with him that what Spinoza calls being is a wholeness without development and therefore without outcome. Spinoza's God is immutable, without affection,[9] without desire, without love for humanity. To me, he thus seemed cold and remote — even bearing in mind his *Deus sive Natura*. Furthermore, it was my impression that for Spinoza passivity is a reduction of being whereas activity is its growth, and that this was too simple, and indeed therefore impossible to practice: it would have sufficed to go from the first to the third kind of knowledge to reach Beatitude, or unadulterated happiness. And when Levinas speaks of the preoriginal passivity, the passivity by which I am responsible to and for the other, I came close to believing that he has reestablished what Spinoza, for his part, had too quickly disposed of.

I was therefore in the process of making of Spinoza not a brother of Hegel — as Levinas was doing — but of Kant: a kind of ascetic, who, by another way, drains human beings of all sensitivity in view of a kind of moral perfection. However, this asepticized and anesthetizing Spinoza is not to be found in either the *Theologico-Political Treatise* or the *Ethics.* I will focus on the *Ethics* because it is the *Ethics* that supplied the purpose and the range of the *Treatise.* And it is in the *Ethics,* specifically where it develops the *conatus,* that one may see that Spinoza's philosophy is a philosophy of desire and consequently of becoming.

"Everything, as much as it can, makes an effort to persevere in its being."[10] What is a thing, on this understanding? Any thing, any body, any part of nature, wherever it is and whatever it is. What is the effort invoked here? It is desire, appetite, or impulse. Spinoza explains himself most clearly in the definition of *desire* offered in the *Definition of the Affects,* which concludes the third part of the *Ethics:* "Desire is the essence of man in so far it is conceived as defined by any of its liking to accomplish an action."[11] In other words, as soon as a body is influenced by another body, that is to say as soon as it is in any relationship with this other body, it starts acting, either to preserve this other body, or to use it. Now this presupposes that no body can exist by itself: being only a part of nature, it needs other bodies to regenerate itself, as shown by the most common experience. The term "desire" sums up all moves made by bodies during this constant regeneration. Whether we human beings know it or not, we obey our desires: "I understand under Desire all efforts, impulsion, appetites and volitions of man, which vary depending on the condition of a given man, and it is not rare to see them so opposed to each other that man, torn in different directions, does not know where to turn."[12] This permits us to conclude: every being, in nature, desires to persevere in its being. But is this persevering the lasting-without-end and thus the remaining-identical that Levinas takes it to be? Not for Spinoza, because "to persevere in one's being" means to increase one's power to act, which is being less passive and more active, less sad and more joyful, less heinous and more loving, less in conflict with others and more in union with them, and consequently more able to establish diversified relations with the rest of nature, deploy multiple talents, and practice a great diversity of activities. For Spinoza, perseverance in being is about a continuous movement, without an end that would have been assigned to it or that can be reached: Spinoza's Beatitude is not a self-satisfied state where a body/spirit that has been satiated digests its success, but rather is the ability to act raised to its highest level, when our activity goes widely beyond our passivity, when we act based on informed decisions. Because Spinoza insists on this understanding, it is not rare for commentators to state that for Spinoza the accomplishment of the self — what he calls perfections and satisfactions — are purely intellectual. This is again a misinterpretation: any knowledge comes only from the affection of bodies for each other; there is no such thing as purely intellectual knowledge, if by this one understands a knowledge that would be characteristic of a spiritual substance, a soul, that could act in any way independently of the body. For Spinoza, the body is not the support of the activity of the spirit, it *is* the spirit. We can only know what the body feels and endures. Because nature is infinite, because the human body is made up of many "individuals" — today, we would say of "elements" — the capacities of the human body are diversified and give us access to many elements of nature, in a potentially unlimited manner. "To persevere in one's being" is this uninterrupted increase, in an unlimited duration (but not infinite, because we are mortal) in so far as our capacities allow for it. But these capacities are not unlimited, because we are only, and always only will be, a part of Nature, which in itself is not organized for us or for anything else. According to Spinoza, Nature follows no goal, has no desire to fulfill, no appetite. God, he says, is impassive. And if everyone tends to persevere in his being, there is no general intention provoking complementarity or harmony among all the beings. It is therefore *as much as it can* that every thing makes an effort to persevere in its being. *As much as it can:* in other words, as much as it depends on its power, and as much as it can affect other things. This means at the same time that no thing has the tendency to destroy or limit itself and that many other things can contribute to its destruction or diminution; and it is of no purpose to accuse them of bad intentions.

Spinoza's *conatus essendi* does not, therefore, have the characteristics ascribed to it by Levinas: the war of all against all, the refusal of the Other, solipsism, pure existence, and, in the end, the *there is*. For a being with desire — and every being has desire — nothing is satisfied with the there is, with being without singular existence. However, though for Levinas desire is subordinated to responsibility, to the penetration of the other (and of the Other — God) in me, for Spinoza, desire well understood is responsibility, because, after all, whatever human beings have in common increases their power to act. If for Levinas, virtue is the consequence of dis-interest, for Spinoza virtue is simply what is useful to human beings, useful in making us understand, when we sees the essence of things, that we live better in harmony than in discord, better in concrete plurality than in solitude. For Levinas, human desire comes from a transcendent God; for Spinoza, desire is part of everything, though only human beings have awareness of it.

It is probably this lack of an exceptional place for the human being within the whole of Nature, in any strong sense, that most upsets Levinas–indeed, this is probably that which underlies the strong misinterpretation he proposes when saying that Spinoza suppresses affectivity and sensitivity when he reduces will to reason. After all, when Spinoza tells us that "will and understanding are one and the very same thing,"[13] he does not subordinate will to reason, and does not make reason the supreme guide for human history (as Hegel later did). Spinoza only says that will and understanding are nothing outside of their practice (as there is no thinking substance), which is always made up of single volitions and ideas. These ideas and wills have no other possible origin than the affections of the body, which is to say, consequently, that an idea about something is nothing other than the expression of willing it, since to will something is to affirm something or negate something — or, finally, to make it an object of attraction or aversion. For Spinoza, again, body and spirit are one and the same thing: will is not a decision of the spirit, which would be applicable to the body or through the body. It is an intrinsic element of desire, an awareness of craving. And it is craving that directs us toward a given thing, whatever it is, or else moves us away from it. This attraction or removal constitutes knowledge, as there is no other way to know but in the craving of the body for something. What I do not desire, I have no way of knowing as a thing or an object, since in that case nothing connects me to it.

To properly understand this identification of will and understanding — which, it may fairly be said, runs against the grain of everything we are commonly taught — it is essential to understand the status of words, images and ideas for Spinoza; or, in more technical terms, it is essential to better understand what he means by the three kinds of knowledge. Nothing exists outside of the things themselves: "The essence of images and words is formed only by the movements of the bodies, which do not in any way involve the concept of thinking."[14] By the movements of the body we can feel an infinity of things, give them or our agreement or withhold it — in short, know them. Things we cannot feel we cannot want; they are beyond our reach. But one can object that it is possible to suspend one's judgment, therefore to dissociate oneself from what one knows and wants. Wrong, says Spinoza, because when the judgment is suspended it is only in uncertainty, as when perception is inadequate and we know that it is inadequate. When a child invents a horse with wings, and nothing stands in the way to of his inventing it, he will consider this horse as existing, even if he does not have experiential certainty. Regarding real beings, things, we cannot suspend our judgment, because knowledge has action as a consequence. We can only doubt in two cases: when we know that we are dealing with ideas (words, images, memories), and when we know that our knowledge of a real thing is maimed or confused. This shows that *will* cannot be dissociated from *understanding.*

We are always in the process of imagining (be it the past, the present or the future), because we only can know things through the way they affect us. Still, we can also go beyond the images by searching for the causes of what affects us, in other words by attempting to understand Nature, which is the same in us and outside of us (as there only are bodies). By knowing how things affect each other and notably engender each other, we go beyond this imaginary knowledge (that is, knowledge of the first kind), to reach adequate, rational knowledge (knowledge of the second kind). When we have become capable in certain situations of grasping without reflection — as it were, "in a glimpse" — some affects, we thus practice a strictly intuitive knowledge (knowledge of the third kind). Spinoza's examples are famously centered on geometrical intuition, but one might just as well consider any activity that one accomplishes easily and without hesitation because one already has good knowledge of the underlying sequence of causes and effects: movements of a skill or craft, in sports and ritual, in use of a common language, and so forth. In any case, if we know through the third kind, insofar as the knowledge relates to an action (including *doing* mathematics, speaking a language, etc.), we do want what we know, which means that the understanding we have of one or the other affection is identical to this affection. Since all affections that we can understand pass through what affects our body, it is the case that each affection either does not move it (because our body is not touched) or moves us (because our body is touched). To all of this, Spinoza adds that the will is not free but constrained through the linking of all things to one another, things of which we truly are a part, yet without being their possessors or masters.

Far from exalting reason, as do Descartes (because it overcomes the erring of the body), Kant (because it regulates, in any regard), and Hegel (because it assigns the goals of universal history), Spinoza in fact takes away its substance, for reason is nothing but the human effort, precisely insofar as this effort is aware of itself, to persevere in its being. Once again, Spirit and Body are one and the same thing and it is for this reason that understanding and will are also one and the same thing: "The Spirit only knows itself as far as it perceives the ideas of the affections of the Body."[15] From this perspective, Spinoza appears much closer to Levinas than Levinas seems to think, if only in his opposition to the idealistic and rational philosophies they both condemn.

Perhaps then it is specifically with regard to eternity that Levinas is truly "at the antipodes" of Spinozism? For Spinoza, eternity is not a status but the result — the *immediate* result — of an understanding of Nature as it is. Eternity thus corresponds to human activity when this activity is unencumbered from any passivity, when we act based on fully informed decisions in such a way that nothing diminishes our power to act. Accordingly, there is nothing mysterious about the infinite, and indeed there can be no opposition to it (that is, in its immobility), because it is, on the contrary, our proximity with infinity, our ability to experience infinity, which gives us access to eternity. This is not simple to understand. For Spinoza, the more we experiment with the infinite possibilities of our active bodies (and spirits), the more we are part of Nature (God), the more we understand It (Him), and love It (Him). This kind of active infinity or infinity in action gives us a real (that is, *formal* in the vocabulary of the seventeenth century) access to the very nature of Nature; and *this* is eternity. "Eternity" for Spinoza is not a painted image, an immutable world or an immutable God (like the Aristotelian one), but the continuous re-creation of Nature (or God), endlessly. Speaking of eternity is not fixing everything in a perfect state but looking at (or sensing) everything in its real — and not imaginary — transformations. I know that this is the most difficult part to understand in Spinoza's Opera, but it is the major key of its construction. Eternity is not some kind of state; it is continuous, endless, infinite transformation of Nature.

This does not at all resemble a "logical ideality in which the individual is absorbed" (see above, n. 4) or the "idea of a mode of being where the multiple is one, and which would center on the present its

full sense" (*TO* 31), such as would be approached as such by the intellect, outside of any lived experience. For Spinoza, all knowledge results
from affections of the Body; pure knowledge does not make sense, and
if we are able to perceive the essence of things, this is only by way of
apprehending them through their causal links — and not strictly
through our imagination or preference. Eternity is not a world hidden behind the temporal world. In fact, it cannot be distinguished from
it. Eternity is a way of apprehending the experience of things, God and
ourselves. Hence the famous sentence in the *Ethics:* "The Spirit of the
one whose Body has many abilities is to a significant extent eternal."[16]
It is the diversity and multiplicity of the activities of the body that gives
the spirit its eternity. Because for Spinoza the Spirit has no substance,
there is no given quantity of the Spirit that would somehow be marked
with the label of eternity. Eternity is rather the dynamism of the Spirit,
which is much more drawn toward the essence of things than to the
individual whose Body is endowed with few abilities. Idealizing abstraction, pure *a priori* intellectual knowledge, does not allow us to take a
single step into eternity.

> We live in a continuous change and it is depending on whether we change
> for the better or for the worse that we are called happy or unhappy. In
> fact, who from being a baby or an infant becomes a cadaver, is said to
> be unhappy, and in the opposite one qualifies as happiness to have been
> able to live the entire duration of a life with a sane Spirit and a healthy
> Body.[17]

Beatitude or life in Eternity is not ecstasy — it is not a unique experience that overcomes a fortunate few — but an experience everyone
can have: it is a matter of increasing one's ability to act, one's joy, one's
virtue, and one's understanding of nature. And all of this would appear
to concentrate itself in what Spinoza calls the "Love for God," which
cannot be distinguished from the understanding of Nature according
to the third kind of knowledge. Eternity is the result of the permanent
effort of understanding and an acceptance of things as they are, while
inadequate knowledge condemns us to the erosion of time inasmuch
as it diminishes us, renders us sad, diminishes our power to act, and

leaves us at the mercy of affects contrary to those helping us to persevere in our being. In short, it is not by removing ourselves from the
world or time or human activity in general that we reach eternity, but
through an increase in activity, by unfolding as widely as possible all
our skills, in any field, giving us a wider access to the infinity of the
world to which we belong — to the infinity, finally, of God.

This, then, is how to understand Levinas's somewhat ungenerous
reading of Spinoza: a mistaken assimilation of him with Hegel and in
general with idealistic philosophy, in which case Spinoza would be
exposed to all of the metaphysical mortification that Levinas inflicts
on those other philosophies. Now we have also just observed, quickly
and easily, that Spinoza does not truly belong in that company. The
entire thrust of the *Ethics* is one of a search for a happy life, which can
only consist in knowing things (God or nature, oneself and the other
human beings) as they are, whereupon we may increase in our activity and decrease in the passivity that makes us prey of the adverse parts
of nature and leads to our diminution or destruction. Spinoza invites
us therefore to a discipline of the moment, indeed of each and any
moment, a discipline consisting in trying all the time to apprehend things
as they are — as a part of the infinite Nature.

Intellection and Revelation: Spinoza, the Unforgivable

Let us return to the question: What is the true significance of
Levinas's animosity towards Spinoza? What, from his perspective,
would be Spinoza's real crime? Evidently enough, since the difference
in ethics and metaphysics are considerably less than one might at first
suppose, it must be a matter of source, or inspiration. It is to betray
the Jewish spirit in favor of the Greek one, or rather to relinquish the

Jewish spirit in favor of another that is exclusively Greek: in Spinoza's philosophy, there is no essential recourse to revelation, no principal response to a transcendental God who would speak to us through the prophets. In the *Ethics* one instead finds a knowledge of God that is accessible to everyone (even if it is difficult), a knowledge that has no private domain and does not pass through any notion of the ineffability of the divine substance: God can be reached through the smallest human experience, as long as this experience transpires reflectively, which is perhaps to say advisedly. What Levinas might then object to, even after all of the foregoing ethical and metaphysical nuances, is Spinoza's thoroughgoing attempt to draw rather exclusively on a "Greek" reading of the world. The following remarks could be read as if with Spinoza in mind:

> In Jewish reading, the intelligible is always outlined starting from a spiritual experience or from a word that has always already been spoken, based on a tradition where transmission and renewal always come together. Reading is a spirit that was never noninformed, and without confusing this essential predisposition with the sterile partiality of dogmatism. It remains the secret of creativity and an eternal recommencing of new things, which is, most likely, the indelible trace of a thinking bearing the mark of Revelation. And, on the other hand, Greek reading — books and things — the intelligence of a spirit that is marvelously non-informed, thanks to which symbols attempt to reveal themselves and, at least, to state themselves with clarity, has become our university parlance.[18]

To be informed means to be warned, it is to know about the true nature of things, about their divine essence, to which no human experience can lead. Ethics is therefore a movement against nature, a deep alteration of nature, the irruption of absolute Otherness manifested by the Face of the other (human). For Levinas there is Revelation — and Election, because not everyone is able to receive the Revelation.

For Spinoza, there can be no light higher than that of nature and no authority other than that of humanity itself. The relationship between a human being and God is without mediation; those who understand the eternal essence of Spirit, which is part of Nature (in other words, God), know God. There is no task imposed on human beings except the ones they discover by themselves as useful for their own preservation. And as the similar is useful to the similar, nothing is more useful to human beings than other humans. It is therefore not by obligation, by coercion — not as a hostage of the other — that we become responsible: it is through our perceptiveness, which cannot be separated from the love for the good. Spinoza would surely not have liked the sentence from Dostoyevsky that Levinas, for his part, "always" quotes: "Each of us is guilty before all for all and everything, and I more than the others."[19] For Levinas, this culpability is the very basis of the ethical I who, each alone and irrecusably, "is the unique point that supports the universe" (GCM 84). And this, of course, is the very root of the idea of substitution: I am responsible for the other, in an unlimited and preoriginal manner.

For Levinas, nature is created and longs for its Creator; for Spinoza, nature is an auto-creation and longs for nothing. Therefore, all that Spinoza can say about the infinite, beatitude, joy, love, the perfecting of self, the indefinite augmentation of the power to act — and all of this constitutes the substructure of ethics — is simply unacceptable to Levinas: Spinoza is not well-informed, he reads God's word as a child, he has no access to the true knowledge of God, therefore anything he can say and write is a caricature of the divine. It is virtually bound to become idealistic, rigid, negating subjectivity and personality, and inclined to erase any true thought of becoming in favor of one or another vision of disincarnated being, of an existing without existence. If all of this testifies to Levinas's incapacity to understand Spinoza, perhaps that is because siding with him would imply giving up the transcendent God, the experience of election, and indeed the grandeur of the Jewish tradition in which Levinas himself finds so much comfort, even and perhaps especially after the abomination of the Holocaust.

What then of Spinoza's freedom of spirit and his idea of an impassive God? Would they have withstood such a trial? One must at least entertain the possibility that they would have, since, according to Spinoza himself, "Who loves God cannot strive to have God love him back."[20] After all, on his reasoning anything else would commit one to a God who is passive, a God could be perfected and therefore would not be God at all, for "God has no passion and is not touched by any state of mind of Joy or Sadness."[21] God is the sum of the individuals composing Nature, which for its part is infinite: God thus lacks nothing and does not feel anything. This was and remains a scandal for Jews, and for that matter Christians as well: with Spinoza, one wants to know what has become of *God* once the God of justice and mercy disappears. If God has vanished, then it remains an open question whether God *is* God at all anymore — in which case Spinoza will have been the father of atheism and the many negations of the subject that have followed. And it would be for this that Spinoza could not be forgiven, even if one were compelled to admit the rest of his philosophy.

Schelling and Levinas: The Harrowing of Hell

Joseph P. Lawrence

When Emmanuel Levinas writes (in the preface of *Totality and Infinity*) that Franz Rosenzweig's *Stern der Erlösung* is "a work too often present in this book to be cited," he effectively names his debt to F. W. J. Schelling as well, for Rosenzweig's work was a sustained attempt to carry to completion Schelling's great philosophical fragment, the *Weltalter*. Scholars of Levinas have explored Levinas's relationship to Schelling,[1] but I confess that, as a Schelling scholar, I knew nothing of this connection until rather recently. I credit above all the energetic work of Jason Wirth for helping me see its importance — and more generally the importance of reading Schelling in the context of recent work in continental philosophy.[2] None of this has been easy. The very thing that Schelling and Levinas have in common, their resistance to the implicit solipsism of overcoming mystery with clarity, make them poor candidates for quick appropriation and comparison. Indeed, Schelling anticipated Nietzsche by openly mocking the scholars who make it their business to "appropriate and compare."[3] Mockery and ridicule is, of course, not Levinas's way of going about things. Even so, he too is so relentless in his polemic against the totalizing desire to know that he forces his reader to pause and question just what a proper scholarly response to his work might be. As such, the very first result of taking up the question of Schelling and Levinas might be that we are forced to set aside the scholarly mask, testimony of one's acquiescence to the order of the same, in order to step forth as the human beings that we are. Whether this is an act of humility or of arrogance is not at all clear. Dispensing with the pretense of knowledge takes a kind of boldness on our part — for what but knowledge might give us a claim to the attention of others?

On the other hand, obscurity aside, the difference between Schelling and Levinas seems clear enough. Levinas would have us start with the face of the other. For Schelling, in contrast, philosophy is *anamnesis,* precisely that maieutic project of self-discovery and self-recovery that Levinas warns us against. If Schelling knows any "other" it is the other within the self. Although Levinas uses similar language in *Otherwise than Being,* it remains to be seen whether this is enough to establish meaningful contact between the two thinkers. As for nature, Levinas almost ignores it, while Schelling discusses it on a broad and even grandiose scale, but only insofar as it is understood as the implicit (or the slumbering) self. To this degree, Schelling is Cartesian: the sole path to the other proceeds through the God who is situated at the root of the self. For Levinas this is the idea of the infinity — but understood as the ground of other human beings, not of nature.

Levinas's God appears only within the rupture of externality where the face of the other stops me in my tracks and announces the limit of my sovereign right to feed and to enjoy. What humbles me is the discovery that you and I are not carved off the same block. In the "I don't truly know you" I find both the call to battle and the invitation to set all battle aside, the lingering trace of a God not simply one, but infinite. It is here that we find Levinas's version of Cartesian doubt. Do I recognize God first through the human other — or is my very ability to see the other not itself bound up with an awareness of my own finitude? With the certainty that I did not create myself, do I not posit a relationship to an infinite that serves as my ground? It is here, in the intuition that being itself is fundamentally *suffered,* that we find the nodal point of a comparison between Schelling and Levinas. Let me begin by putting forth an abstract rendition of the thought itself. But, because the thought demands concretization, I will follow it toward the end of this essay, into the court of the suffering Job himself.

Life attains its characteristic density and intensity (yes, its pain), only when the ethical encounter with the other displaces the ontological quest for knowledge, which, masquerading as an alternative to violence ("see, we are all at heart the same"), is really just a more subtle way of seeking conquest and control. This thought belonged to Schelling long before it was taken up by Levinas.[4] Less a thought than an experience (consciousness turned away from its natural impulse toward objectification), it cannot serve as the bridge that unites the two thinkers: Schelling was not Levinas. Yet to understand the source of Schelling's famously Protean restlessness is to understand how deeply immersed he was in the difficulty that was later to consume Levinas, the difficulty of thinking the Good *beyond* Being. It is here that we glimpse the strange proximity that places both of these thinkers before us. In some very fundamental way, it is the proximity of the Christian and the Jew — or of the Christian and the Jew who have been released from orthodoxy and thus freed from the tyranny of the same. Just as genuine friendship is the meeting of those who have remained true to their own path, the community of religion requires the courage of the heretic.

For the young Schelling the idea of the Good beyond Being began with an insight that he shared with Fichte, the realization that the very quest for reality forces one to philosophize from the standpoint of practical rather than theoretical reason.[5] There is, in a word, no theoretical refutation of solipsism, but a perfectly adequate practical refutation: to the degree that I treat others as real, they disclose themselves as real to me. The other in question is, moreover, no mere object that I encounter: "for where objects are, there am I also, and even the space in which I intuit them is originally only in myself. The sole original *outside me* is an *intuition* outside me, and this is the point at which the idealism we start with is first transformed into a realism."[6] Taken in itself, this is an insight that points more to Habermas (whereby the free and independent intuition outside me is assumed to be an intelligence that reasons just as I do) than it does to Levinas (whereby the intuition is exceeded by a face that strikes me at a pre-intentional level that no intelligence could ever absorb). Nevertheless, this passage is an appropriate place to start the evaluation of his relation to Levinas, for it took Schelling years to realize not only the extent of the otherness of the other, but the claim it makes upon us. Not until after his marriage with Caroline Schlegel does he deliver the stunning observation that becomes the centerpiece for his middle and late philosophy: "This is the secret of love, that it unites such beings as could each exist in itself, and nonetheless neither is nor can be without the other."[7]

While Schelling frequently depicted philosophy as a purely internal attempt to recover knowledge lost in the catastrophe of the primordial fall,[8] he at the same time displayed the disposition and sensibility of a philologist (his father was a classical Orientalist), well disposed to learn from others. In his lectures on the *Philosophy of Mythology* (delivered in his old age), Schelling showed that he had kept alive the languages learned in his youth, including Greek, Latin, French, English, Spanish, Italian, Hebrew, Arabic, and Sanskrit. Whatever "co-knowledge" he may have claimed of the creation,[9] it was knowledge that required a constant move outward in clear renunciation of the will to appropriate, colonize, or domesticate. Schelling and Hegel are not the same.

In the tension between philosophy and philology, which for Schelling ultimately grew into the tension between negative and positive philosophy (between what can be constructed and what cannot), we find a suitable opening for an attempt to read him side by side with Levinas.

Levinas does not simply forbid ontology. His thinking, in fact, unfolds from a penetrating ontological insight that, by way of Rosenzweig, he may have derived from Schelling. Already in *Time and the Other* (1947), we find him reaching into a "to be" so profound that it would still prevail even if beings themselves had never come to be:

> The existing that I am trying to approach is the very work of being, which cannot be expressed by a substantive but is verbal. This existing cannot be purely and simply affirmed, because one always affirms a *being* [*étant*]. But it imposes itself because one cannot deny it. Behind every negation this ambience of being, this being as a "field of forces," reappears, as the field of every affirmation and negation. It is never attached to an *object that is,* and because of this I call it anonymous. (*TO* 48)

As Fiona Steinkamp has recently pointed out,[10] the imprint of Schelling's *Weltalter* (by way of Rosenzweig) is unmistakable, not simply as the thought of being that is utterly necessary and thus always already prior, but in the specific form that is attributed to it, as the field of "forces," particularly those of "affirmation and negation" (*TO* 48).

The necessity at issue goes much deeper than the idea of necessity that constitutes the tradition from Parmenides to Hegel, for (as made clear in the ontological argument for the necessity of God's existence) the traditional idea is first and foremost precisely that: an idea. If being is seen as flowing forth from the concept of being, then it presupposes that concept, which in turn is given only insofar as being itself is given. This represents the limit of the ontological argument: if "God" is, then God is eternally, by virtue of the very concept. While this is true, it nevertheless begs the question of whether or not God *is.* To understand this thought is to understand the priority of the female over the male (even the creator God has always already had being bestowed upon him). Theologically construed (as by Schelling himself), this becomes the basis for an elaborate vision of a suffering God, who is eternally called upon to extract himself from the "unprethinkability" (*Unvordenklichkeit*) of his own existence. One finds this very thought in Levinas's notion of a Being "which leaves no hole and permits no

escape." Irremissibly given, it is "without exit." It is not consciousness, for it is not mine (though I may indeed sink into it). In its eternal "vigilance" it is utterly and painfully aware of itself as a kind of eternal
imprisonment. Lost in anonymity, it knows only that it is, but never
who it is. As the "impossibility of nothingness," it is the other side of
death, that into which we eternally "return." As such, it "deprives sui-
cide, which is the final mastery one can have over being, of its function of mastery."[11] What Levinas paints here is a bleak vision of eternal
recurrence, thought not first by Nietzsche, but by Schelling in the
Weltalter. It is a horror that can never be abolished but only mitigated
in the sleep called consciousness, the illusion of self.

When Levinas distances himself from Heidegger's "Being" it is not
because he has no access to it, but because he recognizes its emptiness
and anonymity. Textually derived from Schelling and Rosenzweig,
what he has in mind receives phenomenological verification in such
experiences as insomnia. The real contrast with Heidegger lies in the
fact that Levinas discerns in Being no god to rescue us. There is no
"rupture of the anonymous vigilance of the *there is*" apart from the
hypostasis of human consciousness itself. This consciousness in its
turn stands alone ("it is a monad"),[12] breaking through its solitude only
by encountering the face of the human other. Thus the rupture from
the eternal that constitutes the self is repeated in the rupture from the
self that is the gift of the other, who thus affords release from monadic
closure. All of this is grounded in an even deeper (and irredeemable)
aloneness. Levinas alludes to it by evoking the solipsism of reason (not
to be mistaken for the divine understanding).[13] Schelling speaks it
directly: "For a person helps another person and even God helps a person. But nothing can help the first nature in its terrible loneliness. It
must struggle through this state alone and for itself."[14]

Creation is the (eternal) birth of God through the harrowing of the inner hell of predivinity (the eternal past). This is the basic conception that Schelling develops in the *Weltalter*. The eternal recurrence of force chasing force (and of will devouring will) is in a sense given even where there is nothing (insofar as nothing is simultaneously "smaller than the smallest" and "larger than the largest"). For that very reason, the *there is* is eternal. In Schelling's account, the fact that each force (affirmation, negation, and the unity of the two) has an equal claim to being results in a circular rotation that can be broken only where the claim is voluntarily renounced. This foundational act of self-sacrifice emerges through an encounter with something higher. Within the eternally awakening godhood, the cycle of potencies (which as potencies manifest themselves as the "will" to affirm and the "will" to negate) is broken open through the encounter with an "Other that is outside of it and wholly independent of it and exalted above it."[15] Beyond the twofold nothing of expansion and contraction is the still more primordial nothing of the neither-nor: the possibility of a joyfully creating God is grounded in a God deeper still, the one who never steps forth from the bliss of eternal oblivion. In contrast to Aristotle, who posited a specific activity (thought-thinking-thought) in the self-encapsulated godhead, Schelling focuses solely on the actuality that makes it function as an unmoved mover. If being as such is will, then this is the "will that wills nothing."[16] It is the happiness that does not know itself, the bliss that thinks nothing. Not something that is good, it is the Good itself, the Good thus *beyond* Being. Creation is rupture and radical departure. Not until his middle period does Schelling understand it positively as a hymn of praise sung in the honor of one who eternally hides. Earlier proclamations echo a kind of gnosticism: God sleeps while the world engages in demonic dance. Levinas never goes quite so far, but he does identify evil with a "surplus of the world."[17] By resisting any move to theodicy, he simultaneously makes it clear that the Good we yearn for once we have been stung by evil is a Good that will never triumph within the world as such.

And, just as Schelling did in his early essay *Philosophie und Religion* (1804), Levinas in *Time and the Other* gives expression to perhaps the core contention of Gnosticism: the idea that we ourselves are the creators of our own being, that creation is cataclysmic fall (or rupture). Levinas speaks in this vein of a "freedom of beginning," a freedom that "enchains" the self to itself, causing even the heaviness of materiality (*TO* 54–56). For the early Schelling, the real guilt we bear is for having taken on existence.[18] In Levinas's formulation, "a free being is already no longer free, because it is responsible for itself" (*TO* 55), a thought reaffirmed in *Otherwise than Being*, where Levinas speaks of an "irremissible guilt" (*OB* 108–09). "Shut up within the captivity of its identity" (*TO* 57), it is self-enchainment, it is matter. Death is its promise of release (*TO* 74). Time itself provides the only redemption from time. The other can be encountered as other, only by one able to die. The "illusion" of hypostatic self-beginning has to be stripped away if the self is to enter fully into the stream of life. Here too hell has to be harrowed — which is possible only through the suffering of it. The reward for learning passivity is a genuine future, in opposition to the future that we construct for ourselves. Such a future is "absolutely other and new," in it, one "never again meets with time as a 'moving image of eternity'" (*TO* 80). The self-created self of hypostasis is literally saved by the approach of death — that over which it is completely powerless. This constitutes the condition for the encounter with the other — which has to be something I receive, not something I posit.

What is undone here is a Kantian conception of experience — and of morality. The dia-chrony of the past (evocative of Schelling's idea of an "eternal past") refers to its irreducibility (even through the longest possible chain of causes) to the present or to the unity of self-consciousness. In *Otherwise than Being*, Levinas refers to an "immemorial past" (*OB* 38), a phrase that not only evokes a strong sense of the "eternal," but renders it "unconvertible into a memory" (*OB* 105). And yet precisely this is put directly before me by the appearance of the other, to whom I am responsible without bearing any responsibility whatsoever for having brought him or her into the world.[19]

While all of this seems incompatible with Schelling's consistent under-standing of philosophy as *anamnesis*, whereby the basis for knowledge is given entirely in the self, we discover that the movement is in fact much the same: the ego, the synthesizing subject of experience, has to be dislodged from its position as knower of objects and thereby brought to ecstatic self-abandonment by the eruption *within the self* of that which is absolutely other to it.[20] This makes possible a kind of "doubling" in which there are "two beings, a questioning being and an answering being, an unknowing being that seeks knowledge and an unknowing being that does not know its knowledge," which gives rise to the inner dialogue that is "the authentic mystery of the philoso-pher."[21] While Schelling's description directly evokes the Platonic trope of interior discourse, it explicitly declines to do so under the figure of a new synchrony. This is not "the *other* already apperceived as the *same* through a reason that is universal from the start" (*TO* 103). Philosophy is not "demonstrative science," does not "proceed from something known, to something else known," and thus has as its first step not knowledge at all, but "ignorance": "It is the surrender of all that is *knowledge* to man."[22] Within this ecstatically opened, unknow-ing consciousness, that other great "unknower" appears, not the one who deludes himself into thinking he knows, but the unconscious one whose knowing is sheer emptiness, correspondence with the naked sim-plicity of what is itself beyond all attribute: the happiness which does not "know" that it is happy. And to this other, the God lost in eter-nal nirvana, finite consciousness bears an infinite responsibility, for only through its self-sacrifice, its ecstatic rupture, does the unknowing God awaken to self-knowledge.

How utterly different from the landscape traversed by Levinas, where there seems to be no "awakening" of God in subjective consciousness itself or, for that matter, anywhere in this world. And yet, palpably, one thought is utterly the same: the unveiling of transcendence stripped of all transcendentality, which is what Levinas has in mind when he writes: "This anteriority is 'older' than the a priori" (*OB* 101). An "anarchy" more primordial than the *arche,* an anteriority older than the a priori, these are tropes for Schellingian "unprethinkability" (*Unvordenklichkeit*), necessity that precedes all concept. The worry that Levinas's strictures against maieutic philosophy exclude any significant dialogue with Schelling dissolve once one sees that the point of philosophical *anamnesis* for the latter is not to recover a deepest layer of consciousness that knowingly posited the totality of being, but, to the contrary, the point is to recover the recollection that consciousness began in fear, the response to being that has been thrust upon it, anterior to its own awakening. What Schelling posits as the ground of divine existence, within the deepest possible moment of interiority (recoverable only through an inner dialogue that withdraws from all things in this world), Levinas locates in the field of exteriority: primordial anarchy is *persecution,* the refusal of the other to regard me as anything but grist for its own mill, the suffering victim of its will to sovereignty. The responsibility I feel to the other, the need to save the other, is bound up with my own will for survival and is thus contaminated by my own guilt. The eternal recurrence is not first and foremost the hell that God has always already climbed out of, but the hell in which we ourselves are still irredeemably entangled. We live so emphatically in the divine past, that God is a future infinitely remote, little more than the hope that an eschatological event could one day eradicate the relentless nightmare of history.

Here, again, we have stumbled upon a startling proximity. Anyone familiar with Schelling's late period will recall how thoroughly he disassociates himself from Hegel's effort to find redemption in history, how decisively he regards the state as incapable of eradicating the principle of warfare that constitutes its own internal condition, how consistently he places humanity's only hope in religion — and a religion so thoroughly stripped of idolatry that, as tied as it is to the history of

Christianity, it nonetheless completes itself as nonsectarian, philosophical religion. Schelling links such religion to the future realization of the ecumenical Church of John, named for the "one Jesus loved," a church that would offset the rampant individualism of Protestant Christianity (the Church of Paul) while avoiding the implicit totalitarianism of traditional Catholicism (the Church of Peter). Christianity, up until this completion, Schelling understands as the "religion of the gentiles," emphasizing its pagan roots to the point of describing Jesus Christ as Dionysus become real, the culmination of the mythological process that has unfolded in a wide span incorporating all of the cultures of the world.[23] Once the "potencies" (religion's own immersion in power) play themselves out, the pure godhead is made manifest. Idolatry thus overcome, Judaism can finally be incorporated within the framework of a Christianity so thoroughly "Christian" that the name itself fades away: religion as such — excluding no one — is all that remains.[24] The final act of grace (the pagan-Pauline impulse) is an insight into law (the concern of Jews, Muslims, and Catholics)[25] so penetrating that it no longer threatens reduction of the other to the same: what can this be but the ethical command read directly off the face of the human other?

A follower of Levinas would presumably find appealing the moment of radical openness that distinguishes Schelling's philosophy of history from Hegel's. Even so, much remains suspect: above all, the idea of a philosophy of history as such. The story Schelling has to tell errs first of all simply by virtue of being a story. If we are embedded in an elaborate journey of the spirit, then we have a distant mythical future in which responsibility for the other will be placed squarely on our shoulders: all else is preparation for and anticipation of that future. For Levinas, reading history as a story is to debase the memory of the past, just as when the "Old" Testament is read as a prefiguration of the New. What comes first, a scripted account of ourselves or the past from which it becomes possible? "Are we on a stage, or are we in the world? Does obeying God involve receiving a role from Him or receiving an order?" (*DF* 121). Whether or not we rise to it, responsibility is placed before us now. The question of God may as yet be unresolved, but my neighbor stands before me as I speak.

Schelling's God is discovered in the emphatic "I don't know," which is the discovery of one's own vulnerability (the strangeness of one's own being); Levinas's God is discovered in the face of the other, in its naked exteriority, that is to say, in *its* vulnerability and *its* strangeness. Amidst all of that vulnerability, we discover the God who shows himself precisely by *not* showing himself. This is not only a warning against idolatry (all the way down to the nation or machine that would save us), but it is a way of thinking futurity in its full radicality. The idea of an eternal past, a dia-chrony so fundamental that it resists every foray of the "I think," is completed by the idea of an eternal future. As the source of eschatological renewal, the future strips away any possible reduction of the other to the same. It is not the coming event that will one day finally be "accomplished" by the sacrifice to it of all that is present; instead, it is a withholding so complete that it fills every present with the significance of deep alterity, awakening the capacity for true speech in "a relation with the infinity of being which exceeds the totality" (*TI* 23). The Kingdom of God is given here and now, but only insofar as it is not given at all: thus the priority of ethics over ontology.

To understand the scope of this transcendence is to understand how completely the ethical must be held free from the quest for empire. The Kantian promise of "Perpetual Peace" through a universal federation of states turns out to be as thoroughly counter to the ethical as is the demand of Dostoevsky's Grand Inquisitor that power be seized for the sake of suffering humanity. The point is not Heidegger's point that we must undo Prometheus's theft of fire from the heavens in order to return it into the hands of the "faceless gods" who rule over the things we enjoy. Better that we accept the "death of these gods" as the way "back to atheism and the true transcendence" (*TI* 142). This is as true for Schelling, purportedly a neopagan, as it is for Levinas. If Schelling's Christ is the quintessence of pagan power, he is simultaneously the will to sacrifice that power by subordinating it to the will of the Father, even unto death itself.[26] The world is redeemed not by the benevolent emperor of the world, but only by the emperor's renunciation of power. Schelling and Levinas stand together with Dostoevsky on this most fundamental issue, aware that the eschatological opening presupposes the rupture of the totality.

And yet they differ profoundly. Schelling philosophizes out of an intellectual intuition that purports to unveil the God who stands at the root of the self: a God to be known. Levinas finds his God only in the godless world of the atheist, where emphatically there is no God to be known. If "the dimension of the divine opens forth from the human face" (*TI* 78), it is a dimension to be traversed not through the disclosure of some hitherto hidden attribute (as if God is there to be *seen*), but only through the mode of one's response: God exists only in goodness itself, only in the resolve to lay down oneself for the sake of the other. The root of this resolve is indeed Schelling's "will that wills nothing," but it is extended into divinity only insofar as it wills nothing for the self and everything for the other. The God in such goodness can only be an absent God.

For Levinas, the world of nature is a world to be enjoyed — and consumed. Its unreliable instability calls forth first the false gods of paganism and then, more reliably, the willingness to labor and the determination to possess. This determination encounters its limit in the face of the other, which opens the full range of possible moral response: murder, enslavement of the other, the free gift of oneself to the other. In the properly ethical response, the world of sense enjoyment is not to be renounced, but shared. The door of one's home, one's deepest interiority, is to be thrown open. The self-enclosed autonomy of the Aristotelian unmoved mover is incompatible with the ethical. Gyges' ring corrupts the soul and has to be tossed aside. The *appearance* of morality fostered by institutions, which has continuity and preservation of totality as its highest goal, has to be replaced by a morality that is so interior as to be hidden — with an interiority, moreover, that renders it absolutely exterior to the totality. By keeping its moral intention hidden, while disruptively seeking to free infinity from totality, such morality invites persecution. It is, moreover, necessarily an atheistic morality. For a God-enclosed universe leaves the story of salvation to God, not to me. The Hegelian universe replicates the problem in the ineluctable march of history. Only a godless universe summons me, not to a hubristic act of pride, but to an act of obedience to the moral imperative written on the face of the other: "Everything that cannot be reduced to an interhuman relation represents not the superior form but the forever primitive form of religion" (*TI* 79). Such "superior" religiosity requires the courage of the heretic.

Schelling, too, was an anarchist at heart, despite his occasional protestations of orthodoxy — and despite his concession that the violence of the state is rendered justifiable by the violence of a humanity caught in self-will. As an anarchist, he looked beyond the state to religion, fully aware that the salvation of singularity before the judgment of God brings with it a limitation on freedom infinitely more severe than the limitation imposed by universal law: "The state, regardless of how powerful it is, can lead only to an external, matter-of-fact kind of justice. In contrast, regardless of how weak the state might be, even if it were to dissolve away entirely, the inner law, the one written into the heart itself, remains, and asserts itself with unremitting urgency."[27] This is where Schelling locates the transition from negative to positive philosophy, for it is the interior and vulnerable self which discovers that the life of God must extend beyond reason. This is an event of truth, moreover, that arises from a purely ethical standpoint (*"durchaus praktisch entsteht"*).[28]

Negative philosophy ends with the unmasking of its highest practical project, the rational state. The political resolution of the problem of justice does not afford a resolution to the problem of life. Here Schelling and Levinas think the same. But where they differ is that for

Schelling the state, reduced to a mere means, serves the purpose of higher contemplation: the discovery of the living God. For Levinas, the parallel discussion of the limit of the state ends not with the contemplative quest for God, but with the erotic quest for true love.[29] Even so, a deep structural similarity still prevails, for love desires no less than an absolute future, a "not-yet-being" that is precisely not "a possible that would only be more remote than other possibles" (*TI* 263). In this thought of Levinas, the Schellingian godhead can clearly be discerned. All love aims ultimately beyond being. Levinas puts it most poetically: "Alongside of the night as anonymous rustling of the *there is* extends the night of the erotic, behind the night of insomnia the night of the hidden, the clandestine, the mysterious, land of the virgin" (*TI* 258–59). This is the real mystery of the other: infinity retreats infinitely into the empty form of the purely infinite — deep in the eyes of the beloved, one finds the invitation to nirvana.

We are not speaking of mystical oblivion. Just as the ascent passage in Plato's *Symposium* ends not with dissolution into pure unity, but with its fruit, the genesis of virtue,[30] so the erotic surge into the full height of the other is more than orgasmic death: it is the birth of the son, actualized futurity. Precisely here, at the hermeneutical culmination of *Totality and Infinity,* Levinas for the first time explicitly names Schelling, who in the *Weltalter* "was able for theological needs to deduce filiality from the identity of Being" (*TI* 267). As a quick aside written by a self-proclaimed "metaphysical atheist," who regards theology as a barrier to the ethical relation to the other (*TI* 78), the remark could be viewed as dismissal — until one notes the consistently Schellingian nature of Levinas's concluding sections on fecundity.

The birth of the Son out of the absolute beyond of the virginally feminine grants him such decisive independence that he is infinitely more than a "projection" of the Father. And yet one knows the Father only by knowing the Son[31] — which must include the knowledge that the Son could have yielded to the devil's temptation to become lord of nature and emperor of the world.[32] The "theological" speculation pivots around the ethical dilemma: do we insist upon the broadest

possible extension of our own spontaneity — or do we surrender ourselves over to the will and authority of the Father? And by what prior
decision has the Father won such authority over us? From the viewpoint of the *Weltalter*, divinity was never simply given but had to
be eternally accomplished. That the Son was left finally in God-
abandonment so that hell became his to harrow was itself a repetition
of what first made the Father into the God he was: creation itself the
eternal accomplishment of the abandonment of self-will. What keeps
this repetition from being repetition of the same (the reason the Son
is not simply an "avatar") is that "ever recommencing being" cannot
"bypass subjectivity" (*TI* 268): the repetition is renewal and rebirth
only to the degree that a genuine ethical choice is placed before the
Son. Power wants control, perpetuation of the same in and through
history. Fecundity wants love, release into death not as an end in itself,
but as a way of acquiescing to the mystery of the ever-renewed other.
Time renewing itself in fecundity is the profound discontinuity between
Father and Son — and of what Schelling calls the "ages" of the world.
The present moment dies that in its resurrection as the entirely other
it can once again command the full attention of what is *present*. In
Levinas's parting words, "Messianic triumph is the pure triumph; it is
secured against the revenge of evil whose return the infinite time does
not prohibit" (*TI* 285).

Once again, we have announced an essential difference between
Schelling and Levinas, only in order as quickly to lose it. It is time to
adopt a new strategy if we are ever to be released from the labor of
Sisyphos. But first some questions. Does Levinas push the creator-cre-
ated distinction so far that God must remain infinitely removed? Is this
not the point of his metaphysical atheism — and the presupposition
whereby any ontology (as ontology of a godless reality) *must* yield to

ethics? What of the relationship between creation and fecundity? How are we to understand his passing remark that "creation as a relation of transcendence, of union and fecundity, conditions the positing of a unique being" (*TI* 279)? Are we, in other words, to understand ourselves as the creatures of God — or as the *children* of God? While Levinas clearly would not hold out for children who might be coddled and shorn of the crushing responsibility of being human, he still might have envisioned the hope that a human is destined for a divinity more soothing than the good conscience which provides ballast to a life wracked with pain — and for a relation more lasting than the gentle caress granted by the female other. Or does he? And what, finally, are we to make of the vast nonhuman world of nature? Is it mere fodder for our enjoyment, or a potential partner in the most inclusive fraternity of all?

If time is death and resurrection, it is also the turning in the between, the opening up of the anonymous "there is," to which I consistently refer as the "harrowing of hell." The Savior reveals the possibility of salvation; he does not simply accomplish it for us. The poet Dante is not the only one who passed through the gates of hopeless despair. According to Schelling, anyone who pursues philosophy begins with the same descent.[33] Indeed, to have grasped the basic intuition of the *Weltalter* is to realize that all of humanity must still traverse the hell of God's eternal past — but with the solace mentioned above: "at least we have one another." The original divine solipsism was broken open forever once the potencies bowed before the majesty of the godhead, the entirely Other, that pure emptiness which is sublime beyond all possibility.

For us, though, divinity remains irrevocably future — from the perspective of history, infinitely and unattainably so. As for death, Schelling considers the possibility of a rainbow-bedecked spirit-world (citing Socrates' myth of the true earth along the way),[34] a projection of what it is to live in the spirit here on this fallen earth. It is the life which begins with the ethical act of self-sacrifice.[35] It is somehow brought simultaneously to its end and its true beginning in the death that opens where the horror of dying ceases, the death, in fact, to which one looks in order to accomplish the patience of dying that at our darkest hour becomes the most perfect form of virtue accessible to us. Schelling considers, in other words, a possibility that Levinas kept shrouded in silence, the possibility that the eschatological opening beyond history is identical with the opening beyond our individual lives.

Yet, whether the hope be framed in terms of final release from being into the Good, or, more radically perhaps, as the Good of concrete virtue into which we are compelled by the very absence of God,[36] we are still turned toward it, for hell has to be traversed. The need to harrow hell is what enables us to understand why Rosenzweig made the *Weltalter* (Schelling's response to the death of his beloved Caroline) his solitary reading in the trenches of World War I — and why, in turn, Levinas read Rosenzweig's *Stern der Erlösung* in a life "dominated by the presentiment and the memory of the Nazi horror" (*DF* 291).[37]

In his afterword to Zvi Kolitz's *Yosl Rakover Talks to God,* Levinas responds to a proclamation of faith delivered in the last hours of fighting in the Warsaw Ghetto. The Holocaust is humanity's ultimate crime: as the systematic murder, down to the last child, of an entire *people,* it constitutes an attempt to uproot fecundity itself, which for Levinas is the only possible vehicle of salvation. But because the Holocaust exposed the refusal of God to intervene in history, it simultaneously stands for the final obliteration of the magician God of idolatry and paganism. This is the case, at any rate, for one who has thought hard enough to have come free of the lure of imperial power (the last vestige of paganism) that still reverberates in our own age. Beyond the scurrilous promise that this state or that machine will save us is the realization that nothing whatsoever will save us. Only in this realization of the truth is the existence of God to be experienced.[38] It is the torture of children, of all who are innocent, that proves how completely God has hidden his face.

Levinas applauds Yosl Rakover's assertion that, while he may somehow still love the God who lets evil be, he "loves His Torah more." The supremacy of the Torah above God is the ultimate proof of the supremacy of ethics above ontology: the need that *we ourselves* work to achieve justice is the gift of a God who manifests himself "not by incarnation but by absence."[39] In the same context, Levinas has some remarkably harsh words to say about Simone Weil — and seems to have set aside Rosenzweig's old hope for a rapprochement between Christian and Jew. Too much evil has been done in the name of the incarnate God. In the name of the God of love, the Jew has always been slaughtered. The viewpoint is clear and compelling: God delivers justice to us only by hiding his face. We are not to stand before God simply as debtors, but as creditors: taking upon ourselves the proof of God's existence. Simone Weil and her ilk, those who want their God to come to *them*, who recognize their God only in feeling, must yield to the cerebral bearers of Jewish learning, those who recognize no God outside the Torah. Not only has the Messiah not come already, but he will never come: we will have to accept the responsibility for saving ourselves.

Yet, as clear, indeed, as austere and beautiful as this view is, Levinas sets it aside once he fully articulates it. He is too deeply touched by Yosl Rakover's cry of anguish, "You should not pull the rope too tight." In Levinas's own words, "A religious life cannot be achieved in such heroic circumstances. God must reveal His face, justice and power must be reconnected, there must be just institutions on this earth. Only he who has recognized the veiled face of God can demand that it be unveiled." Levinas abandons the austerity of his position in order to call attention to a place *between* "the warm, almost palpable communion with the Divine" and "the despairing pride of the atheist."[40] The Messiah has not come. He will perhaps never come. But in his absence, we ourselves will have to build him a sufficient dwelling. Politics trumps religion.

What Levinas fails to mention in his afterword is that Yosl Rakover's talk to God is self-consciously a repetition of the apology delivered by

Job so many centuries before. The only difference is that the declaration of innocence has now been rendered complete: "I do not say, like Job, that God should lay His finger on my sins so that I may know how I have earned this. For greater and better men than I are convinced that it is no longer a question of punishment for sins and transgressions."[41] To point this out is simultaneously to be reminded of why Levinas does not mention the connection: his own view is that Job is to be reproached for not realizing that one must "be responsible over and beyond one's freedom" — that it is our lot to support the crushing weight of the universe even if we were not there at its making (*OB* 121–22).[42]

In his critique of Philippe Nemo's *Job and the Excess of Evil*, Levinas is intent upon destroying any last residue of theodicy.[43] Immanuel Kant, in a similar vein, suggested that the real point of the book of Job is to reprimand the friends of Job for suggesting that Job's sufferings might be a punishment — and thus subsumable under a theodicy.[44] This is an idea that Levinas takes up and radicalizes by pointing out that Job, by insisting upon his innocence, embraced the same naïve picture of a God who metes out justice for us.[45] He faults Nemo with replicating this naivety by appealing to a "beatific encounter with God" as recompense for the excess of evil.[46] According to Levinas's critique, Nemo reproduces yet another error of Job, one that goes beyond the insistence that God should be just by calling attention to Job's own failure to achieve that justice himself, his inability (blinded as he was by his own tragedy) to see the suffering of others.[47]

There is undoubtedly much to make of this critique. Even first-time readers of the book of Job are disturbed by Job's seeming indifference to the horrific fate of his own sons and daughters. But perhaps Levinas himself was too blinded by the suffering of humanity as a whole to see something that he should have seen, what Schelling calls divine indifference or "the will that wills nothing." God's silence is not to be understood as a ruse. The absent God is not using absence to goad humanity to morality, for God *remains* absent. Justice and power are only connected as a result of the greatest effort on our part; undoubtedly they *should* always be connected, but this is our affair not God's. On some very sublime level, the connection does not even matter. We are ephemeral beings.

What Schelling helps us see is that even here (or precisely here), *in a transcendence more radical than the one maintained by Levinas,* an incarnational hope can be rescued. It is the one given, in the book of Job, by the God whom Levinas passes over, the one who breaks silence and *speaks.* This speaking does not violate divine indifference, for it is clearly a word that arises directly from it. "Who are you," the voice demands, "to curse me for your sufferings?" "Who are you to think that the world is supposed to be just?" With an eye to Levinas, the question can be varied: "Who are you to think that I am the cause of your persecution, that it is my concern to drive you toward justice?"

The incarnation is an incarnation of beauty beyond goodness.[48] If the friends of Job err by asserting that God is bound by our own narrow conception of justice, Job errs by saying that God is not bound — but should be. Against this, the voice in the whirlwind suggests that justice is a human affair. From the divine point of view the beauty of creation is enough. The last word is the word of tragedy: self-assertion, down to the simple step into existence, never goes unpunished — precisely because it is the whole itself that is beautiful and good. God's justice is not ours. As an alternative to the human quest for justice, the voice in the whirlwind delivers the role call of the animals: the lioness and her cubs, the antelope and the wild ass. A hawk, vulture, and an ostrich make their appearance as well. Most impressive, perhaps, is the majestic stallion, who "leaps like a locust and snorts like a blast of thunder," as he "champs at the bit and charges into battle," (Job 39) contemptuous of the smell of death and the spectacle of blood and gore. Here, where the whirlwind disclosed a world teeming with life, Job was finally silenced. The question of justice evaporates before the power of God. Humanity is eternally invited to live in the affirmation of what is (which includes the human while yet going beyond it). If we fail to do as we should, we can destroy our own world — but God's world remains untouched. The invitation extends from there and reaches as far into nature as it needs to reach. Not to see this is to fear the catastrophe. To fear the catastrophe is to bring it on. To be reconciled to it is to be freed from it. The voice in the whirlwind concludes by evoking the great Beast and Serpent who, between themselves, complete the work of creation by gnawing everything into dust. It is there, in the dust, that Job finds his comfort — as will we all.

What is peculiar about the indifference with which Job's God says, "let suffering also be," is that it delivers solace. Only if the depth of spirit remains sealed in the nirvana of absolute indifference can the full glory of Creation be made manifest, a glory that spans the divide between what humans call good and evil, revealing a love that reaches out to absolutely everything that could or should be.

The word for what is thus affirmed is an old one. It is *nature*, both the claw of the tiger and the delicate neck of the doe. To let nature be, we have to rise above the obsession with justice that is the source of so much injustice. What humanity needs above all else is wisdom. This is the true goal of both religion and responsible philosophy. The only world worth saving is the one we can let go of. This is a terrible wisdom, but strangely reassuring. Schelling's response to Levinas would have sounded something like this.

From Politics to Ethics (Hegel) or From Ethics to Politics (Levinas)?

Adriaan T. Peperzak

odern philosophy has had difficulty attempting to show the unbreakable unity of the individual with communal aspects of human existence. A number of modern thinkers began their treatises by rationally, even geometrically, constructing a more or less real or ideal community based on a multiplicity of individuals. Yet others, convinced that no form of individualism could ever supply insight into the communal structure of human life, saw all individuals from the outset as members — or even as organs — of a collective whole. While the former struggled in vain to show that contracts or other forms of freely chosen exchange necessarily mutate into communal dispositions and institutions, the latter had to cope with the modern dogma that all philosophy must begin from an autonomous (individual or transcendental) ego. Modern philosophy, then, has not produced a wholly satisfactory synthesis of individualism and communitarianism. This failure could be a symptom of a faulty start, which may be due to the initial questions: Can individuality and commonality be opposed? Does their distinction concern two aspects, two levels, two dimensions of one reality? How do they evoke, provoke, imply, and fortify one another?

Instead of directly meditating on these and associated questions —
or rather, as preparation for such a meditation — I will focus here on
two masters of thought who may be seen as diametrically opposed with
regard to social philosophy: Hegel and Levinas. Because of Hegel's
proximity to the Greeks and Levinas's proximity to Jewish thought,
neither of them can be paradigmatic for modernity or postmodernity.
Nevertheless, both have enough links with the modern ego to challenge each other's philosophy as well as the moral, social, and political ethos of our time.

FROM POLITICS TO ETHICS WITH HEGEL

Hegel's social philosophy is known as a summit and synthesis of the
development that leads from Hobbes and Spinoza to Marx and twentieth century philosophers of the human community. The protagonist
of his ethics is the all-encompassing Spirit, who reveals itself on all levels of the human universe: as idea in logic, as life in nature, as subjective spirit in all humans, as objective spirit in families, states, and world
history, and as absolute spirit in art, religion, and philosophy. This Spirit
cannot be identified with one or more human minds or mentalities
because, from its beginning to its end, it is one all-embracing and all-
permeating movement that unfolds its embryonic Idea through its revelation in nature and human civilization into the absolute self-knowledge
of its religious and philosophical wisdom. Certainly, Hegel treats the
life of individuals, their interaction, and their historical adventures as
relatively autonomous components of that ongoing dynamism, which
he also calls "the whole," but the final truth of all individuals lies in
their realization of a synthetic universe.

Hegel's Spirit is the dynamic and self-knowing universe of all universes, the autarchic and absolutely free universal that encompasses all
genera, species, and individuals. Hegel calls this whole of wholes
"God." Hegel's Spirit is God, but God has a structure that mirrors
the structure of a human individual. God's structure, though infinite,

resembles the structure of a corporeal, self-conscious, intellectual, and freely willing being that develops into a person, a moral subject, a family member, and a citizen of states. These beings have their own histories and cultures, while together constituting the universal history of politics, art, religion, and knowledge. The all-originating and all-embracing Spirit that rules this development is quasi-human, insofar as it concretizes itself in a humanized, socialized nature and a manifold of political bodies that produce several cultures, while being engaged in one encompassing world history. But God is also divine, for God's universality transcends all individual effort, without which, however, God cannot exist.[1]

Within the grandiose framework of the Spirit's unfolding, the self-unfolding of human individuals is delimited by legal, moral, social, and political functions and regulations of their communities. To safeguard their freedom, however, Hegel shows that the true freedom of finite individuals has the same essence and existence as the freedom of the absolute Spirit. An individual's will is fundamentally nothing else than an instantiation of the absolutely free and universal Spirit.[2]

Hegel identifies Rousseau's "general will" (*la volonté générale*) with the "will of all" (*la volonté de tous*). According to its true idea, which is also its ideal, the will of a human individual *is* the individualized freedom of the Spirit that generates, assembles, and inspires the individuals who form historical communities. Because this Idea is not a positivistic generalization of facts but an originary and normative Ideal, Hegel's conceptual reconstruction of the human community is not a mere description. It is the normative, though at the same time historically realistic, project of what a free human life will be, if it realizes its constitutive, innate, essential, or ideal purpose.

The fundamental (or ideal) identity of the individuals' freedom (or free will) with the general, or rather universal, free will of their community is unfolded in a system of communal dynamisms and structures — a common life regulated by legal, political, and socioeconomic institutions and mores. Such a system offers its individual members the possibility of being at home in the world while developing their own talents, working in useful ways, being honored for their contributions to the society, having a say in the direction of their community, and realizing their own happiness and that of their family. The totality that conditions, but also issues from, their cooperation, has a syllogistic structure:[3] the *universal* will — that is, the will of the community as one whole — diversifies itself in the *particular* components of the community's overall constitution (its specific mores, laws, regulations, representative bodies, and so on), through which the *singular* members of the community participate in the orientation and the decisions of its government, which guarantees the encompassing unity of the whole. As instantiations of the whole, the individuals must occupy their appropriate place and play their roles within the totality whose life at the same time conditions and is conditioned by their lives. These places and roles are spelled out in the rights and duties that are inherent to membership in a truly free community. Duties and rights are thus nothing else than inherent aspects of the free will that founds and permeates the social whole. Once there is more than one will, freedom differentiates itself into demands and obligations, as well as into the need for balancing, reconciling, and unifying places, functions, rules, and roles. If the members of the community accomplish the tasks that belong to their various roles, freedom is realized on all the levels of their encompassing system. The universal will of the whole and the individual wills of its components imply one another, thus composing an objective but subjectively willed and integrated world, which has the character of a "second" — i.e., humanized and habitual — *nature*.

What is the meaning that is realized in this second nature, which we also could call the *body politic* of the Spirit? As worldly, and thus corporeal, realization of spiritual freedom, it does not exhaust the Spirit's possibilities, but it realizes the human scene for the highest, no longer merely political, form of human and divine self-realization and self-knowledge: the contemplative mastery of the (natural and human) universe in the forms of art, religion, science, and philosophy.

As objective Spirit, the ethico-political world is the system of incorporated freedom that is presupposed by that contemplation.

But what exactly is freedom? Like Kant, Hegel offers a very formal and abstract definition of free will, which he too sees as another name for practical reason: free will is *the (rational) will that wills itself*.[4] However, the unfolding of this initial definition in Hegel's philosophy of right is concretized by deriving from it the complete pattern of a free community's rational organization. The main lines of right, morality, the family, the socioeconomic order, politics, and world history thus emerge as constitutive elements of real freedom. In doing so, all the components of Hegel's *Politica* receive their various functions as integral moments of one shared totality.

"The will that wills itself" is Hegel's formula for reason's autonomy on the level of human praxis. The syllogistic structure of the system that follows from it implies that individual freedom cannot be fully realized unless it fits into the freedom that is objectified as a second nature of the community within which all individuals concretize their autonomy. Outside any community, there is only a savage, atomistic, nonuniversal, and irrational form of wishing, wanting, acting, and arbitrariness or pseudo-willing. Individual morality, thus, is only a moment (or component) of the overall practice that Hegel characterizes as "ethical" (*sittlich*). Although the principles of morality remind the ethical community of certain individual rights that the community may not ignore, individuals cannot make themselves judges of their community, unless they can appeal to a better or higher community whose standards are more rational or more encompassing. It is always a whole that has the decisive voice. If there is no whole — for example, in a Hobbesian state of nature or during a civil war — individuals fall back on their personal conscience, but this opens the door to arbitrariness and evil, if it is not embedded in a common ethos and a moral tradition that has already realized at least some form of commonality.

Thus far, I have avoided the words "nation" and "nation-state," because Hegel's theory of the state confronts us with a profound ambiguity. On the one hand, it presents a quite coherent theory of the state's syllogistic constitution, whereas, on the other hand, in his treatise on international law, it sins against Hegel's own logic and basic theory of freedom. Indeed, Hegel presents the ethical totality of the (nation-)state as the ultimate form of concrete freedom, which cannot be transcended by a higher whole in the dimension of human praxis. The claim that some nations of Hegel's time were autarchic totalities, could perhaps be defended, and Hegel's analysis does this with great skill; but the claim that the state necessarily is the supreme framework of ethical — that is, political and moral — life, is a mistake for which Hegel has not given philosophically valid arguments. He even contradicts his own logic, when he holds that a supranational tribunal or government are not only nonexistent but impossible, and that therefore wars will remain inevitable.[5] Hegel's philosophical (re-)construction of the nation-state is a monument of demonstration, if seen from the perspective of his logic,[6] but his theory of international law seems to be a dead end. Let us now look more closely at these issues.

Because Hegel sees free individuals as integral (*aufgehoben*) components of the freedom that is being realized by their fully rational community, the norms that rule their morality coincide with — and are merely the subjective aspect of — the norms, rights, and duties that rule their community. If this community is completely realized in the state, then the rights and duties and, in general, all norms that the individuals must obey are realized by being good citizens of a good state.[7] Patriotism is then the encompassing framework within which we must live. What is good for a well-organized state is good for every human individual.

However, can the definition of free will as *universal* will be realized in a *particular* nation? That Hegel concretizes the abstraction of a universal will in a real community — like Kant, who concretized it in a "realm of ends" — follows from his logic, but why does he believe that this "realm" can be realized in one nation or empire? He knows very well that (a) no existing state of his time was fully rational and free, and that (b) there are many states and peoples whose cultures divide the world in different "realms"; but his theory of a free world, in which the freedom of (rational) individuals coincides with the freedom of (rational) states, is a theory of the singular state. The competition between states — the history of rivalry, wars, truces, and periods of peace — "ought to" (*soll*) be ruled by mutual respect, but this norm remains abstract and ineffective because there is not, and Hegel holds that there cannot be, any supranational institution that would enforce it. The only hope that states will stop warring lies in the mores (*Sitten*) that historically seem to direct their choices, but existing habits are often set aside when national interest overrides them.[8]

Not only does the basic principle of Hegel's theory of international law remain too abstract and powerless to orient world history toward an all-human peace, it is also completely silent about the moral, legal, and economic relations between individual citizens of different nations and, in general, about worldwide trade and cultural exchanges. No word is spent on immediate relations between individual citizens of the world, and humanity-as-a-whole does not seem to have any place in his political philosophy. The consequence of Hegel's ethical perspective on the morality of singular individuals is that their lives must be called rational and free to the extent in which they are law-abiding citizens of a rational — that is, well-organized and well-governed — state. Individuals are good or "just" (*rechtschaffen*) when they act and think in agreement with the spirit of their country, as expressed in its rationally justifiable institutions.

In his theory of absolute spirit, Hegel shows that human individuals must also develop their aesthetic, religious and theoretical talents, but he will not dwell on practical relations of universal respect, proximity, fraternity, solidarity, help, compassion, or charity with regard to strangers.[9] To be a good, patriotic citizen and to enjoy philosophy were the main goals of Aristotle's *eudaimonia*. Hegel seems to be a good Aristotelian.

Elsewhere I have argued that Hegel's identification of the state as the summit of ethical life contradicts the principles of his own logic.[10] These principles demand that the multiplicity of singular states be unified and integrated in a higher totality *on the ethical* (that is, *political*) *level* of human life. It is quite possible to amend Hegel's philosophy of right by deducing — in agreement with his logic of multiplicity and unity — a synthetic and world-encompassing framework of legal, moral, economic, and political institutions, as well as virtues that would do justice to humanity as a whole. However, even so, we would stumble on another fundamental thesis of his logic. According to Hegel, the universal will, being the will of the all-originating and all-encompassing Spirit, realizes itself as a *substance,* which is also a *subject* that precedes and summarizes the individual wills in which it is instantiated. Their community — in the form of a family, a state, a realm, or the whole of humanity — is the ground, the substance, the subject, the idea, and the spirit that differentiates and singularizes itself in instances, which it also gathers and integrates as moments of one totality, outside of which there is no other willing or practice. The independence and superiority of the community with regard to its members explains many problematic features of Hegel's moral and political philosophy, but they follow directly from his logic, according to which the truth lies in the complete unfolding of an originary principle that necessarily differentiates itself into a synthetic unity or totality. From the outset, individuals are seen as instances of a universal genus that particularizes itself in order to generate *and integrate* its own singularizations. God realizes (materializes, incarnates, socializes, and comprehends) itself by becoming a host of singular human individuals, who are driven toward material and spiritual cooperation for a world-encompassing civilization that testifies to the one, original, and conclusive, that is, absolute, Spirit.

Hegel's system presupposes not only an originating and all-encompassing or, as Hegel calls it, "infinite" Spirit, which precedes, develops, and crowns the practices and products of human history; it also presupposes human thinkers who condition, produce, and reproduce it. What kind of intentionality characterizes a Hegelian thinker who (re)produces the system of which this paper sketches a few lines? Such a thinker is a subject who (1) from a free-standing viewpoint (2) displays the universe of all universes in a panoramic overview, (3) identifies the origin and the ultimate end of this universe, (4) sees all persons, things, formations, events, and histories as moments of grounding and encompassing wholes, and (5) reduces their entire being and meaning to their being constitutive of the meaning of the ultimate whole composed by them. Hegel's philosophy of human praxis illustrates this intentionality by considering persons and all their relations, rights, duties, actions, and adventures as functions of true or deficient communities. The unicity of individuals is reduced to their contingency, except for those individuals who embody and enact an idea whose outstanding relevance can be demonstrated as a key function of the overall system and its history.

The thinker who unfolds such a system looks always from above; his/her *cogito* is constantly on top of things, which thereby are flattened, just as mountains become flat when seen from a high flying plane. There are many thinkers who think that they occupy a freestanding viewpoint, from which all individuals can be seen as pieces of an all-encompassing chess game. The panorama they observe is motivated by competition, rivalry and polemics, but the point of view seems to be good, because it makes everything and everyone visible for observation — as in science. Or do I overlook the most important fact: the transformation of myself (that is, *my* empirical, conceptual, transcendental, or pseudodivine *cogito*) into a phantastic "I" that, due to its sovereignty, has become estranged from all (myself included), who are involved in the humble chores and responsibilities of everybody's daily life?

FROM ETHICS TO POLITICS WITH LEVINAS

It is clear that Levinas's position, with regard to the universe, is different from that of most post-Cartesian philosophers, including Hegel. Looking from the top suits a treatment of underlings; it does not go well with looking up, as described from the perspective of one's involvement with the Other, who allows me neither time nor distance to leave him/her alone among the many others who populate my universe. I cannot abandon the Other in order to concentrate on more important topics, such as nature, culture, language, the universe, or any other totality. The Other has always already awakened me to a primordial responsibility for him or her. Even when I, for example, as a philosopher, must concentrate on the cosmos, this concentration is only an element of my being-for, listening-to, and thinking-on-behalf-of others. Thinking without teaching might be a form of narcissism; but if all concentration is subordinate to being for Others, how can we justify what philosophy does and how does it differ from the manner of thought that is illustrated by Hegel's system?

FACING

Levinas has shown that the Other's *face* — another's addressing me by facing or speaking to me — comes forward as an exceptional mode of existence. "The face" surprises and impresses me by its unique "height" (*hauteur*). It inspires in me a kind of awe; it makes me look up; it forbids murder and it calls for respect, welcoming, hospitality. By addressing me, the Other awakens me to a fundamental concern and responsibility for you. It is not possible to describe the experience of a face-to-face encounter in merely descriptive terms; moral connotations cannot be neglected to faithfully state how the Other's facing-me appears. Appearance *is* here a command. The fact of someone looking at me makes me immediately aware of the fact that I cannot murder this person — you. I ought to offer you space and time. Your presence forbids any monopoly. Your emergence summons me to share nature, food, education, culture, language, and civilization with you. The precise extension of my responsibility for your life — the concrete duties implied in my being-for-the-other — is not immediately obvious, but further experience and analysis will bring clarification.

At least one element of Levinas's analyses can be clearly ascertained: the existence of other humans reveals to me that I cannot be defined as an isolated monad, because I am constitutively linked by care, concern, responsibility with every other human that I may encounter. An individual is never alone. As responsibility for others — as intersubjective normativity — ethics is an essential part of each individual's existence. To be me is to be *always-already* involved in a nonchosen dedication to you.

This beginning refutes the centrism of Hegel's philosophy of self-consciousness, spirit, and will. To the extent that responsibility precedes and dominates freedom, the will is not its own possession, but for-you. I am free-*for* others, free to affirm and confirm and serve their lives in a world they own as much as I, perhaps even more than I. Whether I should also be responsibly serving myself — or my true Self — has still to be seen, but in any case, my responsibility cannot reduce the Other to a subordinate moment of my own self-realization.

When we reflect upon the question of what exactly causes the normative character that the other's face reveals to me, we come to the amazing conclusion that it does not lie in any specific feature, quality, form, or aspect of the various faces that look at me. The reason why the other commands me is not the other's beauty or kindness or health or lovability. "The face" is unqualified, naked, wholly abstract; it is everybody's face, though it is not at all indifferent, because everybody is unique. Though all faces are similar, each face is absolutely unique; and yet this unicity — and thus its radical difference from all other faces — is a universal fact. This fact cannot be reduced to a kind of similarity or dissimilarity because the face transcends all qualifications and properties.

The other's universally unique command is undeniable, although the other has neither the status of a master, nor that of a servant or slave. We cannot capture your addressing me by describing the context in which you appear or the role you play. The absoluteness of your facing me does not depend on any text, context, framework, or totality. If I try to contextualize or integrate a face, it changes into a component of an encompassing whole, which then immediately effaces your facing-me. Here lies the root of a radical difference between Levinas and Hegel:

human individuals cannot be reduced to functions, members, organs, or moments of any community. Insofar as a face is caught in a context or world, or any other kind of totality, it hides behind a more or less successful but always partial, shadowy, or stylized mask, which makes it part of a natural, cultural, linguistic, and historical whole. Such a mask differs from other masks through its lines and colors, its beauty, and its emotional expressions; but it has lost its ethical force, even if it is still aesthetically pleasing, scientifically interesting, or erotically lovable.

SAYING

In order to "see" what Levinas describes, it is helpful to be aware of the epistemological conditions of such a seeing. This can be eased by the consideration of an element that is overlooked too often in Western philosophy.

In studying the essence of knowledge, truth, science, or philosophy, we often focus on propositions or theories as examples of a structure that Aristotle summarized in the formula *legein ti kata tinos*, "to say something about something." However, in doing so, most often we forget or neglect the fact that there cannot be any *saying* at all, unless there is someone, *tis*, who presents the proposition to someone else, *tini* (in the dative), who is a real or possible interlocutor.[11] If I take the place of *tis*, the speaker, my speaking is a first-person-speaking, which reaches out to a listener, who thereby necessarily becomes a respondent. In addressing my words, I challenge and provoke the other to a response (even if the listener refuses to react otherwise than by silently ignoring the speaker). Often, my speaking (*legein*) says something about something; but it is not necessary that speaking or any other act of addressing concentrate on an object or context. The addressing itself is what connects you and me. Communication establishes a bond, even if we hardly speak *about* anything. One can address another even without words by a simple gesture or a meaningful look. The difference between speaking *to* and speaking *about* something or someone is radical, because it radically differentiates the position and orientation — the intention — of the speaker. By speaking *about* things or persons, I oversee, gather, and display them in a context which I oversee and control as the supreme observer. In speaking *to* someone, however, I propose and offer myself to the other's attitude, whose character I cannot determine or calculate. My addressing you is a link within — or, sometimes, the beginning of — a temporal process through which you and I provoke each other to engage in a duo-personal history of listening and responding.

It is obvious that speaking-about lends itself easily to an egological and panoramic thematization of things, events, and persons, whereas speaking-to involves me in a dialogue with someone who constantly responds in a way of his own and thus maintains me in a noncentral, up-looking, and serving place. If saying *precedes* the said, Hegel's systematic thought can no longer be fundamental or all-encompassing. Totality characterizes all that can be gathered and synthesized, whereas addressing keeps you and me separate through a communion that is not a self-same unity.

Levinas's distinction between Saying (*le Dire*) and the Said (*le Dit*) can be developed into a theory that respects both the communal and the individual dimensions of our belonging together as two irreducible but inseparable dimensions of human existence. We are at the same time (1) situated and sharing members of a community and (2) personally responsible for our own destiny and that of others. As involved in other lives, we, at the same time, develop our own personal destinies; together we share the common goods that permit us to be citizens of the world, while transcending the world by being radically separate and unique.

To develop such a theory, we could provisionally use the traditional contrast of form and content (or matter) in order to unfold the distinction between the *towardness* involved in all varieties of addressing, on the one hand, and the *aboutness* of the message that is addressed. The matter would then stand for all those contents and contexts you and I can share with one another, that is, all that which any you and I have or can have in common: customs, institutions, documents, texts, and so on. This constitutes us as a *we* and its structure can be summarized by the expression *being-with* (*Mitsein*). If community is a synonym of this we, it means that aspect of our lives we share or have in common: the network of roles, functions, duties, and rights, which all of us recognize as ours.

The form, however, would indicate the always unique face-to-face relationship and its many varieties of addressing, personal engagement and devotion that go from a simple provocation to mutual care and friendship. It cannot be reduced to a variety of being-with as realized in sharing, because it has the dialogical, personally committed and devotional structure of being-*toward* or being-*for*. The full meaning of this relationship can be perceived only from a first-person perspective that is neither panoramically objective nor subjectively arbitrary. It simultaneously distances and unites you and me through a bond that focuses on your utterly abstract (naked) unicity, while it also must be meaningfully filled by sharing goods that can enrich your and my own existence. Although our connection does not absolutely depend on any specific matter or content (*ultimately* it doesn't matter what we share), you and I desire to express our mutual service in the commonality of a language, a culture, a people, a religion, an ethos, a story, or a history, even if we can hardly share anything unless we transform our differences into a new blend and brand of our own making. In any case, your and my attempts in making our linkage concrete by expressing it in a common way of behaving and speaking will always owe most of its content and style to the traditions to which we have been introduced by our education.

For a full analysis of our participation in the traditions of communities to which you and I now belong, we can learn a lot from all those authors who have analyzed and synthesized the historical, sociological, linguistic, religious, and hermeneutical aspects of humanity from a panoramic perspective. For the analysis of the mutual devotion that is implied in all initiation, education, teaching, conversation, friendship, and contention, however, we must retrieve the hints and suggestions that Aristotle and others have left us concerning friendship, dialogue, and personal commitment, but much has still to be done before we can fully understand the fundamental role of the dialogical aspect of human action. One of the mistakes we can make in this respect is to replace the dialogical structure by a dialectical logic that reduces all voices to one supervoice with the pretension that it possesses the final synthesis. For that would kill the universal unicity of each and every voice.

Just as in our understanding of Kant's ethics, we must insist on the unbreakable tie that unites form and matter into one inseparable dynamism. Devotion to one another — developed into an adventurous history of personal commitments — needs concretization through concerted sharing in the ongoing civilization that has not waited for us to be ruled, although it invites us to emendate it as much as we are able to. Looking from the perspective of the larger community with its institutions and traditions, we must be aware that this community inevitably dies unless it is kept alive by individuals who, in various degrees of friendship and dialogue, constantly appropriate and recreate their heritage as an essential part of their own, exceptional, uncommon and unique destinies. Like a score that is never performed, a community is dead, if it is not perpetually resurrected by individuals who adjust its structures and traditions to their communication with all the others who face them within or without familiar contexts and horizons.

Philosophy as Service

Whereas Hegel's dialectical perspective gathers all persons from the outset as moments of one whole, Levinas begins by recognizing that you, in speaking to me, decenter my care and concern. Hegel, too, recognizes that to be oneself implies that one is also related to and *for* another, but this exteriorization is only a moment of a necessary return to and recentering of the initial unity, whereas Levinas's analysis of my relation to you shows that its characteristic asymmetry holds me in the position of a servant.[12] It is true that my service presupposes and demands that I develop my talents in order to serve you well — and

this presupposes my responsibility and freedom for my own development — but this self-realization does not transform you into a part of
me or any other whole: you and I remain separated despite our — mutu-
ally asymmetric — communication.[13] Insofar as we form a *we*, we form
a community, but this is only the milieu and the shared part of our different but interwoven and unique destinies.

The difference between a dialogical and a dialectical relation issues
an important consequence for the perspective and method of philosophy. Hegel's panoramic scene presupposes an all-seeing I in the name
of whom the philosopher speaks. To whom does such a philosopher
speak? To an audience of other ego's who imagine themselves to be
other potential representatives or prophets of the all-encompassing and
transcendental I. If Levinas is right in stating that my speaking is dominated by your epiphany, I speak always in my own name, but primarily for any you, to whom I look up, while listening and responding.
When you speak, you instruct me; when I respond, I might instruct
you, but I do this as a servant, even if you recognize me as your master. Even if I am an original philosopher in my own right, I cannot
proclaim my thought as if it were the conclusive Word that comes from
the top of the earth. I can only offer it as a proposal to all of you whom
I invite to use it in your own critical and creative work of speaking philosophically. If I *am* for-you, I also *think* and *speak* (and listen and rumi-
nate) *for you*. Hopefully, once in a while, my speaking is useful, but it
does not have to come back to me. Teaching is a gift. Whether research
is also generous depends on its being oriented to teaching or other
kinds of service.

COMMONALITY

It is obvious that Levinas cannot enclose philosophy within a framework that embraces all that matters in one whole of all wholes, whether
this whole is characterized as Being, Substance, Subject, Concept,
Universality, Totality, Idea, Spirit, God, the Infinite, or the Absolute.
When Levinas calls the Other "infinite," while opposing him/her/you

to the totality, he indicates that it is not possible to enclose the Other within the limits of any whole. All totalities are finite, not only because they are composed, but also because they can be embraced by some ego. To be other in the emphatic sense revealed in your face, is to fall outside any whole or universe, to interrupt all dialectical summation, to be incomparable and utterly irreducible. If the Other cannot be reduced to any form of the *Same,* if he or she or God cannot be integrated (*aufgehoben*) in any higher or more profound union, the community of the Other and the I (of any you and me) cannot constitute one substance, subject, spirit, or god. You and I *can* be seen as moments of a social whole, but such a vision does not see what you and I ultimately are and *do not share:* your and my unique destinies, even if these are intertwined in many ways. And yet, we need to think about and act within the horizons of encompassing, social, economic, and political wholes. Sociology, history, political theory and practice are necessary, if we do not want to restrict the horizon of our lives to the personal or most intimate rapports that link each of us to family or friends. Social justice, the freedom and well-being of a country, and other communal constellations demand general overviews, statistics, general measures, institutions, legal and political equality, and so on. But how can we justify such generalities without recourse to some sort of general will and a subject of such a will?

To show that the asymmetric relation between the Other and me cannot provide the complete foundation of politics and social responsibility, Levinas refers us to *the third* (*le tiers*): he, she, all of them who do not immediately come to the fore in my unique experience of life. In some passages on "the third," the expression seems to evoke the anonymous multitude without face or voice that hides behind you, or looks at me through your eyes and thus indirectly regards me. However, the only real difference between you, whom I know, and all others whom I have not yet encountered lies in the fact that each of them can, but has not or not yet, faced me.[14] Because the Other's face commands me not by any particular feature but as a naked face, all faces — whether I have already seen them or not — have the same significance. The hidden faces are not different from your face that keeps me awake, except that the hidden ones have not yet shown up, but still might face me — they are awaiting me, and I already know that and how they will summon me to be for them as soon as I become aware of their existence. I do not need to wait for a real encounter: their demand is clear; I am responsible for all who can become and virtually are already you. The difference between one Other and all others is not radical, insofar as *any* Other has a face.

You, who face me here and now, speak to me in the name of all humans — as if you were also the face of all faces, the holy face that every time reveals the truth of each other's commanding nakedness. Humanity is present in your face — not as Kant's human essence (*Menschheit*), but as the uniquely unique, and yet profoundly universal you, who are incomparably comparable, simultaneously identical with and different from any other you. The contradictions I now am writing down summon me to withdraw from the theoretical framework I am formulating, but how can I do this otherwise than by undercutting that framework in a gesture that offers myself as being for any you whose unique destiny affects my own unicity?[15]

NOTES

NOTES TO EDITOR'S INTRODUCTION

1. E. Levinas, *De l'évasion* (Montpellier: Fata Morgana, 1982), 104; the note is supplied by J. Rolland.
2. This is the proper point of entry for an investigation of "place" in Levinas's thinking. In "Place and Utopia" (1950), attachment to a place is the indispensable condition for ethical action. See *DF* 99–102. Whether this conception remains intact within *Totality and Infinity*'s scheme of radical responsibility deserves separate treatment.
3. A. de Waelhens, *La philosophie et les expériences naturelles* (La Haye: Martinus Nihjoff, 1961), 11; my translation.

NOTES TO TAMINIAUX, "LEVINAS AND THE HISTORY OF PHILOSOPHY"

1. Emmanuel Levinas, "La ruine de la representation," in *EDE* 125. Translated as "The Ruin of Representation," in *Discovering Existence with Husserl,* ed. and trans. Richard A. Cohen and Michael B. Smith (Evanston, Ill: Northwestern University Press, 1998), 112. This essay will henceforth be abbreviated as *RR* and cited in the body of my text, with the French reference following the English translation. I note that it was originally published in *Edmund Husserl 1859–1959* (La Haye: Martinus Nijhoff, 1959), 73–85.
2. Martin Heidegger, *Being and Time,* trans. Joan Stambaugh (Albany: State University of New York Press, 1996), 22; modified translation.
3. Ibid.

NOTES TO NARBONNE, "GOD AND PHILOSOPHY ACCORDING TO LEVINAS"

1. Emmanuel Levinas, "The Trace of the Other," trans. Alphonso Lingis, *Deconstruction in Context,* ed. Mark Taylor (Chicago: University of Chicago Press, 1986), 345–59. [Here, and throughout my translation of this essay, I have, for the convenience of the English reader, modified the existing English translations whenever I thought the author's intent could be more clearly rendered. — Translator]
2. This essay is a summary, not without some additions, of the arguments of a more ample exposition in Jean-Marc Narbonne's *Lévinas et l'héritage grec,* which is contained in Jean-Marc Narbonne and Wayne Hankey, *Lévinas et l'héritage grec, suivi de, Cent ans de néoplatonisme en France. Une brève histoire philosophique,*

Collection *Zétézis* (Paris: Librairie philosophique J. Vrin; Québec: Presses de l'Université Laval, 2004). An English translation of this work was published by Peeters Press in 2006, as *Levinas and the Greek heritage*.

3. So for example in *GCM* 92: "You know, when I pay homage to Heidegger, it is always costly to me, not because of his incontestable brilliance, as you also know."

4. "That subjectivity is the temple or the theater of transcendence, and that the intelligibility of transcendence takes on an ethical sense, certainly does not contradict the idea of the Good beyond being. This is an idea that guarantees the philosophical dignity of an enterprise in which the signifying of meaning separates from the manifestation or the presence of being. But one can only wonder whether Western philosophy has been faithful to this Platonism." *GCM* 76.

5. *Emmanuel Levinas: Basic Philosophical Writings*, ed. Adriaan Peperzak, Simon Critchley, and Robert Bernasconi (Bloomington: Indiana University Press, 1996), 21. Henceforth *BPW*.

6. Jean-François Mattéi, "Platon et Lévinas: au-delà de l'essence," *Emmanuel Lévinas. Positivité et transcendance,* suivi de *Lévinas et la phénoménologie,* ed. Jean-Luc Marion (Paris: Presses Universités de France [Épiméthée], 2000), 79.

7. Levinas, "Trace of the Other," 347.

8. *BPW* 58.

9. I borrow this term from Jean-Luc Marion in *Sur le prisme métaphysique de Descartes* (Paris: Presses Universitaires de France, 1986), in which he speaks of the "destitution" of metaphysics in charity or by the charity worked by Pascal: "By destitution, what is meant is that disqualification that does not criticize metaphysics in its order, but that warns against its unjust excesses in the 'order of charity . . .'" (359).

10. In this sense, *otherwise than being* certainly goes further than the Platonic *beyond being* or *essence,* but it is especially opposed to and totally at a distance from *essence,* i.e. the Heideggerian understanding of Being. The title of the book *Otherwise than Being, or Beyond Essence,* as Levinas himself points out in his "Preliminary Note" (*OB* xli), could have been: *Otherwise than Being, or Beyond Essance.* That *essance* is the understanding of Being specific to Heidegger that Levinas tries to transcend, and not, first and foremost, the Platonic *essence.* But as Levinas confides, "we have not ventured" (*OB* xli) to go that far.

11. For the Greek edition, see V, 5 [32], 12, lines 37ff. For an English translation with Greek on facing pages, see *Plotinus, Ennead V,* Trans. A. H. Armstrong (Cambridge: Harvard University Press, 1984), 192, 943.

12. [Emmanuel Levinas, preface to the second edition of *De l'existence à l'existant* (Paris: Vrin, 1986), p. 12 (unnumbered), my translation. This important four-page preface was not included in *EE* (see above, note 9), and has not, to my knowledge, been previously translated into English. — Translator]

13. *De caelo,* book 1 chapter 1, 268b1.

14. "On the Usefulness of Insomnia," an interview conducted by Bertrand Révillon in 1987, *Is It Righteous to Be? Interviews with Emmanuel Levinas,* ed. Jill Robbins (Stanford: Stanford University Press, 2001), 236. Henceforth *IR.*

15. Levinas, "Meaning and Sense," *CPP* 103.

16. *OB* 140.
17. *IR* 236.
18. Emmanuel Levinas, *Les imprévus de l'histoire* (Fontfroide-le-Haut: Fata Morgana, 1994), 204. *Unforeseen History,* trans. Nidra Poller (Urbana: University of Illinois Press, 2004).
19. *Charmides,* 174b–c. Only a simplistic version, which Levinas's precisely is not, could lead one to think that Judeo-Christianity has neither more nor less than a monopoly on altruism. Does not Proclus, at the close of antiquity, emphasize that "that which is perfectly good possesses plenitude, not by the mere preservation of itself, but because it also desires, by its gift to others and through the ungrudging abundance of its activity, to benefit all things and make them similar to itself"? (*On the Existence of Evils,* trans. Jan Opsomer and Carlos G. Steel [Ithaca: Cornell University Press, 2003] sections 23, 21–25). On this point, see also Narbonne, *Lévinas et l'héritage grec,* 105ff. (see note 1 above).

NOTES TO MESKIN, "THE ROLE OF LURIANIC KABBALAH"

I want to thank my colleagues in Hebrew College's Philosopher's Project for 2004–05 who read and offered valuable suggestions on what turned out to be the earliest drafts of this paper: Avi Bernstein, Harvey Shapiro, Barry Mesch, Bernie Steinberg, and Alan Zaitchik. I also want to thank my colleague Nehemia Polen for his helpful insights and encouragement as my work on this project evolved. I am grateful to Martin Kavka for his comments and editorial suggestions which have helped me to make significant improvements at several key points in the text. A considerably abridged version of this paper was presented in December 2005 in Washington DC at the annual meeting of the Association for Jewish Studies.
1. *Philosophy and Theology* 4, no. 2 (Winter 1989): 105–18; citation, 107. The explanatory material in square brackets was added by the interviewer, Edith Wyschogrod.
2. Perhaps the single best book on Rabbi Luria's life and thought is Lawrence Fine's recent *Physician of the Soul, Healer of the Cosmos: Isaac Luria and His Kabbalistic Fellowship* (Stanford: Stanford University Press, 2003). See in particular Fine's discussion of tzimtzum in chapter 4, pp. 128–34. A classic discussion of tzimtzum is found in Gershom Scholem's *Major Trends In Jewish Mysticism* (New York: Schocken Books, 1978), 260–64 (section 4 of the chapter devoted to Lurianic Kabbalah). See also his *Kabbalah* (New York: Dorset Press, 1987), 128–35; and Isaiah Tishby, *The Doctrine of Evil and the 'Kelipah' in Lurianic Kabbalism* [in Hebrew] (Jerusalem: Magnes Press, 1991), 52–61. In the works cited here Scholem famously argued for a historical connection between the Lurianic conception of God's withdrawal, and the traumatic expulsion of the Jews from Spain at the end of the fifteenth century. Scholem was, in another words, interpreting Lurianic divine self-contraction as God's self-exile, a notion he takes to reflect the historical exile of the Jews from Spain a mere 70 or so years before Rabbi Luria's creative work. As Fine points out (*Physician of the Soul,* 394–95,

n. 29), although this posited historical connection has been seriously challenged by Moshe Idel in a series of important writings, it is hard to deny the centrality of exile as a category in the lives and thoughts of Rabbi Luria and his circle.

3. Secondary works on Boehme point both to general resemblances between Boehme and the Kabbalah, and also to a similarity between Boehme's understanding of God's "self-concentration in Himself" prior to expanding outward and the Lurianic doctrine of tzimtzum. See for example Robert F. Brown, *The Later Philosophy of Schelling: The Influence of Boehme on the Works of 1809–1815* (Lewisburg, PA: Bucknell University Press, 1977), esp. 52–64; Gershom Scholem, *Major Trends in Jewish Mysticism* (New York: Schocken Books, 1978), 237–38; and Andrew Weeks, *Boehme: An Intellectual Biography of the Seventeenth-Century Philosopher and Mystic* (Albany: State University of New York Press, 1991), 102ff. (Weeks also records the interesting speculation that Boehme (1575–1624), who claimed to have experienced his life-altering mystical revelation in the town of Görlitz in the year 1600, may have met and spent time with a certain Rabbi Löw who apparently visited Görlitz that very same year! Students of Jewish history will, of course, immediately identify this rabbinic figure as Rabbi Judah Loew ben Bezalel, the Maharal of Prague (1525–1609). Whether or not he would have been well-acquainted specifically with Lurianic Kabbalah at that time remains unclear.) For Schelling, in addition to Brown's work, see Jürgen Habermas's famous essay "Dialectical Idealism in Transition to Materialism: Schelling's Idea of a Contraction of God and its Consequences for the Philosophy of History," in *The New Schelling*, ed. Judith Norman and Alistair Welchman (New York: Continuum, 2004), 43–89; Christoph Schulte, "Zimzum in the Works of Schelling," *Iyyun* 41 (January 1992): 21–40. For Rosenzweig, see Stephane Moses, *System and Revelation* (Detroit: Wayne State University Press, 1992); and Robert Gibbs, *Correlations in Rosenzweig and Levinas* (Princeton: Princeton University Press, 1992).

4. The works (cited in the last note) of Habermas and Schulte, and to a lesser extent Moses and Gibbs, all make this point. For the most part western thinkers in the modern era have historically acquired their knowledge of Kabbalah in general and Lurianic Kabbalah in particular from the work of Christian kabbalists, *as transmitted and adapted by* hermetic, mystical, and theosophical figures in the eighteenth and nineteenth centuries, such as Oettinger and Molitor. On this see both Schulte, *Zimzum*, and Ernst Benz, *The Mystical Sources of German Romantic Philosophy*, trans. Blair R. Reynolds and Eunice M. Paul (Allison Park, PA: Pickwick Publications, 1983). Matters remain less clear for the lone figure of Boehme, the nature of whose real contact with Kabbalah, if any, has stayed shrouded in obscurity.

5. The works on this question from which I benefited most in writing and revising this paper are: Charles Mopsik, "La pensée d'Emmanuel Lévinas et la cabale," *Cahier de l'Herne: Emmanuel Levinas* (Paris: Éditions de l'Herne, 1991), 378–86; and Oona Ajzenstat (Eisenstadt), *Driven Back To The Text: The Premodern Sources of Levinas's Postmodernism* (Pittsburgh: Duquesne University Press, 2001), esp. 139–99. Another work that bears directly on this question is Elliot Wolfson, "Secrecy, Modesty, and the Feminine: Kabbalistic Traces in the Thought of

Levinas," *Journal of Jewish Thought and Philosophy* 14 (2006): 1–2. Also of interest are: Richard Cohen, "The Face of Truth and Jewish Mysticism," *Elevations* (Chicago: University of Chicago Press, 1994), 241–73; and more generally, Susan Handelman, *Fragments of Redemption* (Bloomington: Indiana University Press, 1991). Three additional studies, which touch on this question indirectly through comparisons between Levinas's thought and the early nineteenth century, ethico-kabbalistic text *Nefesh ha Hayyim* (The Soul of Life) of Rabbi Hayyim of Volozhin are: Catherine Chalier, "L'âme de la vie: Lévinas, lecteur de R. Haïm de Volozin," *L'Herne: Emmanuel Levinas* (Paris: L'Herne, 1991), 387–98; Stéphane Moses, "L'idée de l'infini en nous," in *Répondre d'autrui: Emmanuel Levinas* (Boudry-Neuchâtel (Suisse), 1989), 41–51; and my own "Toward a New Understanding of the Work of Emmanuel Levinas," *Modern Judaism* 20, no. 1 (February 2000): 78–102.

   6. The pioneering works in this field are the dissertation of Ronit Meroz, "The Teachings of Redemption in Lurianic Kabbalah" [in Hebrew] (Hebrew University, 1988); and Joseph Avivi, *Binyan Ariel: Introduction to the Homilies of R. Isaac Luria* [in Hebrew] (Jerusalem: Misgav Yerushalayim, 1987). A good summary of the history and current state of research in this field can be found in Pinchas Giller, *Reading the Zohar: The Sacred Text of the Kabbalah* (Oxford: Oxford University Press, 2001), 21ff. See also Fine, *Physician of the Soul* (see note 3 above).

   7. I will return later to consider the work of these scholars. Of course, I will be arguing here that Lurianic material both exerts influence on, and does real conceptual work in Levinas's philosophy, and so must respectfully disagree with Mopsik's way of reading Levinas and the conclusions which flow from it. Ajzenstat's important work on the other hand opens up many fruitful possibilities for exploration.

   8. Ludwig Wittgenstein, *Philosophical Investigations*, 3rd ed., ed. G. E. M. Anscombe (New York: Macmillan, 1968), remarks 6 and 12.

   9. This paper is an excerpt from a larger research project, on which I have been working for some time, devoted to the role that traditional Jewish sources in general and kabbalistic sources in particular play in Levinas's *philosophical* work. I hope to have a chance in the context of a full-length treatment to expand both the analysis, responses, and remarks which must be offered here in an abbreviated form.

   10. I have based this part of the paper on the following sources: Elie Wiesel, *Legends of Our Times* (New York: Avon Books, 1968); Elie Wiesel, *All Rivers Run To The Sea: Memoirs* (New York: Knopf, 1995); Salomon Malka, *Monsieur Chouchani: L'énigme d'un maître du XXᵉ siècle* (Paris: J.C. Lattès, 1994); Yair Sheleg, "A Jewish Enigma of the Twentieth Century," [in Hebrew] *Ha-Aretz*, September 26, 2003; Yair Sheleg, "Goodbye Mr. Chouchani," *Ha-Aretz English edition*, September 26, 2003; Channah Amit, (Untitled Recollections of Shoshani, in Hebrew), *'Amudim*, 1995, pp. 133–34; Shalom Rosenberg, (Untitled Recollections of Shoshani, in Hebrew), *'Amudim*, 1995, pp. 135–37.

11. Shmuel Wygoda, "Le maître et son disciple: Chouchani et Lévinas," *Cahiers D'Etudes Lévinassiennes* (2002), no. 1: 149–84.

12. Malka, *Monsieur Chouchani*, 206ff.

13. I would like to thank Professor Hanoch Ben Pazi for the significant comments he offered on an earlier version of this paper presented at the AJS conference in 2005. Professor Ben Pazi made three important points. First of all he indicated that, as Professor Shalom Rosenberg's remarks above suggest, Shoshani may well have been learned in Kabbalah — but this says nothing about his attitude toward Kabbalah, which seems to have been at least somewhat skeptical. Secondly, there is an additional conduit through which Levinas might easily have learned something about kabbalistic tradition, namely the writings of Gershom Scholem, which certainly provide enough information to have furnished Levinas with an understanding of Lurianic Kabbalah. Finally Ben Pazi repeated an anecdote that has made its way around the scholarly world, concerning a meeting and conversation between Levinas and Scholem when the latter visited Paris sometime between 1960 and 1962. Levinas reportedly asked Scholem for kabbalistic texts he might study that bore on matters ethical. Scholem recommended three books: the *Shomer 'Emunim* (The Keeper of Faithfulness) of the famous Hasidic Rebbe Aharon Rokeach (1880–1957, also known as Reb Arele), a pietistic and mystical exploration of the nature of faith and religious devotion; the *Nefesh ha Hayyim* already mentioned above in note 5, and perhaps most suggestive of all, the *Sefer Likutei 'Amarim* (known colloquially as the *Tanya*) of R. Schneur Zalman of Liadi (1745–1812) the founder of the Chabad-Lubavitch Hasidic movement, a text which remains absolutely central to this group today. While kabbalistic references can be found on nearly every page of each one of these texts, R. Schneur Zalman's *Tanya* directly and profoundly reworks many Lurianic themes into a new psychological and spiritual Hasidic vision. Levinas was reputed to have followed Scholem's advice and to have read all three texts! (What he made of the first and third texts remains a tantalizing mystery.) This anecdote may be taken as additional support for my claim that Levinas had at least some knowledge of kabbalah in general and Lurianic kabbalah in particular (and that he came by it through more or less traditional Jewish channels of transmission). While I am grateful to Professor Ben Pazi for his invaluable observations, he cannot be held responsible for the use I make of them.

14. Despite our very different approaches to this issue, at this point my argument begins to converge with that of Martin Kavka in his analysis of the differences between Rosenzweig and Levinas. See his *Jewish Messianism and the History of Philosophy* (Cambridge: Cambridge University Press, 2004), chapter 4.

15. *TI* 109–74; *Totalité et Infini* (La Haye: Martinus Nijhoff, 1980), 81–148; hereafter all page references to the French original will follow that of the English translation.

16. *TI* 190–92; 165–67.

17. *TI* 198, 200; 172, 174.

18. Levinas does not mean, of course, that the encounter with the face of the other makes me in fact more moral. Rather, this encounter jars me out of my

egocentric complacency, even if I disregard the other's appeal, because another has addressed me and I have, in some sense, addressed myself to him or her.

19. *TI* 204; 179.

20. Rudi Visker, *Truth and Singularity* (Dordrecht: Kluwer Academic Publishers, 1999), 284.

21. Ibid.

22. Ibid., 286.

23. I thank David Raffeld for this felicitous formulation of Levinas's position.

24. Visker, *Truth and Singularity*, 303.

25. Shaul Magid, "Origin and Overcoming the Beginning: Zimzum as Trope of Reading in Post-Lurianic Kabbalah," in *Beginning Again: Toward a Hermeneutics of Jewish Texts*, ed. Aryeh Cohen and Shaul Magid (New York: Seven Bridges Press, 2002), 163–214. After a resourceful and wide-ranging introduction to the topic, Magid focuses on three figures in the ongoing creation of Lurianic (Magid prefers to call it "post-Lurianic") Kabbalah: R. Moshe Hayyim Luzzato (the "Ramchal"), R. Yitzhak Isaac Haver Waldman, and R. Dov Baer Schneurson (known in Lubavitch tradition as the Mittler Rebbe). Among other things, Magid's valuable essay helps make a strong case for thinking of Lurianic or post-Lurianic Kabbalah not merely as a series of historically connected individuals and texts, but rather as a living Jewish religious *tradition* or sub-tradition, a whole greater than the sum of its parts. Pachter's detailed work (see Appendix) adds even more strength to this case.

26. Charles Mopsik, "La pensée d'Emmanuel Lévinas et la cabale," 378–86. An internet site dedicated to Mopsik offers a bibliography which lists 19 separate books and almost 50 articles, http://www.charlesmopsik.com. This site also contains a link to Mopsik's own history of the influence and dissemination of Kabbalah among post World War II French intellectuals, "Les formes multiples de la cabale en France au vingtième siècle", http://www.chez.com/jec2/artmop.htm.

27. Ibid., 380.

28. Francis Oakley, "'Anxieties of Influence': Skinner, Figgis, Conciliarism and Early Modern Constitutionalism," *Past & Present* 151 (May 1996): 60–110.

29. This distinction originated with Hans Reichenbach. See his *The Rise of Scientific Philosophy* (Berkeley and Los Angeles: University of California Press, 1968), 231. It was adopted by a generation of philosophers of science, including Hempel and Popper, and then came to be challenged by Kuhn and Feyerabend. The so-called science wars can be viewed as a fight between those who take this distinction to capture the nature of valid scientific work, and those who take it to be an illegitimate abstraction after the fact from that work. Recent efforts to move beyond the polarization of the science wars argue that this distinction introduces an overly strong dichotomy between elements that may in fact be more closely bound together in valid scientific work. On this see Ian Hacking, *The Social Construction of What?* (Cambridge: Harvard University Press, 1999); and, from a different angle, Helen E. Longino, *The Fate of Knowledge* (Princeton: Princeton University Press, 2002).

30. Two important examples are: John Caputo, *The Mystical Element in Heidegger's Thought* (New York: Fordham University Press, 1986); and Sonya Sikka, *Forms of Transcendence: Heidegger and Medieval Mystical Theology* (Albany: State University of New York Press, 1997).

31. The most important impetus for this trend was the publication in 1968 in French (English translation, 1983) of Ernst Benz's *The Mystical Sources of German Romantic Philosophy* (see note 5 above). On Hegel see Glenn Alexander Magee's impressive *Hegel and the Hermetic Tradition* (Ithaca: Cornell University Press, 2001); David Walsh, "The Historical Dialectic of Spirit: Jacob Boehme's Influence on Hegel," in *History and System: Hegel's Philosophy of History*, ed. Robert L. Perkins (New York: State University of New York Press, 1982), 15–46; and Cyril O'Regan, "Hegelian Philosophy of Religion and Eckhartian Mysticism," in *New Perspectives on Hegel's Philosophy of Religion*, ed. David Kolb (New York: State University of New York Press, 1992), 109–29. On Schelling see Brown, *Later Philosophy of Schelling* (see note 4 above); Edward Allen Beach, *The Potencies of the Gods: Schelling's Philosophy of Mythology* (New York: State University of New York Press, 1994); and Friedemann Horn, *Schelling and Swedenborg: Mysticism and German Idealism*, trans. George F. Dole (West Chester, PA: Swedenborg Foundation, 1997).

32. See Charles Taylor, *Sources of The Self* (Cambridge: Harvard University Press, 1989), esp. 18–19, 57ff, 91ff, 307, and 374. Taylor had already discussed the concept of articulation in his 1977 essay "What Is Human Agency?", reprinted as chapter 1 of *Human Agency and Language* (Cambridge: Cambridge University Press, 1985), esp. 24–26, and 34–40. I have found two essays on Taylor very helpful in thinking about articulation: Michael Morgan, "Religion, History, and Moral Discourse," in *Philosophy In An Age of Pluralism: The Philosophy of Charles Taylor In Question*, ed. James Tully (Cambridge: Cambridge University Press, 1994), 49–66; and William Connolly, "Catholicism and Philosophy: A Nontheistic Appreciation," in *Charles Taylor*, ed. Ruth Abbey (Cambridge: Cambridge University Press, 2004), 166–86. Also of use was Nicholas Smith's *Charles Taylor: Meaning, Morals and Modernity* (Cambridge: Polity Press, 2002).

33. Taylor, *Sources of the Self*, 96–97.

34. Taylor, "What Is Human Agency?", 36.

35. Indeed, one might well go further here and say that we must stop reading Levinas by dividing his work up into "philosophical" or "Jewish", and then applying the *appropriate* discipline to the appropriate bit. We need a holistic reading of Levinas; I have offered such a reading here.

36. Mordechai Pachter, "Circles and Straightness: The History of an Idea From Lurianic Kabbalah To The Teaching of Rav Kook," [in Hebrew], *Da'at* 18 (Winter 1987): 59–90; English translation in chapter 2 of Mordechai Pachter, *Roots of Faith and Devequt: Studies in the History of Kabbalistic Ideas* (Los Angeles: Cherub Press, 2004).

37. His extensive survey includes the writings of R. Emmanuel Hai Rikki, R. Moshe Hayyim Luzzato, the Gaon of Vilna, R. Hayyim of Volozhin, R. Isaac

Yitzhak Chaver, R. Shlomo Eliashiv (the author of *Leshem Shvo v' Achlama*), and Rav Kook.

38. This convergence starts with the Ramchal and proceeds through the Gaon of Vilna and his school into Rav Kook. In researching this paper I found the work of Joëlle Hansel invaluable for understanding the originality and enduring contribution of the Ramchal to this and many other issues in the formation of Lurianic tradition. See her "Défense et illustration de la cabale: *Le philosophe et le cabaliste de Moïse Hayyim Luzzatto*," *Pardès* 12 (1990): 44–66; *Moïse Hayyim Luzzatto: Kabbale et philosophie* (Paris: Cerf, 2004); and "La lettre ou l'allégorie: La controverse sur l'interprétation du 'Simsum' dans la cabale italienne du XVIIIᵉ siècle," in *La controverse religieuse et ses formes,* ed. Alain Le Boulluec (Paris: Cerf, 1995), 99–125.

39. *TI* 130–42; 103–15.

40. *TI* 192–93; 167.

41. This resonance suggests that there may, unexpectedly, be strong lines of affiliation between Levinas and Rav Kook. I hope to have an opportunity to explore this possibility in another venue.

NOTES TO KAVKA, "LEVINAS BETWEEN MONOTHEISM AND COSMOTHEISM"

1. See Samuel Moyn, "Judaism Against Paganism: Emmanuel Levinas's Response to Heidegger and Nazism in the 1930s," *History and Memory* 10:1 (1998), 25–58, esp. 46f. I say "apparent emphasis" because the distinction between transcendental phenomenology and existential phenomenology is often exaggerated; for an account of Heidegger as a transcendental phenomenologist à la Husserl, see Steven Galt Crowell, *Husserl, Heidegger and the Space of Meaning: Paths toward Transcendental Phenomenology* (Evanston, IL: Northwestern University Press, 2001), esp. 115–28.

2. Zygmunt Bauman, *Modernity and the Holocaust* (Ithaca, NY: Cornell University Press, 1989).

3. For more on the antisecularist arguments of Heschel, see Martin Kavka, "The Meaning Of That Hour: Prophecy, Phenomenology and the Public Sphere in the Early Writings of Abraham Joshua Heschel," in *Religion and the Secular in a Violent World: Politics, Terror, Ruins,* ed. Clayton Crockett (Charlottesville: University of Virginia Press, 2006). See also Shaul Magid, "A Monk, A Rabbi, and 'The Meaning of This Hour': War and Nonviolence in Abraham Joshua Heschel and Thomas Merton," *Cross Currents* 55:2 (Summer 2005), 184–213.

4. Adriaan Theodoor Peperzak, *Beyond: The Thought of Emmanuel Levinas* (Evanston, IL: Northwestern University Press, 1997), 15.

5. Howard Caygill, *Levinas and the Political* (London and New York: Routledge, 2002), 150.

6. Emmanuel Levinas, "Politique après," in *L'au-delà du verset: Lectures et discourse talmudiques* (Paris: Minuit, 1982), 218. See the somewhat different

translation at "Politics After!," in *Beyond the Verse: Talmudic Readings and Lectures*, trans. Gary D. Mole (Bloomington: Indiana University Press, 1994), 194.

7. Caygill, 93.

8. For another critique of Levinas's politics, see Leora Batnitzky, *Leo Strauss and Emmanuel Levinas: Philosophy and the Politics of Revelation* (Cambridge: Cambridge University Press, 2006), chapter 7.

9. Caygill, 203.

10. Critchley, "Five Problems in Levinas's View of Politics and the Sketch of a Solution to Them," *Political Theory* 32:2 (April 2004), 172–85, quotations from 174–75.

11. Ibid., 182.

12. Jeffrey Goldberg, "A Little Learning," *The New Yorker* 81:12 (May 9, 2005), 36–41.

13. For more on this, see Hilary Putnam, "Levinas and Judaism," in *The Cambridge Companion to Emmanuel Levinas*, eds. Robert Bernasconi and Simon Critchley (Cambridge: Cambridge University Press, 2002), 33–62.

14. See the rest of the paragraph following the sentence quoted from EN. Neoplatonism, for Levinas, is both progress and return; a full accounting of this would require patient reconstructions of the use of "hypostasis" and "trace" in Levinas's early and middle periods, in addition to a very close reading of these remarks from the 1980s on Neoplatonism. For my thoughts on the ambiguous relationship between Levinas and Plotinus, I am indebted to Christy Flanagan.

15. In claiming that this hybrid position can be found both in both Levinas and the Hebrew Bible, I am admittedly re-establishing a Levinas-Judaism axis, but with the important addendum that religious traditions occlude the porousness of their own boundaries. See, for example, the character of "Abram the Hebrew" in Genesis 14, a man who is described as a member of an ethnos that does not yet exist — and when that ethnos does come into existence, it is no longer rooted in a man named "Abram," but rather a man named "Abraham." The ethnic marker of "Hebrew" is therefore unessentializable, radically contingent and open. Danger erupts when the occlusion of this openness is used to prejudge the contours of philosophical arguments.

16. As a result, I think it is imprecise to describe Levinas as a negative theologian who would argue, along with Maimonides, that "we are only able to apprehend the fact that He is and cannot apprehend his quiddity." [Moses Maimonides, *Guide of the Perplexed*, trans. Shlomo Pines (Chicago: University of Chicago Press, 1963), 135.] Levinas, unlike Maimonides, argues that manifestation is the condition of the possibility for apprehending the fact that God is.

17. Jan Assmann, *Moses the Egyptian: The Memory of Egypt in Western Monotheism* (Cambridge, MA: Harvard University Press, 1997), 1.

18. Assmann, *Die Mosaische Unterscheidung, oder der Preis des Monotheismus* (München: Carl Hanser Verlag, 2003), 19–22.

19. Assmann, *The Search for God in Ancient Egypt*, trans. David Lorton (Ithaca, NY: Cornell University Press, 2001), 199.

20. Ibid., 68.
21. Assmann, *Die Mosaische Unterscheidung*, 61.
22. Ibid., 62.
23. For more on the link between matter and privation in the history of Jewish philosophy, see Kavka, *Jewish Messianism and the History of Philosophy* (Cambridge: Cambridge University Press, 2004).
24. Assmann, *Die Mosaische Unterscheidung*, 147.
25. Ibid., 63.
26. Assmann, *Moses the Egyptian*, 199.
27. Assmann, *Die Mosaische Unterscheidung*, 28.
28. Assmann, *Moses the Egyptian*, 191.
29. Assmann, *Die Mosaische Unterscheidung*, 28 (see also 158).
30. Assmann, *Moses the Egyptian*, 45.
31. Assmann, *Die Mosaische Unterscheidung*, 33.
32. Ibid., 28.
33. Ibid., 67.
34. Assmann, "State and Religion in the New Kingdom," in *Religion and Philosophy in Ancient Egypt*, ed. W. K. Simpson (Yale Egyptological Studies 3) (New Haven: Yale UP, 1989), 73.
35. Assmann, *Die Mosaische Unterscheidung*, 68.
36. Ibid., 78.
37. Peter Schäfer, "Das jüdische Monopol: Jan Assmann und der Monotheismus," *Süddeutsche Zeitung* 184 (August 11, 2004), 12.
38. Indeed, at a public talk at Princeton University in the fall of 2005, a quite famous European scholar of intellectual history decried Assmann's work (but not Assmann himself) as antisemitic, and went on to invoke the pluralism of rabbinic/midrashic reading as proof that Judaism was essentially liberal in a way to which Assmann was simply blind. In addition, he claimed that Levinas had demonstrated this point. Whatever the merits of the point about Levinas, arguments about midrash such as these have been largely, and rightly, out of style in America for two decades as a result of David Stern's debate with Susan Handelman. See David Stern, "Literary Criticism or Literary Homilies? Susan Handelman and the Contemporary Study of Midrash," *Prooftexts* 5 (January 1985), 96–103.
39. For the interview, see Levinas, "Ethics and Politics," trans. Jonathan Romney, in *The Levinas Reader*, ed. Seán Hand (Oxford: Blackwell, 1989), 289–97.
40. Levinas, "Is Ontology Fundamental?," trans. Peter Atterton, Simon Critchley and Adriaan Peperzak in *Basic Philosophical Writings*, eds. Peperzak, Critchley, and Robert Bernasconi (Bloomington: Indiana University Press, 1996), 7/*En* 19.
41. Levinas, "La trace de l'autre," in *En découvrant l'existence avec Husserl et Heidegger* (Paris: Vrin, 1967), 198; Levinas, "The Trace of the Other," trans. Alphonso Lingis, in *Deconstruction in Context*, ed. Mark C. Taylor (Chicago: University of Chicago Press, 1986), 355.

42. Levinas, "La trace," 199; Levinas, "The trace," 356.
43. Edith Wyschogrod, *Emmanuel Levinas: The Problem of Ethical Metaphysics,* 2nd ed. (New York: Fordham University Press, 2000), 159.
44. Levinas, "La trace," 194; Levinas, "The Trace," 351–52.
45. See Edmund Husserl, *Ideen zu einer reinen Phänomenologie und phänomenologischen Philosophie. I. Buch: Allgemeine Einführung in die reine Phänomenologie* (Halle: Niemeyer, 1913??), 185–88; Husserl, *Ideas Pertaining to a Pure Phenomenology and to a Phenomenological Philosophy. First Book: General Introduction to a Pure Phenomenology,* trans. F. Kersten (The Hague: Martinus Nijhoff, 1983), 217–21; James Mensch, "Manifestation and the Paradox of Subjectivity," *Husserl Studies* 21 (2005), 35–53, esp. 40–43.
46. Levinas, "La trace," 201; Levinas, "The Trace," 358; Levinas, "La signification et le sens," in *Humanisme de l'autre homme* (Montpellier: Fata Morgana, 1972), 68; Levinas, "Meaning and Sense," trans. Alphonso Lingis, Simon Critchley and Adriaan Peperzak in *Basic Philosophical Writings,* 63.
47. *AT* 7 / *AeT* 31; compare the translation at "From The One to the Other," 134 ("as if the One were anticipated by that deprivation itself").
48. Levinas, *TI* 110ff/*TeI* 82ff., where Levinas argues that objects of enjoyment are not objects of representations, and the somewhat different version of this argument at *OB* 63–68, 72–74/*AE* 80–86, 91–94. For recent work on the role of sensibility in Levinas's arguments, see Kavka, *Jewish Messianism and the History of Philosophy* 157–88, as well as Leslie MacAvoy's "The Other Side of Intentionality" and Diane Perpich's "Sensible Subjects: Levinas and Irigaray on Incarnation and Ethics," both in *Addressing Levinas,* eds. Eric Sean Nelson, Antje Kapust, and Kent Still (Evanston, IL: Northwestern University Press, 2005), 109–18 and 296–309.
49. A different example: I have never been able to articulate why I do not like chocolate. I have never felt confident making claims in which I talk about its bitterness, or associate it with raw eggplant. Such claims have never led to understanding; the former usually is met with "What about milk chocolate?" (answer: still disgustingly bitter) and the latter met with calls for my institutionalization. If enjoyment were indeed associated with representations, the predicates that others enjoy and that I do not could be more easily picked out, and my conversations about chocolate would not end as awkwardly as they do.
50. Martin Heidegger, *Being and Time,* § 17–18.
51. See also Jan Patočka, *Plato and Europe,* trans. Petr Lom (Stanford, CA: Stanford University Press, 2002), 24 — "What I am constantly explaining here has one sole purpose: that we realize that manifesting in itself, in that which makes it manifesting, is not reducible, cannot be converted into anything *that* manifests itself in manifesting. Manifesting is, in itself, something completely original" — and the discussion of Patočka in Mensch, "Manifestation and the Paradox of Subjectivity."
52. Husserl, *Ideen* 172; *Ideas* 204.
53. See also the description of the face at *OB* 88/*AE* 112 ("The face of a neighbor signifies for me an irrecusable responsibility . . . it escapes representation"),

which links up with the manifestation of manifestation itself because the face signifies without representing.

54. I could not have articulated this point without extensive conversations and team-taught seminars on Levinas with my colleague David Kangas.

55. The stronger path out of this is rooted in the nature of language. The phenomenology of conversation in which Levinas engages in "Is Ontology Fundamental?", "Freedom and Command," and *Totality and Infinity* delineates a structure in which the self abjures itself while the other attests him- or herself in various propositions. Because consciousness is, as it were, turned off during these moments in conversations, the other person is not seen in terms of predicates and categories, or, as Levinas says in "Freedom and Command," in the indicative. When we are silent, we are faced with the choice of either continuing the conversation, or walking away. This choice is free; the fact of choosing is not. For this reason, Levinas writes in "Freedom and Command" that "the face is the fact that a being affects us in the imperative." Even if a reader of Levinas were to point to the milder language of invitation that he uses in this essay ("expression invites one to speak to someone"), an invitee cannot choose whether or not she or he will respond to an invitation. Not responding is already to turn the invitation down. As a result, the phenomenology of conversation shows that there is no hard and fast distinction between facts and norms. *CPP* 21. I have learned much on this point from Bob Gibbs, *Why Ethics?: Signs of Responsibilities* (Princeton: Princeton University Press, 2000), chapter 1, and more recently, Leslie MacAvoy, "The Force of Obligation in Levinas" (unpub. ms.). The milder way to get Levinas out of the is/ought problem is to read Levinas as claiming that the ethic of substitution has a pragmatic interest behind it; its articulation is a possible (and perhaps the best possible) way of showing that we are not duped by morality. While grounding it in an account of selfhood opens it up to philosophical problems if it is to be a universally binding ethic, the Levinasian analysis at least justifies that the ethic of substitution is worth pursuing; it makes life worth living in an age that has repeatedly failed to demonstrate that point. Such an account would also admit that an ethic based on hope, if this is really what the ethic of substitution is, must be open to revision, based on unforeseen effects.

In any case, viewing the ethic of substitution as really being a divine command theory, as some interpreters are wont to do, seems to open up more problems than it solves unless "divine command" is recast either as natural law or in terms of a community's pragmatic testing of its fallible understanding of the divine will. For more on this, see Martin Kavka and Randi Rashkover, "A Jewish Modified Divine Command Theory," *Journal of Religious Ethics* 32:2 (Summer 2004), 387–414.

56. For Levinas on entrusting [*confier*], see *OB* 79/*AE* 99.

57. Franz Rosenzweig has a somewhat similar — though failed, because he utterly neglects to analyze the body that soul animates — account of soul in *The Star of Redemption*.

58. My interpretation here is admittedly tendentious. I agree with Claire Katz (in her *Levinas, Judaism, and the Feminine: The Silent Footsteps of Rebecca*

[Bloomington: Indiana University Press, 2003], 138) that maternity exemplifies the giving of oneself in another. But further claims about the necessity of exposure to real women for being an ethical agent, such as when she claims that "Levinas's philosophy is life-affirming, and the feminine, as *both empirical figure and metaphorical attribute* [emphasis mine], plays a key role in achieving that end" (155), seem less philosophically sure to me. Such a claim about real women makes Katz's analysis appear essentially heteronormative, implying that gay men might not be able to be ethical agents because there are not necessarily women in their dwellings, and because only women can be feminine. It is this latter point, on which Katz seems to agree with Levinas (59), which seems to me to be patently false. (To be fair, there is the implication, in her chapter on "Abraham and the Tempering of Virility," that Katz sees Abraham as a feminine figure. But this is not as clear as it could be.) The homophobic implications of Katz's argument are unnecessary for her own project of rescuing biblical women as Levinasian figures who should therefore no longer reside at the margins of the biblical tradition, and are unnecessary in articulations of *Levinasian* philosophy because "female" is not coextensive with "feminine." Nevertheless, such homophobia may fairly surface in intellectual-historical articulations of *Levinas's* philosophy.

59. For example, the claim that the signifyingness of Levinasian subjectivity "refers to an irrecuperable pre-ontological past, that of maternity" at *OB* 78/*AE* 99.

60. For the link between wounding and enjoyment, see *OB* 64/*AE* 81.

61. Assmann, *Moses the Egyptian*, 196.

62. Ibid., 197. See my remarks about Levinas and Neoplatonism above, esp. on p. 82 of this volume.

63. Assmann, *Die Mosaische Unterscheidung*, 70.

64. Assmann, *Moses the Egyptian*, 201; ibid., 70.

65. Caygill 203.

66. See S. Rawidowicz and B. C. I. Ravid (eds.), *Israel: The Ever-Dying People and Other Essays*. Sara F. Yoseloff Memorial Publications in Judaism and Jewish Affairs, (Madison, NJ: Fairleigh Dickinson Press, 1986).

67. See Andrew Heinze, *Adapting to Abundance* (New York: Columbia University Press, 1992), 69–79.

68. An earlier version of this paper was presented at the annual meeting of the International Association for Philosophy and Literature in 2005, at a panel on Levinas and the ancients. My thanks to Silvia Benso for organizing the panel, and for the comments from the other panelists and the audience, especially Deborah Achtenberg, Brian Schroeder, and Wayne Froman. Throughout the process of writing and revising this paper, conversations with Bob Erlewine about Assmann's work have been immensely helpful. And, as noted in earlier footnotes, I am also indebted to David Kangas and Christy Flanagan. Responsibility for the paper's remaining weaknesses remains mine alone.

NOTES TO ATTERTON, "ART, RELIGION, AND ETHICS POST MORTEM DEI"

1. The exception here is Andrius Valevicius, "Afterword: Emmanuel Levinas, the Multicultural Philosopher," *Continental Philosophy Review* 31, no. 1 (1998): 11–14.

2. For a detailed biography of Levinas, see Marie-Anne Lescourret, *Emmanuel Levinas* (Paris: Flammarion, 1994); Salomon Malka, *Emmanuel Lévinas: La vie et la trace* (Paris: Jean-Claude Lattès, 2002). See also *DF*, 291–95; *IR*, 23–28; and *EI*, 21–33.

3. Malka, *Emmanuel Lévinas,* 27.

4. Vassily Grossman, *Life and Fate,* trans. Robert Chandler (New York: HarperCollins, 1995).

5. See Emmanuel Levinas, "A quoi pensent les philosophes?" *Autrement* 102 (1988): 58–59; "Peace and Proximity," *Basic Philosophical Writings,* ed. Robert Bernasconi, Simon Critchley, and Adriaan Peperzak (Bloomington: Indiana University Press, 1996), 167; see also *IR* 80–81, 89–92, 106, 120, 132, 191, 192, 206–07, 208, 216–18.

6. Although *Life and Fate* was completed in 1954, it was confiscated by the KGB in 1961, and did not again see the light of day until it was smuggled out of the USSR and published in Switzerland in 1981. The earliest reference Levinas makes to the novel is 1986, so we can assume that he did not possess a copy prior to 1981, by which time, needless to say, his thinking had already achieved full flower.

7. Friedrich Nietzsche, *Twilight of the Idols* in *The Portable Nietzsche,* trans. Walter Kaufmann (London: Penguin, 1976), 549.

8. See Friedrich Nietzsche, *The Will to Power,* trans. Walter Kaufmann (New York: Vintage Books, 1968): "Truth is a kind of error without which a certain species of life could not live" (272). This aphorism was penned in 1885.

9. See Herbert Lottman, *Albert Camus: A Biography* (New York: Doubleday, 1979), 54.

10. See the introduction by John Cruickshank to the English translation of Albert Camus, *Caligula; Cross Purpose; The Just; The Possessed* (London: Penguin, 1984), 29.

11. "Her figure gave promise of becoming in form a Venus de Milo" (*BK* 174). Dostoyevsky's description of Grushenka, as first seen through the eyes of Alyosha (*BK* 172–74), should be compared to Levinas's depiction of the feminine in section II, part D, and section IV, part B of *Totality and Infinity.*

12. Samuel Beckett once said of James Joyce, "he never rebelled; he was detached; he accepted everything. For him, there was no difference between the fall of a bomb and the fall of a leaf. . . ." Beckett quoted in E. M. Cioran, *Anathemas and Admirations,* trans. Richard Howard (London: Quartet Book, 1992), 133.

13. See Immanuel Kant, *The Critique of Judgment,* trans. J. H. Bernard (Amherst, NY: Prometheus Books, 2000) part 1, sections 1–5.

14. Levinas's essay was criticized by the editors of *Les Temps Modernes* when it first appeared for ignoring Sartre's views on art and the possibility of social and political engagement. See Seàn Hand's introduction to "Reality and Its Shadow," in *The Levinas Reader* (Oxford: Blackwell Publishers, 1990), 29–30.

15. Clement Greenberg, "Modernist Painting," *Art and Literature* 4 (Spring 1965): 193.

16. See Friedrich Nietzsche, *The Gay Science,* trans. Walter Kaufmann (New York: Vintage, 1974), esp. sections 108, 125, and 358.

17. Nietzsche, *The Will to Power,* 853.

18. Friedrich Nietzsche, *The Birth of Tragedy,* trans. Walter Kaufmann (New York: Vintage, 1967), 83. In the same work, Nietzsche writes: "it is only as an aesthetic phenomenon that existence and the world are eternally justified" (52; see also 141). For Nietzsche, art is a great stimulant to life and thus functions as an antidote to the negative will to power that subordinates instinctual life to the will to truth.

19. Nietzsche, *The Gay Science,* 182, section 125.

20. Sigmund Freud, "Dostoevsky and Parricide," *Writings on Art and Literature* (Stanford: Stanford University Press, 1997).

21. Emmanuel Levinas, "A Conversation with André Dalmas," *Proper Names,* trans. Michael B. Smith (Stanford: Stanford, 1996), 154. For further references to Ivan's thesis, see Emmanuel Levinas, "The Old and the New," *TO* 124, 126.

22. "We propose to call 'religion' the bond that is established between the same and the other without constituting a totality" (*TI* 40).

23. Dying, Mr. Verkhovensky, father of Peter, says, "God is necessary to me if only because he is the only being whom one can love eternally" (*D* 655). This should not be confused with genuine piety. For Mr. Verkhovensky, God is the only being whom one can love for eternity, and since God cannot extinguish love, God cannot therefore extinguish one who really loves him.

24. Compare Ivan's refusal to justify the suffering of an innocent if it leads to the greatest good with Raskolnikov's position: "Well, don't you think that one little crime could be expiated and wiped out by thousands of good deeds?" (*CP* 84)

25. See also Levinas, "A quoi pensent les philosophes?" 58; and *PL* 175.

26. Emanuel Levinas, *Autrement que savoir* (Paris: Editions Osiris, 1988).

27. The locus classicus of "the problem of evil" is Hume's *Dialogues Concerning Natural Religion:* "Is God willing to prevent evil, but not able? Then he is impotent. Is he able, but not willing? Then he is malevolent. Is he both able and willing? Whence then is evil?" (David Hume, *Dialogues Concerning Natural Religion,* part 10, ed. Norman Kemp Smith [New York: Bobbs-Merrill, 1947], 198.) Hume attributes these questions to Epicurus. (See Sextus Empiricus, *Physics,* 3.42.9–12, *Hellenistic Philosophy,* ed. Brad Inwood and L. P. Gerson [Indianapolis: Hackett, 1988], 364.) Since Levinas almost never refers to Hume (the exception is *CPP*

76), we may suppose that Hume's version of the problem failed to impress him, or, frankly, left him cold. I submit that the problem with Hume's rendition is not due to any lack of rigor, but its lacking in the expressive power to expound what its demonstrates. Hume's argument is no more likely to disturb the good conscience of the theodicist than is Smerdyakov's observation in *The Brothers Karamazov* that the book of Genesis contains a contradiction (*BK* 144). However, when we encounter what is essentially the same argument in Dostoyevsky's "Rebellion" — and this is the best argument I know in defense of literature's ability to make epistemic claims — it becomes very powerful indeed.

28. See Emil Fackenheim, *Quest for Past and Future* (Boston: Beacon Press, 1968); *God's Presence in History* (New York: Harper and Row, 1970); *The Jewish Return Into History* (New York: Schocken Books, 1978).

29. Michael Wyschogrod, "Faith and the Holocaust," *Judaism* 20 (1971): 286–94; reprinted in *A Holocaust Reader*, ed. Michael L. Morgan (Oxford: Oxford University Press, 2001), 164–71.

30. See Immanuel Kant, "On the Miscarriage of All Philosophical Trials at Theodicy," trans. George di Giovanni, *Religion and Rational Theology* (*The Cambridge Edition of the Works of Immanuel Kant*), ed. Allen W. Wood (Cambridge: Cambridge University Press, 2001). Levinas quotes this "quite extraordinary short treatise of 1791" at *PL* 167 n. 8.

31. See, for example, Richard Kearney, "Dialogue with Emmanuel Levinas," *Dialogues with Contemporary Continental Thinkers* (Manchester: Manchester University Press, 1984), 31; *GCM* 84; Emmanuel Levinas, *Autrement que savoir*, 72, 92; *PL* 179; *CPP* 168; *IR* 56, 72, 100, 113, 133, 161, 169, 229; *EI* 98, 101; and *OB* 146.

32. Peter Atterton, "Face-to-Face with the Other Animal?" *Levinas and Buber: Dialogue and Difference*, ed. Peter Atterton, Matthew Calarco, and Maurice Friedman (Pittsburgh: Duquesne University Press, 2004), 262–81; "Ethical Cynicism," *Animal Philosophy: Essential Readings in Continental Thought*, ed. Peter Atterton and Matthew Calarco (New York: Continuum, 2004), 51–61.

33. Etymologically the word "criminal" derives from the Latin *crimen*, meaning "accusation."

34. See, for example, Søren Kierkegaard, *Either/Or*, volume II, trans. Walter Lowrie (New Jersey: Princeton, 1971), 198, 223.

35. Irving Greenberg quoted in David R. Harrington in "Time and Weighing: Theodicies of Everyday Life," (conference presentation, *Psychology for the Other: A Seminar on Emmanuel Levinas*, Seattle University, October 28, 2006, (http://www.seattleu.edu/artsci/psychology/conference/papers/harrington.doc).

36. I wish to thank Mary McCalman and Robin Prior for their criticisms of an earlier version of this paper.

NOTES TO KATZ, "EDUCATING THE SOLITARY MAN"

I benefited greatly from conversations with Daniel Conway, Catherine Kemp, and Mitchell Aboulafia about the themes in this paper. In particular, Cathy Kemp's insights regarding the plurality of "Enlightenments" protected the integrity of my claims, and her wit, when it came to discussing Rousseau's eccentric behavior, provided an important perspective while I wrote this paper. The argument is better than it would have been without these philosophical insights. I would also like to thank Martin Kavka for his much needed criticism — and for encouragement where due. Finally, John Seery reminded me that philosophers are not the only academics who read Rousseau's *Emile* and that the political scientist approaches this book with a very different attitude.

1. Jean-Jacques Rousseau, *The Social Contract*, in *"The Social Contract" and Other Later Political Writings*, ed. V. Gourevitch (Cambridge: Cambridge University Press, 1997), 41.

2. I realize that some will see Rousseau as late for the Enlightenment, but I nonetheless place him within this tradition of thought.

3. Pufendorf also held this view.

4. Jean-Jacques Rousseau, *Emile*, trans. (London: Everyman, 1993). Although published in the same year as his *Social Contract*, *Emile* was published several months later.

5. I need to make two points here. First, I am aware that the Enlightenment is not the monolithic philosophical or intellectual movement that often characterizes or caricatures it. See, for example, Jonathan Israel, *Radical Enlightenment* (Oxford: Oxford University Press, 2002); and Roy Porter, *Enlightenment in a National Context* (Cambridge: Cambridge University Press, 1981). Second, my point here is not about the truth of *the* Enlightenment per se, but rather to address how Levinas would have viewed this philosophical movement and the influence it had on our own way of thinking.

6. For a compelling account of the positive role of dependency in Jewish philosophy, see Leora Batnitzky, "Dependency and Vulnerability: Jewish and Feminist Existentialist Constructions of the Human," in *Women and Gender in Jewish Philosophy*, ed. Hava Tirosh-Samuelson (Bloomington: Indiana University Press, 2004), 127–52.

7. For more on the education of women during this time period, see also Mary Wollstonecraft, *A Vindication of the Rights of Women* (London: Penguin, 1993).

8. Rousseau, *Emile*, 5.

9. Certainly this is not the first time a philosophical treatise encounters the problem of origins. We also find this in Plato's *Republic* and Aristotle's *Nicomachean Ethics*.

10. Rousseau, *Emile*, 393.

11. Ibid., 387.

12. The scope of this paper does not allow me to address several other related questions to the one cited above. For example, *how* does Sophie come to know these things; what does her epistemic privilege mean with regard to their relative educations and the suggested "superiority" of one sex over the other?

13. Rousseau, *Emile,* 532.

14. Ibid., 533.

15. See *Émile et Sophie ou Les Solitaires* (Paris: Rivages poche Petite Bibliothèque, 1994). The sequel, the story of Emile and Sophie in Paris, indicates that neither Emile nor Sophie nor the two of them as a couple, can function without the presence of the tutor. When Sophie is grieving the loss of their daughter, Emile is unable to console her. He takes her to Paris because he believes she needs the distractions of the city. Emile, however, is corrupted by the temptations of the city. He is not only unable to respond adequately to Sophie's need for an intimate relationship with another person, but he also turns his attentions to women outside of his marriage. Rejected and hurt, Sophie must also turn to another to allay her grief. The story continues to its sad ending — Sophie becomes pregnant by another man and Emile must eventually abandon her. One wonders if the tutor has been successful; one also wonders if Rousseau realizes the failure of his own educational project. See, Susan Moller Okin, "The Fate of Rousseau's Heroines," in *Feminist Interpretations of Jean-Jacques Rousseau* (University Park, PA: Penn State University Press, 2002), 92–93.

16. Emmanuel Levinas, *On Escape,* trans. Bettina Bergo (Stanford: Stanford University Press, 2003).

17. When thinking about Rousseau's *Emile,* it is difficult not to think about one's own practical experience with children. Levinas's insight here could not ring more true. I can think of only too many conversations with my 5-year-old daughter that begin with her complaint that she does not like the rules (as few as there are!) and that she does not have to listen to us. Instead, she tells us, she's going to live in the wild (her exact words). Images of Itard's *The Wild Child* abound. So, we remind her that she will have to find food, clothing, and there are no soft beds in the wild. Although her first inclination is to want to say "so what?", she gets the point — thus providing her with a different sense of who we are as parents, our position, while also one of making rules, affords her a certain freedom insofar as we provide her with clothes, food, and shelter, not to mention love, warmth, and fun.

18. See *TO; TI.*

19. See *OB.*

20. See *DF; NT.*

21. Levinas's conception of ethical subjectivity emphasizes an obligation that is not chosen and from which we cannot recuse ourselves. It emphasizes our obligation and response to the Other that cannot be discussed in terms of failure — we are already obligated. But in spite of this claim, certainly it is the case that this obligation to others is violated, betrayed, and ignored, that is, we often fail in our

response to the Other. And it is not clear how this response occurs or why it fails. I suggest that Levinas's philosophical project needs to be supplemented by a discussion of how to cultivate this response. I thus turn to themes in education and schooling, in particular. If Levinas's view of subjectivity is "universal," that is, if it applies to everyone, and if this conception of response can be or needs to be cultivated, then we need a conception of that cultivation that is also universally applicable.

22. Originally published in *Les Cahiers de l'Alliance Israélite Universelle*, the publication of the *Alliance*, in which Levinas published frequently.

23. *DF* 277–88. This essay was originally published in *Hamoré* — a journal of Jewish teachers and educators.

24. Ibid., 280.

25. Ibid., 280.

26. See Ibid., 280–86.

27. Ibid., 282.

28. Emmanuel Levinas, "The Transcendence of Words," in *Outside the Subject*, trans. Michael B. Smith (Stanford: Stanford University Press, 1993), 148.

29. Levinas is critical of the term "pedagogy" (See *TI*), since for him it signals all that is wrong with education and ethics, primarily that it is simply a didactic relationship. It also has an unfortunate Greek etymology, which ties it to the *paidagógos*, the slave who escorted the children to school. Worse, it can reference a dull or pedantic teacher. But pedagogy can also refer to "instruction" or "learning," which is how I employ this term.

30. Levinas, *Outside the Subject*, 148.

31. I maintain that the subtext of Levinas's ethical project, manifested in Levinas's use of the feminine throughout his work, also serves a pedagogical end. The feminine becomes the example, that to which the masculine, the virile, should aspire to become. A close reading of the feminine from Levinas's earliest work, *Time and the Other*, to his last philosophical book, *Otherwise than Being*, reveals an instructive dimension. For a longer discussion of this point, see Claire Elise Katz, *Levinas, Judaism, and the Feminine: The Silent Footsteps of Rebecca* (Bloomington: Indiana University Press, 2003).

32. In his interview with François Poirié, Levinas tells us that "Judaism is not the Bible; it is the Bible seen through the Talmud, through the rabbinical wisdom, interrogation, and religious life." (*Is It Righteous to Be? Interviews with Emmanuel Levinas*, ed. Jill Robbins [Stanford: Stanford University Press, 2001], 76). In an interview published under the title "On Jewish Philosophy," Levinas tells his interlocutor, "it seems to me essential to consider the fact that the Jewish reading of Scripture is carried out in the anxiety, but also the hopeful expectation, of midrash." Levinas goes on to name Rashi's commentary in particular as that which brings the *Chumash* to light: "the Pentateuch — *Chumash* — never comes to light without Rashi" ("On Jewish Philosophy," in *In the Time of the Nations*, trans. Michael B. Smith. [Bloomington: Indiana University Press, 1994], 169. Reprinted in *Is It Righteous to Be?*, 239–54).

33. See Claire Elise Katz, "Teaching Our Children Well: Pedagogy, Religion and the Future of Philosophy," *Cross Currents* 53, no. 4 (Winter 2004): 530–47; and Katz, "Levinas — Between Philosophy and Rhetoric: The 'Teaching' of Levinas's Scriptural References," *Philosophy and Rhetoric* 38, no. 2: 159–72.

34. In any number of places Levinas refers to midrash as an example of his philosophical term "the saying," that which remains unthematized. In Levinas's view, midrash opens up the voices in the Torah that are muted in the text, either because they are explicitly absent from the narrative structure or because the narrative structure lacks clarity. Midrash lifts these voices out of the text and then brings them to bear on the narrative. By enabling our access to these others, midrash brings us closer to the ethical. To approach the Torah Jewishly, then, is precisely to approach it through the rabbinic commentary on it. Thus, midrash keeps the Torah alive by preventing its easy thematization. And it prevents this thematization by posing questions and offering alternative readings of the text. Further, the interpretative model of midrash is similar to Levinas's saying insofar as the saying is an excess, that which lies beyond the said. In Levinas's words, the saying opens me to the other. The saying expresses the infinite of the other person. Philosophy, then, is derivative of religion because it is what allows us to take the ethical message of Judaism and project it into a universal language. See "God and Philosophy," in *GCM* 74.

35. See Abraham Joshua Heschel, *The Prophets* (New York: Harper and Row, 1965); Levinas, *OB;* Hermann Cohen, *Religion of Reason, Out of the Sources of Judaism,* trans. Simon Kaplan (Oxford: Oxford University Press, 1995) — a publication of the American Academy of Religion. Cohen's discussion of poverty and the social responsibility that a community and each individual in that community has to respond to it, in essence to end it, is quite striking.

36. See *ITN* xiii.

37. See Claire Elise Katz, "'The presence of the Other is a presence that teaches': Levinas, Pragmatism, and Pedagogy," *Journal of Jewish Thought and Philosophy* 14, no. 1–2: 91–108 (forthcoming); See also "Thus Spoke Zarathustra; Thus Listened the Rabbis: Nietzsche, Education, and the Cycle of Enlightenment," *New Nietzsche Studies* (forthcoming).

38. See *DF* 280.

39. See Katz, "'The presence of the Other is a presence that teaches.'"

NOTES TO JUFFÉ, "LEVINAS AS (MIS)READER OF SPINOZA"

1. In *DF* 106–10.
2. In *DF* 111–18.
3. *Dieu, la Mort et le Temps* (Paris: Grasset, 1993), 124.
4. "Franz Rosenzweig: A Modern Jewish Thinker," in *Outside the Subject,* trans. Michael B. Smith (Stanford: Stanford University Press, 1994), 58; "Franz

Rosenzweig: une pensée juive moderne," in *Hors sujet* (Paris: Le Livre de Poche, 1997), 80.
  5. *Outside the Subject*, 3.
  6. *CPP* 137–38; *Humanisme de l'autre homme* (Montpellier: Fata Morgana, 1972), 81.
  7. "The Bible and the Greeks," *ITN* 133.
  8. *Le Mort et la Temps*, 17, 32.
  9. Benedict de Spinoza, *Ethics* in *The Collected Works of Spinoza*, trans. Edwin M. Curley (Princeton: Princeton University Press, 1985), part V, proposition 17; *Éthique*, trans. Robert Misrahi (Paris: PUF, 1990).
  10. Ibid., III, prop. 6.
  11. Ibid., III, prop. 6.
  12. Ibid., III, prop. 6.
  13. Ibid., II, prop. 49, corollary.
  14. Ibid., II, prop. 49, scholium.
  15. Ibid., II, prop. 23.
  16. Ibid., V, prop. 39: "Qui Corpus ad pluram aptum habet, is Mentem habet, cujus maxima pars est aeterna."
  17. Ibid., V, prop. 39, scholium.
  18. Emmanuel Levinas, *Transcendance et intelligibilité* (Genève: Labor et Fides, 1996), 46.
  19. Levinas's relationship to Dostroyevski is treated extensively in the essay contributed by Peter Atterton to this volume. See above, 105–32.
  20. Spinoza, *Ethics*, V, prop. 19.
  21. Ibid., V, prop. 17.

NOTES TO LAWRENCE, "SCHELLING AND LEVINAS"

  1. The relationship to Schelling is discussed in some detail in Robert Gibbs, *Correlations in Rosenzweig and Levinas* (Princeton: Princeton University Press, 1992).
  2. Jason M. Wirth, *The Conspiracy of Life: Meditations on Schelling and His Time* (Albany: State University of New York Press, 2003).
  3. I have in mind the famous "We Scholars" section from Nietzsche, *Beyond Good and Evil* trans. Walter Kaufman (New York: Vintage Books, 1966), 121–41. His critique of contemporary scholarship as representing the viewpoint of the "rabble" (Levinas would speak of "the reduction of the other to the same") was anticipated by Schelling, whose most acerbic formulations can be found in the preface to *Philosophie und Religion* (1804). They are motivated by Schelling's conviction that both philosophy and religion are necessarily "esoteric" — grounded in a truth that can only elude the "spiritless" viewpoint of scholars, whom Schelling likens to "sexless bees," capable of gathering honey but incapable of engendering life: F. W. J. Schelling, *Sämmtliche Werke*, 14 vols. (Stuttgart and Augsburg: Cotta Verlag,

1856–1861), 6:13–15 (hereafter cited as *SW*). The affinity with Nietzsche becomes completely palpable in that famous section at the end of the *Weltalter,* where Schelling writes of philosophy as a controlled form of "madness," distinguished from the passionless attitude of scholars (*Verstandesmenschen*), which he describes as "imbecility" (*Blödsinn*): Schelling, *The Ages of the World,* trans. Jason Wirth (Albany: State University of New York Press, 2000), 103; *SW* 8:339.

4. Jason Wirth develops this thesis in the first chapter ("The Nameless Good") of his *Conspiracy of Life,* 5–31.

5. This is what led Franz Rosenzweig, when he published the *Systemprogramm,* to attribute it to Schelling rather than Hegel — even though the manuscript was in the latter's handwriting. His evidence began with the fragment's opening phrase: "Since in the future all of metaphysics will fall under *ethics.*" A full account of the authorship of the fragment (which is generally included in editions of not only Schelling and Hegel, but of Hölderlin as well) is given in Xavier Tilliette's "Schelling als Verfasser des Systemprogramms?" which can be found in *Materialien zu Schelling's philosophischen Anfängen,* ed. Manfred Frank and Gerhard Kurz (Frankfurt: Suhrkamp Verlag, 1975), 193–211. The *Systemprogramm* itself is included in the same text, 110–12.

6. F. W. J. Schelling, *System of transcendental Idealism,* trans. Peter Heath (Charlottesville: University of Virginia Press, 1978), 173; *SW* 3:555.

7. F. W. J. Schelling, *Philosophical Inquiries into the Nature of Human Freedom,* trans. James Gutmann (Chicago: Open Court, 1989), 90; *SW* 7:408.

8. *Philosophie und Religion* (1804) is the essay that most famously introduces this notion (*SW* 6:11–70), but it is most elegantly and succinctly advanced in the Introduction to the *Weltalter* (*Ages of the World,* xxxv–xl; *SW* 8:199–206).

9. *Ages of the World,* xxxvi; *SW* 8:200.

10. Fiona Steinkamp, "Eternity and Time: Levinas Returns to Schelling," in *Schelling Now: Contemporary Readings,* ed. Jason Wirth (Bloomington: Indiana University Press, 2005), 207–22.

11. These quotations are all found in *TO* 50; cf. Steinkamp, "Eternity and Time," 208.

12. *TO* 52.

13. *TO* 85.

14. *Ages of the World,* 104; *SW* 8:339.

15. *Ages of the World,* 23; *SW* 8:233.

16. *Ages of the World,* 24; *SW* 8:234.

17. Emmanuel Levinas, "Transcendence and Evil," in Philippe Nemo, *Job and the Excess of Evil,* trans. Michael Kigel (Pittsburgh: Duquesne University Press, 1998), 178.

18. *Philosophie und Religion,* in *SW* 6:42, 47, 61.

19. "Diachrony and representation," in *TO* 97–120. It should be pointed out that whereas *Time and the Other* was originally published in 1947, "Diachrony and representation" appeared first in 1983 and was added to the English translation as a supplement.

20. F. W. J. Schelling, "On the Nature of Philosophy as Science," in *German Idealist Philosophy*, ed. Rüdiger Bubner (London: Penguin Books, 1997), 233–37; *SW* 9:234–38.

21. *Ages of the World*, xxxvi; *SW* 8:201.

22. "On the Nature of Philosophy as a Science," 227; *SW* 9:228.

23. This summarizes the argument of volumes 11 through 13 of the *Sämmtliche Werke* that contain the still untranslated "Philosophie der Mythologie" and "Philosophie der Offenbarung." While Schelling does argue that Christ is the culmination of the mythological tradition, he at the same time stresses that he steps out of mythology, hence must be understood as historically real. In this way his vision has to be clearly distinguished from its popularized versions, which can be found, for instance, in Timothy Freke and Peter Gandy, *The Jesus Mysteries* (London: Thorsons, 1999).

24. Once one understands the concept of "philosophical religion," it becomes clear that Schelling's vision of a synthesis of Christianity and Judaism is not to be identified with any final "conversion" of the Jews. What is at issue here is not the battle between religious sects but the eschatological realization of universal religion. See *SW* 14:321–32. I have discussed the concept of philosophical religion in Joseph P. Lawrence, "Philosophical Religion and the Quest for Authenticity," in *Schelling Now*, ed. Jason Wirth, 13–30.

25. I should emphasize that this "grace versus law" schema is Schelling's not mine (*SW* 14:146–47).

26. *SW* 14:187–98.

27. *SW* 11:553. Cf. Levinas, *TI* 245ff.

28. *SW* 11:569.

29. *TI* 240–47.

30. Plato, *Symposium*, 212a.

31. Levinas's rendition of the relationship from the perspective of the Father looking to the Son: "He is me a stranger to myself" (*TI* 267). To complete the thought from the perspective of the Son, one can add the words of Paul Célan that adorn the chapter "Substitution" in *Otherwise than Being*: "Ich bin du, wenn ich ich bin" (*OB* 99). This determines our relationship with all of our fathers, all the way down to Socrates, to Christ, and, yes, to the Lord God Himself. But how much is demanded here, that I truly be I!

32. *SW* 14:225–27.

33. *SW* 9:217.

34. Plato, *Phaedo*, 110b–114c.

35. F. W. J. Schelling, *Clara: or, On Nature's Connection with the Spirit World*, trans. Fiona Steinkamp (Albany: State University of New York Press, 2002), 67–78; *SW* 9:92–110.

36. Emmanuel Levinas, "God and Philosophy" (1975), *Basic Philosophical Writings*, ed. Adriaan Peperzak, Simon Critchley, and Robert Bernasconi (Bloomington: Indiana University Press, 1996), 141.

37. Levinas, "Signature," *DF*, 291.

38. See Levinas's afterward to Zvi Kolitz, *Yosl Rakover Talks to God*, trans. Carol Brown Janeway (New York: Vintage Books, 2000), 81.

39. Ibid., 85.

40. Ibid., 86.

41. Ibid., 9.

42. Cf. *OB* 114.

43. "Transcendence and Evil," 165–82.

44. Kant, *On the Failure of All Attempted Philosophical Theodicies*, published as a supplement to Michael Despland's *Kant on History and Religion* (Montreal: McGill-Queen's University Press, 1973), 283–97.

45. Emmanuel Levinas, *Entre Nous: Thinking-of-the-Other*, trans. Michael Smith and Barbara Harshav (New York: Columbia University Press, 1998), 241–42.

46. "Transcendence and Evil," 179.

47. Ibid., 180.

48. At this point I begin to borrow some of my own words from Joseph P. Lawrence, "Beauty beyond Appearances: Nature and the Transcendent," *Journal of Environmental Philosophy* (Fall 2005). The citations are adapted from Stephen Miller, *The Book of Job* (New York: Harpers Perennial, 1992).

NOTES TO PEPERZAK, "'FROM POLITICS TO ETHICS' OR 'FROM ETHICS TO POLITICS'?"

1. I summarize here the conclusion of my *Selbsterkenntnis des Absoluten: Grundlinien der Hegelschen Philosophie des Geistes*, Spekulation und Erfahrung II, 6 (Stuttgart-Bad Canstatt: Frommann-Holzboog, 1987); and *Modern Freedom: Hegel's Legal, Moral, and Political Philosophy* (Boston: Kluwer, 2001), 110–73.

2. For the demonstration of the following summary, see Peperzak, *Modern Freedom*, 174–222.

3. For the central role of the syllogism, see Hegel's *Logic* (*Gesammelte Werke* [Hamburg: Meiner, 1981], 12:90–126) and his *Enzyklopädie* of 1817, §§ 129–39.

4. Cf. Peperzak, *Modern Freedom*, 188–210; and "Freiheit bei Hegel," in *Geist und Willensfreiheit: Klassische Theorien von der Antike bis zur Moderne*, ed. Edith Düsing, Klaus Düsing, and Hans-Dieter Klein (Würzburg: Königshausen & Neumann, 2006), 153–69.

5. On Hegel's analysis of international law and politics, cf. Peperzak, *Modern Freedom*, 575–98.

6. Cf. ibid., 72–82, 223–74.

7. Cf. ibid., 386–95.

8. There are at least three reasons why Hegel is anticosmopolitan: (1) a positivistic reason: he did not dare to jump over the international factuality of his time by deducing a political constitution for the entire humanity on the basis of his own logic and his definition of free will; (2) a totalitarian one: according to Hegel, it is impossible to develop a moral theory without first unfolding a theory of the

political totality within which the individuals unfold their lives as singularization of an encompassing universality; (3) a systematic reason: the transition from objective spirit to absolute spirit presupposes that the realm of objective spirit, as particular and intermediary between subjective spirit and absolute spirit, must show its lack of totalization. The highest form of community (i.e., the supreme realization of universality on the objective level of reality) "must" be scattered (a multitude of states makes a history of wars and fragile peaces necessary) in order to be *aufgehoben* by one triumphant world culture, whose summit is reached in the true philosophical interpretation of all nature, history, and culture.

9. Cf. Peperzak, *Modern Freedom,* 635–40.

10. Cf. Peperzak, "Hegel contra Hegel in his Philosophy of Right: The Contradictions of International Politics," in *Journal of the History of Philosophy* 32 (1994): 241–64.

11. Cf. Peperzak, "Datief" in *Tijdschrift voor Filosofie* 67 (2005): 435–51.

12. Hegel also states that an individual cannot be alone and that my relation to other persons is a constitutive element of my personality, but this essential connection has a radically different meaning. (1) In Hegel's context, the relation between other persons and me is a concretization of a fundamental law of logic: no x can be what it is without excluding some non-x. This exclusion is a relation and this relation is co-constitutive of x's identity with itself. All otherness is thus an internal and integral moment of any (determinate) being (*Dasein*). (2) In Hegel's view, the necessary relation that ties the other person to me shows that the other from the outset is "for-me," because the orientation of my thought about the other confirms and reinforces my own centrality: the other comes to me from the outside in order to be integrated by me. Levinas's description, on the contrary, shows that the Other changes the orientation of my being- and thinking-for-myself into my being and thinking for you, who, by addressing me, subordinate my self-concern to a startling (commanding, demanding, even accusing) center that contradicts my self-centeredness and calls me out of myself.

13. As I have argued elsewhere, the asymmetry of the relation that the Other's "highness" (*hauteur*) imposes on my being-for-you, cannot be affirmed as basic unless one also affirms that the Other likewise experiences me as high. See, for example, Peperzak, *Beyond: The Philosophy of Emmanuel Levinas* (Evanston, IL: Northwestern University Press, 1997), 125–26.

14. Cf. Peperzak, "You: Universal and Unique," forthcoming in *Le Tiers,* ed. Marcomaria Olivetti.

15. If it is true (1) that belonging to a community means that individuals *share* common features, goods, relations, goals, etc., and thus are members of one body, and (2) that the asymmetric relations between (all of) you and me cannot be understood as parts of a subordinate and synthesizable dimension, which is part of our shared commonality, then (3) the unity of that community and the association (or society) of all individuals is a problem that neither Hegel nor Levinas have fully solved. However, the principle for Levinas's solution lies in his

subordination of the human community (i.e., the totality of our sharing all that can be shared), symbolized by "the third" (cf. note 14), to the each time unique asymmetric relations between you and me. The sociality of the latter, which remains the highest ethico-political dimension, cannot be integrated into a higher human community. The originary and ultimate dimension cannot be found in any synthesis or totality and individuals remain ultimately unique, other, solitary and alone, responsible not only for others' and their own lives, but also for their lonely death, and absolutely unique destiny.

Another version of this rapport between the two dimensions of Levinas's philosophy is found in his conception of (his own) *ontology* and his *ethics*, which, in *Totality and Infinity*, is also called *metaphysics* (cf. Peperzak, *Beyond*, 72–120). One objection against Levinas (and against the preceding lines, which already are too synthetic for his taste) can be formulated thus: If height, asymmetry, otherness, etc. are revealed in all faces, do you not necessarily fall back on the thesis that these are universal characteristics of one and the same reality: the human essence that speaks for itself? The answer is that the objection itself is an expression of the superior, panoramic, and totalizing Hegelian perspective and praxis of modern (and large parts of postmodern) philosophy — a perspective that refuses to abandon its own egological and tautological view and standpoint in order to adopt the first person position of someone who *undergoes* the Other's facing instead of deciding that egological thinking itself is the methodical summit for an adequate approach of human lives. From such a viewpoint (which is one inevitable, but not necessarily supreme, perspective within scholarship), one cannot avoid developing an all-encompassing ontology, but your facing me reveals to me that you are radically different and more important than any philosophy *about* you.

ABOUT THE CONTRIBUTORS

Jeffrey Bloechl is associate professor of philosophy at the College of the Holy Cross and series editor of *Levinas Studies: An Annual Review*. He has written *Liturgy of the Neighbor: Emmanuel Levinas and the Religion of Responsibility* (2000) and edited *Religious Experience and the End of Metaphysics* (2003). Much of his current work is in the area of phenomenological anthropology.

Peter Atterton is assistant professor of philosophy at San Diego State University. He has published articles and translations in the area of Continental philosophy, and is coeditor of several books. He has coedited, with Matthew Calarco and Maurice Friedman, *Levinas and Buber: Dialogue and Difference* (2004). His interests focus on the intersection of Continental philosophy (especially the work of Nietzsche, Heidegger, Foucault, Levinas, and Derrida) with applied ethics, psychoanalysis, and animal rights. He is currently preparing a new book, *Ethics and Beyond: Levinas in Question*.

Michel Juffé was professor of political philosophy at the University of Paris-Marne-la-Vallée and professor of sociology and ethics at the École Nationale des Ponts et Chaussées for several years. In addition to many essays in the areas of psychoanalysis and philosophy (especially Spinoza), he is the author of *Les fondements du lien social* (1995) and *La tragédie en héritage, de Freud à Sophocle* (1999), as well as editor of *Psychanalyse et philosophie* (2001) and director of *Expériences de la porte* (2005).

Claire Katz is associate professor of philosophy and women's studies at Texas A&M University. Her current research focuses on the intersection of philosophy of education, political philosophy, gender, and religion. She is the author of *Levinas, Judaism, and the Feminine: The*

Silent Footsteps of Rebecca (2003) and the editor of *Emmanuel Levinas: Critical Assessments* (2005). She has published essays on Levinas, Merleau-Ponty, Nietzsche, feminist theory, philosophy of education, and philosophy of religion. She is currently at work on a theory of education that assumes Levinas's ethical subject.

Martin Kavka is associate professor of religion at Florida State University. He is the author of *Jewish Messianism and the History of Philosophy* (2004) and the coeditor of *Tradition in the Public Square: A David Novak Reader* (2007) and *The Cambridge History of Jewish Philosophy: The Modern Era* (forthcoming). He is presently coediting a volume of essays in honor of Edith Wyschogrod, and writing a book that revisions American Jewish covenantal theopolitics for the post-9/11 era.

Joseph Lawrence is professor of philosophy at the College of the Holy Cross. He is the author of *Schellings Philosophie des ewigen Anfangs* (1989). In addition to a number of specialized articles on Schelling, he has also written a variety of essays on authors ranging from Socrates to Thomas Mann. Convinced that Schelling's idea of philosophical religion can form the basis for intercultural dialogue, Lawrence is a frequent contributor to the Turkish newspaper *Zaman.*

Jacob Meskin is assistant professor of Jewish thought and education at Hebrew College in Newton, Massachusetts, where he also helps to run a national adult Jewish education program. His article "Modern Jewish Philosophy and Its Background in Nineteenth and Twentieth Century Jewish Tradition" will appear in *The Cambridge History of Jewish Philosophy: The Modern Era* (forthcoming). He is currently working on a manuscript on the pivotal role of traditional Jewish materials in Levinas's philosophy.

Jean-Marc Narbonne is professor of philosophy and member of the Institut d'Éudes Anciennes of the Université de Laval (Québec), president of the Canadian Society of Neoplatonic Studies, editor of the collection *Zétésis,* and with Georges Leroux co-directs *Les œuvres de Plotin* in the Budé Collection of Les Belles Lettres. He has published important studies of Neoplatonic thought, especially on Plotinus, with close attention to its relation with contemporary European thought. His books include *La métaphysique de Plotin* (1994, 2001), *Hénologie, ontology et Ereignis: Plotin, Proclus, Heidegger* (2001), and *Levinas and the Greek Heritage* (2006).

Adriaan Peperzak is Arthur J. Schmitt Chair of Philosophy. He has conducted extensive research on Hegel (*Modern Freedom*, 2001), Plato (*Platonic Transformations*, 1997), and Levinas (*Beyond*, 1998), as well as in the areas of ethics (*Before Ethics*, 1998, and *Elements of Ethics*, 2004) and phenomenological epistemology (*The Quest for Meaning*, 2003, and *Thinking*, 2006). His current work includes a project on Heidegger and one on intersubjectivity and politics.

Jacques Taminiaux, Ph.D., J.D., is professor emeritus of philosophy at Boston College, where he has taught regularly since 1968, and at the Catholic University of Louvain (Louvain-la-Neuve, Belgium), where he was also director of the Center for Phenomenological Studies (Husserl-Archives). He was among the founding members of the editorial board of the *Phaenomenologica* book series in which Levinas's two major books were published. He is the author of many books on German idealism and on the phenomenological movement including, most recently, *The Metamorphoses of the Phenomenological Reduction* (2004).

INDEX

holiness, doctrine of, 86
Holocaust, 106, 118–21, 192
humanism, Jewish, 144–46
Hume, David, 4, 230–31n217
Husserl, Edmund: on being, 6; and
deconstruction, 12; and Descartes,
22–25; and intentionality, 12–14;
Levinas on, 6; and phenomenology,
1–27; works by: *Cartesian Meditations*,
23, 25

illeity, 80, 93. *see also* otherwise than
being
imaginary knowledge, 167
immanent manifestation, 92–99, 135
immortality, 111–16
individualism, 197–99, 208–11, 240n12.
see also communitarianism
infinity and the infinite, 24–25; and being,
53, 59; separateness of, 64–69,
217–18n2; Spinoza on, 168; in *Totality
and Infinity*, 63–69; and transcendence,
64, 69
influences: on philosophy, 70–72
innocence, 115–17, 120–22, 124–29
In Search of Lost Time (Proust), 108
intentionality, 8, 12–14
interethnic violence, 88
interiority, 184
international law, 202–03
intuitive knowledge, 167
"Is Ontology Fundamental" (Levinas),
90–91
Israel, 80–81

Jankelevitch, Vladimir, 1
Jewish humanism, 144–46
Jews. *see* Judaism
Job, 194–96
Job and the Excess of Evil (Nemo), 194
Judaism: and context, 71; Jewish
philosophy, 136, x; lack of
understanding of, 88; Levinas'
philosophical articulation of, 69, 73–75;
and memory, 102; Spinoza and, 154;
survival of the Jews, 121; Talmudic
tradition, 56–57, 150–51, 154–56, x;
and Western philosophy, x. *see also*
education, Jewish
Juffé, Michel, 153–73, ix

justice, philosophy of, 45–46, 195. *see also
tzimtzum*

Kabbalah, 49–77, 217–18n2, 218n4, viii
Kant, Immanuel, 4–5, 122, 194
Karamazov, Alyosha (fictional character),
126–27
Karamazov, Ivan (fictional character), 105,
111–18, 120, 125–27
Katz, Claire, 133–52, 227–28n58, ix
Kavka, Martin, 79–103, viii
kingship, 101–02
knowledge, 166–70, 178
Kolitz, Zvi, 192
Kook, Abraham Isaac (Rav), 57

law, 106, 111–16, 122–25, 181–88,
202–03. *see also* ethics
Lawrence, Joseph P., 175–96, ix
Laws (Plato), 42
Legends of Our Time (Wiesel), 56
Leibniz, Gottfried Wilhelm, 4
Lermontov, Mikhail, 107
Levinas: and communitarianism, 207–14;
and maternity, 98
Levinas, Emmanuel: on art, 108–11; on
atheism, 113, 121, 130; on being,
30–36, 179–80; and communitarianism,
207–14; on dependency, 142–43,
150–51; and Descartes, 17–18, 22–25;
on the Enlightenment, 135–36, 232n5;
and the feminine, 136, 142, 151,
234n31; on God, 118–21, 129–32,
186–87, 193; and Heidegger, 180; and
history of philosophy, 15–27, vii–viii; on
Husserl, 6; influence of Dostoyevsky
on, 105–32, ix; influence of Kabbalah
on, 49–77, 217–18n2, viii; on Jewish
education, 136–37, 142–47, 149–51; on
love, 128; and maternity, 227–28n58;
and monotheism, 79–83, 90; and moral
law, 122–25, 187–88; and ontology, 20,
33–35, 38–46; and phenomenology,
15–27; philosophical articulation of
Judaism, 69, 73–75; and Plato, 37; on
religion, 113–14; and Schelling,
175–96; social philosophy of, 198–214;
on Spinoza, 153–73, ix; on suffering,
125–29; on transcendence, 186–87; use
of Jewish traditions, 56–57, 148–49,